Whatever Works:
Feminists of Faith Speak

A Girl God Anthology

Edited by Trista Hendren and Pat Daly

Preface by Dr. Amina Wadud

Girl God Books

Written by Trista Hendren / Illustrated by Elisabeth Slettnes

The Girl God: A magically illustrated children's book celebrating the Divine Feminine.

Mother Earth: A loving tribute to Mother Earth and a call to action for children, their parents and grandparents.

Tell Me Why: A feminist twist of the creation story told with love from a mother to her son, in hopes of crafting a different world for them both.

Upcoming Girl God Anthologies
edited by Trista Hendren and Pat Daly

Jesus, Mohammed and the Goddess

Single Mothers Speak on Patriarchy

www.thegirlgod.com

Whatever Works: Feminists of Faith Speak

ISBN 978-1-50784-863-0

Cover Design by Trista Hendren and Anders Loberg
Interior Design by Pat Daly and Anders Loberg
Cover Art by Elisabeth Slettnes
Printed in the U.S.A. by CreateSpace

www.thegirlgod.com

Contents

---

*[1] Trigger warning for sexual violence

For *all* the women and girls around the world who continue to work toward the liberation of all women with faith and hope.

"Some beliefs are like walled gardens. They encourage exclusiveness, and the feeling of being especially privileged. Other beliefs are expansive and lead the way into wider and deeper sympathies. Some beliefs are divisive, separating the saved from the unsaved, friends from enemies. Other beliefs are bonds in a world community, where differences beautify the pattern."

Sylvia Fahs

Preface

Dr. Amina Wadud

WOMEN ARE WISE. Some times in the unfolding of human history on this planet, women may have needed to preserve their wisdom in silence: few or no words combined with embodied embrace of the earth and all the inhabitants. We are clear that this is NOT such a time. We have entered into a time of full embrace for the voices of women's wisdom. Women speak. This ancient voice of wisdom will benefit All who listen as it is spoken in abundance, generosity and truth. Now those of traditional dances are making sacred praise. There are new steps and a new beat.

The stories that unfold in this anthology defy those outmoded tendencies toward trivializing the perspectives, experiences and divine light of women amongst us. In this volume, women speak from multiple locations of faith and community. They defy any who might linger in those old stereotypes about women as merely story-tellers. Herein are women who share their visions and reality. They are every woman: in multiple ways—and yet— in no single monolithic way.

Certainly the word "faith" unites them—but it is neither one faith, nor one presence amongst those who share a single faith-tradition. Stories told here have faith as affirmation in sacred presence. Women walk these paths of faith and still create bridges to help all who read to cross over from the stymied manifestations of faith-experience that characterized past overzealous patriarchal interpretation (of faith and religion).

One might also say that feminism frames these women and their stories. Here again, the stories in this volume defy the tendencies towards a narrow sliver of the wide breath of feminisms. It moves beyond simple Western liberal feminist storytelling and spiritual mayhem to bring us back around whole to our multi-variant humanity.

Despite the absence of a single unifying characteristic, this volume is coherent and courageous. Indeed it is its depth and breadth that is most significant to what comes across as a unique contribution to women's voices in our time. As you enter into the pages of this anthology, set aside your pre-conceived notions that women only inhabit the margins of major faith traditions; or that women must mimic men in order to be whole, to be fully human. It was delightful to see how variant was the mandate to tell stories that open to the endless creative possibilities of women within a variety of faith traditions—even some that others condemn as irredeemably patriarchal.

This defiance has been a motivating force in my life. A half century ago, I gave up the idea that "religions" are ONLY what men have made of them. My father, and favorite patriarch, was a Methodist Minister. He was also a poor working-class Black man with a dream about the City of God. From him I learned about devotion and spiritual integrity. From my father I learned that a person cannot live a lie AND be close to the Sacred— however the Sacred is conceived: God, Goddess, gods, energy, change, nature or LIFE itself. We cannot know the Divine until we first encounter our own naked selves through the macabre mirror of our realities.

A lie won't do. False and shallow projections of self reacting to the dictates of "popular" culture won't do. Being true to One's self is the minimum requirement for transformative awakenings. Because this lesson came to me through my father, a man of spirit and engaged struggle, a man of faith—and yet still a man, himself chained by limits in earthly resources, and of racism—I learned early not to bow down to the forces of good and evil as manifest in the adherence to singularity of vision. There is no one place, time or person—including myself—who has a monopoly over Truth. Thus my search has been toward ever more radical pluralism as the hallmark of Truth.

For it is within the very moment you settle for a single iteration of yourself that you kill off the infinite possibilities of self unfolding by that single reality. For while Truth about self is essential for transformation, clinging to any one iteration of that self becomes a prison of one's own making. The magic of this anthology of women is in its radical reflection that "we are every woman," and women are NOT the same. We do not need to pretend to sameness in order to express what is most essential about us—that is—our very existence, and our engaged faith experiences.

This unique collection has the powerful capacity to remind us of the awe and beauty in diversity without itself becoming a sort of pop culture of Self worship. Each of these stories is True, and each is intimately connected to the lives of the women telling them. Read deeply. Enjoy. Then, tell your own story. That is what this volume invites you to do. I did and I am already a better person for it.

"Part of healing the wounded feminine and reclaiming feminine wisdom is for the women to reconnect, to come together as sisters with a common mission rather than stay isolated and reinforce a divisiveness which disempowers us all and weakens our efforts."

Jane Hardwicke Collings

Whatever Works

Trista Hendren

I HAVE A HARD TIME WITH SPEAKING. The mandates of quietness and submissiveness that I grew up with in the church still plague me as a 40-year-old woman. While I *can* speak, when pushed, and often had to while finishing my MBA, it is still something I find extraordinarily difficult. I could actually go days without saying one word to anyone. Having youngish children doesn't make that an option for me; nor does the fact that I am *desperate* to end the patriarchy that has strangled me since birth.

I want a very different life for my daughter.

Writing this introduction has been a challenge. While writing is not technically *speaking*, I often read my words aloud to myself as I compose them, to hear and feel how they sound against the realities of the air. I feel inspired and transformed by the pieces that have come in, and yet, I still feel a cringe factor when it comes to Christianity, my faith of origin. Admittedly, there is still a gaping wound there; my (Christian) father and I have not spoken for more than a year. Our differences in opinion regarding faith and feminism play a big part in that.

In addition, I have been in the midst of a traumatic family court situation that seems like it will never end.

My sisters—of all faiths—sustain me. Muslims, Jews, Goddessians, Atheists, and Christians. Throughout the last six months, I've had conservative Christians and Muslims praying for me and witches casting spells and lighting candles. I've cried my heart out to women of all faith persuasions and been supported in different ways by each of them.

When I went through my second divorce seven years ago, I was at my lowest point ever. I had shrunk in size to a 00, which was representative of how I felt about myself during that time. I was invisible and barely functioning. I had no legal representation and no money. I did the best I could with two young kids and

1

very little help. Due to the condition my former husband's addictions left us in, we lost our family home and I was forced to file for bankruptcy. My children helped me to realize that I needed to become my strongest self again.

I left a 13-year career as a mortgage broker to embark on a new dream. Feminism gave me the vision that I deserved better; my faith gave me the strength to persevere until better came.

Today, I sit in the courtroom with the attorney who has been representing me for the last six months. We have spoken before about his son, who I know he adores, but I have not fully comprehended WHY he agreed to take on my case, now totaling tens of thousands of dollars with my measly $200-a-month payment. He gives me the why in code that I decipher in my head. He mentions singing in a choir, which ultimately leads me to ask him more. I like this style of his; he doesn't beat me over the head with the fact that he's a Lutheran. And so my questions begin.

I'm quite sure he doesn't identify as feminist – but his act of charity to me as someone whose reality is mostly that of a single mother—certainly is. *It is an act that no one else over the last eight years has been willing to do, male or female, feminist or not.*

I sit nervously in my chair, fingering the tiny gold charm inscribed with *Al-Fatiha*[2], silently reciting the verse in my head as I nervously make it through the court proceedings. While I rarely do the things that most people associate with Islam anymore, it is these moments in my life when I rely on my faith to sustain me.

During these last trying months, I often questioned the potency of my feminist work under the rock I felt stuck under. I worried that I was not able to adequately protect my own children— or even me for that matter—under our patriarchal system. I'd ask myself, *who am I to speak of these things when I can barely hold my own head above water?*

---

[2] A prayer at the very beginning of the Quran, also known as "the Mother of the Book".

The truth is that I could not have won my case—or my life back—without the help of this Christian attorney. The truth is that it's unlikely I would have stayed sane these last years without the support of my secular humanist (third) husband. The truth is that I would be utterly lost without the support of my sisters around the world of *all* faith persuasions. Had I locked my heels and refused to be open to the possibilities of who *could* help me, I would likely still be trapped in the same miserable spot.

In those moments in the courtroom I began to question my resentment of Christianity and reconsider what it means to actually be a Christian—or a person of any faith.

I grew up with a pamphlet that listed the supposed beliefs of nine other major religions (summarized in a brief paragraph), followed by detailed explanation about why each belief was *wrong*. My religion was fundamentalist Christianity and I followed it to a T. Looking back, I am embarrassed to say that while I knew people from a variety of cultures and religions, the only reason I ever spoke to them was to convert them.

As a teenager, I read *The Book of Mormon* and started going to Seminary, again with the intention of saving *those poor Mormon kids*. The missionaries came to my home in droves, two-by-two in their white dress shirts and ties, where I often puzzled them. No one could answer my never-ending questions.

I suppose the Muslims were the most concerning to me then, although I didn't read the Qur'an until college, after marrying a Muslim. At that point, I *had* to read it, because everyone was *certain* that my *savage* Arab husband would soon start beating me.

A few years earlier, I had left home to attend a Southern Baptist college with the intention of becoming a minister. It soon dawned on me that the real purpose for girls in that school was to find a husband.

Once I began to study the historical, linguistic, and cultural roots of the Bible in-depth, I felt as though I had been lied to my entire life. I left Florida nine months later an atheist, certain I could never believe in anything again.

3

Back home, I found feminism and a cute Lebanese guy. Both would change the course of my life forever.

I never had any intention of converting to Islam. My new husband encouraged me to think on my own terms and believe in myself – which was something completely new to me after growing up as a submissive church girl. It was that freedom and the kindness of my new family that prompted me to study Islam. It wasn't so much the Qur'an itself I was in love with; I still find it a boring and tedious read. What drew me to Islam was actually Ramadan—and the dream of full equality between all people.

One thing that has always stuck with me since my conversion is that the way people viewed me completely changed. I am still the same person I always was, but suddenly I started hearing that I "deserved to die" and was a "sand nigger." After 9/11, I was also told that all Muslims "should be put into internment camps."

Every single week, I hear racist, shitty comments about Muslims—often from other feminists.

Many people forget that racism and sexism are brothers.

Approximately a quarter of the world's population is Muslim – and few, if any, people ever leave their faith of origin. Islamophobia only guarantees that the majority of Muslim women will be isolated, resentful, and suspicious of the Western world.

There is a general feeling in many Western feminist circles that women of faith cannot be feminists. This is particularly true of Muslim Feminists, but I've certainly seen it with other groups as well. For example, when Kate Kelly was excommunicated from the Mormon Church last year for speaking out on her views about the treatment of women in that church, I often posted to my Girl God Facebook page about her situation in solidarity. Time and time again, I heard a similar response: "She should just leave that church."

I do not share that view. The "should" is deeply concerning to me. Certainly there is value in challenging the patriarchal structures from within, too. I would argue that we have no hope of saving the world via feminism if we ignore the belief structures that saturate the planet.

Faith is often cultural. It involves entire families and communities; hence faith is deeply personal. While I don't regularly practice Islam anymore, it is hurtful when I hear other feminists make comments about Muslims. My first marriage didn't work out, but it had nothing to do with religion and everything to do with getting married too young. My Lebanese in-laws are still family and my first husband remains a dear friend. Over the last 20 years, I have maintained friendships with Muslims in my local community, and increasingly, all over the world thanks to social media. I *love* my extended Ummah.

While there are certainly things that I would challenge about the Muslim faith, it is not helpful to receive such criticisms from those who know little about Islam. I liken this to the dynamic in many families that it is OK to critique your own family members, but when someone outside the family starts shredding the character of a mother or sister, all hell breaks loose.

Religion tends to be divisive and women (especially feminists), cannot afford to be divided anymore. Life is so much harder than the Disney movies many of us grew up watching. It is deeply unfair to women, and particularly unjust to women of color. Nothing prepares most of us for the reality of our daily lives. We need each other now more than ever.

Gerda Lerner wrote that "Men develop ideas and systems of explanation by absorbing past knowledge and critiquing and superseding it. Women, ignorant of their own history [do] not know what women before them had thought and taught. So generation after generation, they [struggle] for insights others had already had before them, [resulting in] the constant inventing of the wheel."

I believe a big part of that problem is that women within feminism are fragmented and don't take the time to listen to each other often enough. There is so much that we can learn from each other to avoid reinventing the wheel every generation. If you tear a blanket up into bits, it no longer functions as a blanket. But if you sew those same pieces back together, you can still keep someone warm.

5

There are obvious remnants of misogyny in all the world's religions. Women, still, for the most part are not equal participants in the leadership of most faiths. The expected submission and subordination of women and girls continues to be the norm worldwide. But instead of clustering ourselves neatly into our own faiths, might we not learn from each other? Might Muslim women learn from female Rabbis and Priests? Might Christians and Hindus learn from the women-only mosques springing up throughout the world?

Women remain 70% of those living in poverty. Those with the least often cling to religion the hardest. So when we tear apart the blanket that religion offers to many of our sisters living in poverty, we are literally taking away one of the few things that is still keeping them warm.

This begs the question: *what sort of feminism do we want?* One that supports the vision of a few privileged white women and leaves the rest of the world behind? Or, a feminism that liberates *everybody*?

I would love to see the definition of "feminist" widened if for no other reason that many of my closest friends don't label themselves as such when their actions say otherwise. If there is a wounding with that particular word, perhaps we need a new word to define our work. Perhaps we need to come back to women's circles and meet each other face-to-face, where we are. We each need an opportunity to speak our stories, our wounds and our triumphs. *All* women must be welcome.

This anthology is meant to widen the circle and inspire listening and reflection. Within each faith tradition there are certainly both wounding and healing attributes. My hope is to find whatever works for each of us so that we can find solutions to the horrific problems plaguing women around the world. We must come together if we are ever to end patriarchy.

Carol P. Christ wrote that, "Even people who no longer 'believe in God' or participate in the institutional structure of patriarchal religion still may not be free of the power of the symbolism of God the Father. A symbol's effect does not depend on rational assent, for a symbol also functions on levels of the psyche other than the rational. Symbol systems cannot simply be rejected;

they must be replaced. Where there is no replacement, the mind will revert to familiar structures at times of crisis, bafflement, or defeat."

This is true of all the patriarchal world religions, although the specific wording may differ. The way I grew up, I listened to the (mostly) male pastors speak and their words were Gospel. I was terrified of being wrong, so I studied the Bible and other books written by men for hours every day to make sure I was geared up with the "right" information.

Audre Lorde once said that "our feelings are our most genuine paths to knowledge." I find these words hopeful as I embark on a new way of sorting out what I believe. Years after leaving behind the image of God the Father, I still struggle to acknowledge my truth over what male spiritual leaders define as "The Truth".

Whatever Works is a collection of writing by feminists of faith from around the world. This anthology contains personal essays, poems and academic musings with the goal of sparking a conversation among women of all faith backgrounds. Religion plays one of the biggest roles in creating and maintaining value systems, and yet it is often disregarded within feminism itself as if we could simply walk away and forget about it.

All of us are limited by our cultural and religious perspectives. As we were finishing this book, I realized I wanted to cover menstruation specifically, as it became clear to me that it was one of the biggest hurdles to full equality within most faith traditions.

I queried the other contributors on our working Facebook group to see if anyone could suggest authors. Rabbi Dahlia Marx suggested Zoharah Noy-meir, who I had asked upfront for a contribution many months ago, but whose schedule at that time had not allowed her to participate. She suggested I try again, and I did. I asked Dahlia to "cross her fingers" that Zoharah would join us.

She immediately replied that Jews *did not do that*. All these years, even growing up with family-like Jewish neighbors across the street and years of interfaith work, I had no idea that crossing fingers was even a Christian reference.

When you think about all the songs we grow up singing and the stories we learn about, our lives are saturated in the religion of our culture, whether we practice that religion or not.

When I read Patricia Lynn Reilly's *A God Who Looks Like Me,* I wished that there was a similar book for Muslim women, but I didn't know of any. When I wrote *The Girl God,* I wasn't sure I'd find the divine feminine within Islam at all. I was pleasantly surprised to find Her everywhere.

My spirituality has changed drastically *many* times over the years as my life has coursed through three husbands, two birthed children, two new stepsons and many other radical changes. I have moved far away from a male God and shifted toward the divine feminine. This book includes selections from women who identify with Her and those who do not.

My mother, Pat Daly, has joined me in editing this project. When I asked her to partner with me, she seemed baffled. She has written two books and thousands of professional resumes over the past 30 years, but a book about *feminism*?

While my mother still does not fully identify as a feminist, she certainly behaves like one. Years ago, when I was left with nearly nothing after my second divorce, it was her actions and generosity that allowed my children and me to survive. In the U.S., there are not many provisions for single mothers who may or may not receive a pittance of child support. I couldn't go back to my previous work and I needed to be near my children so that they could get the support and nurturing they needed to heal. All I had to go on was a dream: to write books that would change the world.

Nearly everyone thought I was *completely* insane.

My mother has been one of the few people who actually believed in me and supported me in word and deed.

The foundations of *The Girl God* have been built with the help of many people; however, I could not have completed any of my projects without the help of my dear mother. And so, it seemed fitting to invite her here to edit our cherished words with her caring touch.

Each of the selections in this anthology has moved something in me—sometimes even a lost part that I wasn't sure was still around anymore. I hope that it will spark a conversation among and between women of all faith—and even those of no faith.

Feminism is also a faith—a faith that someday, somehow, things will improve for at least our daughters and granddaughters. My dream is that life will change for the better for us, too.

Many of us are still learning to speak in our own words. We must be patient with ourselves and with each other as those words come out.

May the speaking, the listening, the dialogue, and the radical change begin!

A Note About Styles and Preferences

Whatever Works contains a variety of writing styles from women around the world. Non-English natives and various forms of English are included in this anthology and we chose to keep spellings of the writers origin to honor (or honour) each woman's unique voice.

It was the expressed intent of the editors to not police standards of citation, transliteration and formatting. Contributors have determined which citation style, italicization policy and transliteration system to adopt in their pieces. The resulting diversity is a reflection of the diversity of academic fields, genres and personal expressions represented by the authors.[3]

If you find that a particular essay doesn't sit well with you, please feel free to use the Al-Anon suggestion that has become so helpful to me:

"Take what you like, leave the rest!"

That said, if there aren't at least several writings here that either challenge you or leave you feeling deeply uncomfortable, I have not accomplished what I set out to do.

– Trista

---

[3] This paragraph is borrowed and adapted with love from *A Jihad for Justice: Honoring the Work and Life of Amina Wadud* – Edited by Kecia Ali, Juliane Hammer and Laury Silvers.

Goddess Spirituality as Liberation Thealogy

Rev. Dr. Karen Tate

A FRIEND OF MINE STARTLED ME one day when she announced she was leaving what we loosely called Goddess Spirituality because it lacked substance. Besides the Wiccan Rede, which left a lot of gray area to rationalize wrong-doing, she felt what we were learning about Goddess Spirituality didn't delve enough into ethics and learning about individual pantheons or the Wheel of the Year was not really providing us adequate guidance as a template for living. She had made the decision to turn to Buddhism to see what it offered. Her decision stuck with me because I believed she had a point – and I kept mulling it over for some time. I also came to believe the spirituality, devotion and inspirational aspects were often absent or in short supply as well. Yes, there was so much to learn – tarot, doing ritual and magic, herstory, astrology, comparative religion, deities, herbology, study of various traditions, sacred sites – but what about making the ancient teachings relevant to help change our patriarchal world? To uplift us and help us become better people. What did Goddess Spirituality offer?

What first jumped out at me was that Wiccans and Pagans and Goddess Advocates may very well have different way-showers, elders and foremothers. While Wiccans and Pagans might turn to Starhawk, Selena Fox, Dion Fortune, Scott Cunningham and Ray Buckland, *to name just a few* well known teachers, Goddess Advocates might also turn to Fox and Starhawk, but certainly were turning to, *again, naming only a few*, Riane Eisler, Mairja Gimbutas, Jean Shinoda Bolen, Clarissa Pinkola Estes, Merlin Stone, academia and feminists. In fact, it was Merlin Stone's *When God Was a Woman* and Riane Eisler's extensive research of history in *The Chalice and the Blade*, that kept me on the path as I discovered herstory was not a feminist fantasy. Eisler's dominator paradigm theory, then her partnership theories from *The Partnership Way*, informed the budding feminist blossoming within and laid some of the ground work leading me toward becoming a social justice activist. I could see that for some there was a fork in the road as some Wiccans and

11

Pagans never took that path of activism that I eventually found most relevant as a Goddess Advocate. Looking back, I see my own books reflect my growth as priestessing became more than making ancient rituals relevant for contemporary devotees or doing Wheel of the Year rituals.

My earliest years as a priestess, discovering the impact of standing in Her sacred sites, culminated in writing *Sacred Places of Goddess: 108 Destinations,* which miraculously got me into mainstream places teaching about Goddess through the back door of "sacred travel and pilgrimage" that I might never have gained entry to had I just been teaching some aspect of Wicca or Paganism. One could easily see the diversity of Goddess by her many names and faces across the globe from ancient times to living traditions – and how to get there if you were an armchair traveler or you actually ventured out with boots on the ground.

Priestessing the community for dozens of years, starting an Iseum within the Fellowship of Isis, then later, the not-for-profit Isis Ancient Cultures Society, resulted in my documenting esoteric and exoteric experiences in *Walking An Ancient Path: Rebirthing Goddess on Planet Earth,* answering my experience of there sometimes being a dearth of offerings available delving into the devotion, inspiration and more spiritual aspects of Goddess Spirituality. But it wasn't until my newest book, *Goddess Calling,* out in early 2014, that I connect all the dots between what I'd learned as a Priestess of Goddess Spirituality with how it all fits in with social justice and politics. Getting beyond Wicca 101, tarot, astrology, ritual making and all the rest, I realized what Goddess taught us was in fact the new liberation thealogy of our time. Goddess set us free from patriarchal oppression!

While Christianity might have once been considered liberation thealogy as slaves and women flocked to this new religion offering them hope from their plight in life, it was now Goddess spirituality offering an alternative to oppression, exploitation and domination. Now I could answer my friends' faulty or perhaps premature conclusion with certainty and find her assessment of Goddess Spirituality being lacking untrue, because the Divine Feminine does in fact teach us quite a lot about how to live a peaceful, joyous, empowered and sustainable life. We just have

12

to go beyond Wicca 101 and the Wheel of the Year. Her many images of divinity and mythology teach us much if we are willing to rethink and reinterpret and courageously tell new stories, some of which I'll gently touch on here and now.

So let us look at several brief examples of the Sacred Feminine as deity, metaphor or myth and how we're given a template for living or advice for values we might embrace.

1) I've hinted at this previously, but let me punctuate: We find under the broad umbrella of Goddess, many faces across continents and cultures, with no mandate that we worship one name, one face. Instead we see a metaphor for plurality, diversity and inclusion in the loving and life-affirming Sacred Feminine, rather than the jealous, One Way, andocentric and exclusionary god of patriarchy keen on asking men to sacrifice their sons to prove their loyalty and a holy book filled with violence. Those embracing Goddess might easily see choosing peace, tolerance, gender equality and peoples of all walks of life; gay, straight, people of all skin colors and religions or no religion at all, as being in alignment with Her diversity, resulting in a more inclusive, just, equal, balanced and sustainable world and society.

2) Consider the mythology of the Inuit Goddess Sedna. She is the gatekeeper between humankind and the sea creatures of the regions near icy waters on which indigenous people depend for their livelihood. If mankind becomes too greedy and exploits the creatures of the sea, Sedna cuts humanity off until he takes only what he needs. Greed and excess are taboo as we are all inter-dependent upon each other. As our environmental Goddess, Sedna, teaches us to be wise stewards of Mother Earth and Her creatures. This is a rejection of excess and exploitation in all forms and She calls us to environmentalism and to be Her spokespeople protecting habitats across the globe. We might be called to be at the forefront fighting against fracking, poisoning our water and air, and depleting our natural resources. We would deplore exploitation of any kind, including wage discrimination, worker exploitation or multi-national corporations decimating local economies and indigenous peoples. We certainly would use our vote to support those

who fight for the 99% and allies who would protect Mother Earth and Sedna's creatures.

3) Egyptian wall carvings clearly show the Egyptian Goddess Isis bestowed upon pharaohs their right to rule and they were to rule their kingdoms governing under the laws of the Goddess Maat, namely truth, balance, order, and justice. Similarly, we see the Hindu Goddess Kali standing atop her consort, Shiva, whose powers must be activated by Her. Clearly this suggests patriarchy, or rule of the father, resulting in rule by the male gender, has not always been the way of the world, nor would it be the way of the world with Goddess restored to center. Neither would we want *patriarchy in a skirt* as absolute power corrupts absolutely. Even a cursory glimpse here shows a call for female leadership and a respect for women's power, both which are sorely lacking in our world as academia, corporate America, religious institutions and politics has less than 20% representation by women in the United States. We must support women who embrace Goddess ideals and support their leadership in these bastions of male control. Isis grants the pharaoh the right to rule, but as can be seen in inscriptions where she extends to him the Goddess Maat, or the laws of Maat, he must rule over the people abiding by her laws. We can interpret that in contemporary times to mean we should expect our leaders to show support for and promote civil rights, voter rights, worker and immigrant rights and consumer protection from powers that might mis-use and exploit the individual or the planet.

4) In the thealogy of the Sacred Feminine, Goddess affirms women's bodies and sexuality. Priestesses of pharmacology, mid-wives and women hold the power over their own bodies and life and death is in their hands. Today the patriarchy dictates to women the parameters of beauty and women fall victims to their standards spending millions with plastic surgeons to live up to some impossible ideal. According to the American Society of Plastic Surgeons, 13.1 million cosmetic procedures were performed in 2010, up 5% from 2009. Beyond physical beauty, the patriarchy wants to control all aspects of women's sexuality and reproduction. Known in the United States as Big Pharma, pharmaceutical companies now hold the power over

women's bodies as they encourage women to disconnect from their menses, that monthly inconvenience, that curse. They say, here, take our pill and see your sacred blood magically disappear. Disconnect from one of the very things that empowers you as a woman! In a not-so veiled culture war, one political party has declared war on women by attempting to de-fund Planned Parenthood, thwarting access to contraception, trying to pass laws to make divorces harder to obtain, trying to legalize the murder of abortion providers, and by having miscarriages investigated and abortions abolished. Women's bodies and lives are the terrain on which this current extremist conservative movement is taking a stand.

5) If we had a feminine face of god at the center of society, or Her ideals affirming life, female authority, sacred sexuality, and leadership, men and their institutions would not control or dictate to women. Equal is equal. Women would understand their sexuality and bodies are sacred and in their own hands and would not be complicit in their own oppression or exploitation. Fortunately many women are catching on to this as they embrace groups like the Red Tent Movement.

6) Goddess thealogy affirms female power. Where Goddess was worshiped, her temples were the centers of wisdom, culture, and financial power and were often presided over by women. The Unitarian Universalist Women's Cakes for the Queen of Heaven curriculum, as well as researchers such as Merlin Stone and Heide Goettner-Abendroth, in her book, *Societies of Peace: Matriarchies Past, Present and Future* point to matrilineal, matrifocal or matriarchal societies where Goddess was venerated and maternal values practiced, women and children were protected and had a spot at the center of the culture, reaping the benefit of that positioning at the center. Not only must we restore women's position in society to that of equal partnership with men but we must once again turn to the attributes of the Feminine, such as caring, sharing, nurturing, negotiation, collaboration, solidarity, partnership and peace – all of which have been marginalized or demonized under patriarchy – and embrace these values so that quality of life is restored for the most of us.

In conclusion, I've touched briefly on but *a few ideas* that show how Sacred Feminine herstory, metaphor and mythology might be reclaimed and reinterpreted to provide a roadmap for a more sustainable future. We have in the feminine images of divinity deities, archetypes and ideals to show us the way. It is up to us to move away from or temper the "authoritarian father" idealogy that shapes our religions and culture and instead heed the advice of the Great She and her Sacred Feminine liberation thealogy as our role model.

Every Altar Girl the Catholic Church Turns Away is a Gift to the Rest of the World

Soraya Chemaly

ONCE EVERY FEW YEARS, since 1994 when girls were first allowed to serve as altar girls in Catholic churches, the issue of banning them comes up. Recently it was a story about Joseph Illo, a San Francisco priest who barred girls from services. He explained in a statement, that boys lose interest because girls do a better job; that the role of altar boy is tied to an all-male priesthood, so it makes no sense to have altar girls; that being an altar boy is what sparks a desire to be a priest; and that, for good "boys will be boys" measure, girls distract the boys who are meant to serve. Altar girls are, in effect, the religious equivalent of a gateway drug. While Pope Francis might be lauded as a champion of liberalization, he also draws a line at girls and women.

The argument articulated by Illo is a standard one, most recently clarified by Raymond Burke, a conservative American Cardinal in Rome. Burke likes to throw around the word "feminized" in the very traditional, pejorative way. He believes, in his patriarchal heart of hearts, that altar girls are to blame for today's dearth of (male) priests. The degree to which girls' abilities, gifts, spiritual ambitions or hopes are quashed is rarely, if ever, directly addressed.

Thing 1: Barring girls from serving and women from the priesthood is sexism and it is indefensible and wrong.

Thing 2: Even religious sexism is still sexism.

Thing 3: Even traditional sexism is still sexism.

Thing 4: If you are a practicing Catholic, and care deeply about equality, the exclusion of altar girls and the messages that exclusion imparts to boys, you have options.

My question isn't about the Church, whose actions are unsurprising and make a lot of sense from a self-serving hierarchy's perspective. My question is, why do people who otherwise do everything they can to provide egalitarian (and often superior) outcomes for their children continue to support this institutional power when there are so many viable spiritual, scriptural and community options?

Banning altar girls because they are girls conveys a great deal of destructive information to children. I have lost count of friends who are genuinely concerned about growing confident, ambitious girls, or are worried about the boy crisis in education, one notably related to overconfidence and hyper-masculinity, who then faithfully take their children into church, catechism and Sunday school. It's confusing to girls to hear one set of "girl power" words and behaviors and then be told that they, and they alone, must set those words and behaviors aside in deference to boys – which is exactly what happens in conservative religious communities.

When girls go to churches where there are no women priests they learn to be quiet. They are taught, through thousands of small interactions, language and rules, that their words cannot and do not have power and that access to God has to be mediated always through boys and men. They learn that some humans are more closely created in God's image and that they are not among them. They learn that expectations about empathy, kindness, forgiveness, self-control and sacrifice are gendered and imbalanced. They learn that their desires must be sublimated so that the desires and destinies of boys and men can be prioritized and fulfilled. This is first true not in a sexual or emotional way, but in the way that young girls, like boys, can and do develop deep faith and a desire for the priesthood – often way before the opportunity to serve at an altar. Really, go back and read Illo's statement. Very deeply implicated in the denial of women in the priesthood are ancient prohibitions regarding women, blood and old beliefs about women's polluting bodies.

Boys learn very different messages. They learn that they are special by comparison. They learn to act and speak publicly. They learn to be authoritative. They learn that their words have power and that they have a unique (compared to their sisters) relationship with those who wield it. They learn that the society they live in values what they have to say, because they are boys saying it. They learn that they will not be held accountable for their actions. They learn that their needs have primacy.

The relationship that the Church cultivates, sometimes dangerously, between priests and altar boys is a very quotidian one of human male fraternal legacy. This is sexism and the practice of barring girls from the altar and women from ministerial roles is a very quotidian practice of sexual discrimination.

When I first read that the reason for this most recent prohibition was that the Church had been dangerously "feminized" I actually burst out laughing. There are no official women priests and no women are allowed in the senior hierarchy of the Vatican. There are no women in position of power or authority in the Church who do not report to a man. There are barely any in the Vatican itself. At last count, out of the city-state's roughly 550 citizens, 32 were women – 1 nun and 31 lay. Since they cannot actual fill ministerial or administrative roles, I imagine they are doing a fair amount of the cooking and cleaning that their ovaries prepare them to for so excellently. There is also the growing influence of the ultra-secretive and conservative lay organization, Opus Dei, known for distinctly sex segregated and gender hierarchical practices. One of the few exceptions to the exclusion of women in senior, influential roles used to be the significant number of women who served as presidents of Catholic colleges and universities, a number that exceeded women's representation in non-Catholic schools. (The majority of Catholic colleges were founded by women religious orders and were sex segregated. Once desegregation began, women lost ground.) Not one woman has been named president in the increasing trend of hiring lay people to head up Catholic colleges and universities.

The shining light in this situation are the American Catholic nuns and Catholic women priests who run their own churches. They are a persistent thorn in the Church's side. A long-awaited report on religious women (which does not include 50,000 current women priests) was published in December, 2013.

The history of religious women is filled with role models, public figures, ecclesiastical and spiritual leaders, but they have always functioned within the frame of patriarchy. The literal outspokenness of women leaders is a central problem. Before they take any action they first violate norms by speaking publicly with confidence, intelligence, expertise, and authority.

During the last election cycle, when Nuns on the Bus (also a great documentary) led by Sister Simone Campbell, took to American highways with a scathing critique of policies supported by the Vatican and Catholic Bishops, it revealed the very gendered nature of social justice, as well as related political fissures, in the Church. Lay people embraced this movement out of a sense of what they perceived to be the authentic message of Christ.

Acts of liberal social justice conducted by smart, respected, charismatic women are the Church's penultimate nightmare. The ultimate nightmare is their public politicization, a substantive threat to all-powerful old boy networks. That politicization makes very clear that the suppression of girls and women's speech and leadership in churches has implications that far exceed Sunday services.

There are 18 cardinals and 449 US bishops, all male, who hold an enormous amount of political sway by audaciously claiming, in the face of obvious difference, that they represent the nation's millions of Catholics. As a matter of doctrine they don't. As a matter of public practice, they are losing ground. There are now more than 100 ordained women priests in the United States. On January 1st of this year, 67-year old Rev. Georgia Walker, a former Sister of St. Joseph, was ordained as a Catholic priest. This isn't, in the words of one prelate, "a current fad."

"They can't take away my baptism, they can't take away my calling to the priesthood. All they can do is deny me their sacraments," she explained. "But now, I am a priest and I can provide those sacraments. Not just to myself but to others." This is a woman, with a constituency, who couldn't care less if she is excommunicated by a sexist Church.

According to the Association of Roman Catholic Women Priests, this is long overdue.

Their stated objectives?

1. We seek equality for women in the church, including decision-making and ordination.

2. We minister to the poor and marginalized.

3. We live the spiritual and social justice tradition of the church serving inclusive communities of equals.

4. We actively and openly participate in non-violent movements for peace and justice.

"Radical feminist movement" is as old as the Church. Its diverse manifestations have made it possible today for women around the world to drive to churches, read the Bible, work for pay in Catholic schools, feed the children that they bring to Sunday school, have sex without the exhaustive and sometimes deadly effects of compulsory pregnancy, live through dangerous childbirths to stay with their families, divorce abusive spouses and challenge the legitimacy of raping priests. It's made it possible for conservative women to blog about their beliefs, get on Fox to defend them, vote for Rick Santorum, and chose life with their families when faced with tragic and catastrophic pregnancies. And, yes, it's made girls think that their words and actions are publicly consequential and can contribute, in a way not related to their reproductive capacities, but to the common good.

What a horrific list of frightening, disruptive and obscene outcomes that we should all abhor. And that's all without touching on the deliberate erasure of a history of women bishops, deacons and priests; Magdalene Laundries; sexual abuse by priests; or global human rights violations resulting from an all-male priesthood's objections to modern public health initiatives. Millions of girls and women, and their families suffer grave harm as a result of these objections.

The ritualized silencing of girls and women by denying them the authority to be priests, or even altar girls, has enormous consequences for individuals and society.

The Church's problem is not girls who want to serve at altars. It's the girls who realize that they are, for no legitimate moral or ethical reason, not respected as equals and as fully human people with the capacity for authority and ministry. Every altar girl this Church turns away is a gift to the rest of the world.

Feminism & God/dess in Judaism

Neorah Garcia

ALWAYS BELIEVED IN WOMEN'S RIGHTS and equality, but it wasn't until the last two years that I have become more vocal, and officially identified myself as a feminist – and a Jewish feminist. A major factor in my passion for feminism (and the rights of girls and women around the world) has been social media. Through social media, I have "met" some pretty amazing women, of various cultures and religions, all with rich "herstories" and experiences. I have become aware of the writings of some awesome Jewish feminists and Jewish women Rabbis, and they have opened my eyes to the impact our ancient Jewish Matriarchs and sisters made in our religion and culture. I have also become so much more aware of the suffering of girls and women worldwide at the hands of misogynist cultures and religions. I have also become so much more aware that the women of these cultures and religions are rising up and speaking out against the violence and hatred toward them. I cannot personally fight their battle for them, or tell them how they should do it, but I can support my sisters wherever they are because we are all fighting for the same core issues.

As an American woman in the Western world, I cannot impose my views and beliefs as a feminist on women of different cultures and faiths, even though I have problems with the Western World culture and don't necessarily identify with it, mostly because of my faith as a Jew. As a Jewish woman, my views, beliefs, and goals as a feminist differ from mainstream American culture, and we have different issues within our religion that need to be addressed.

I will fight my own battle, within my own world, culture, and religion, in my own way. All women are fighting for the same issues, but in different ways that relate to our own unique situation. We are all fighting for equality for all girls and women, and for us to be recognized as human beings – who have minds and voices, and who have a lot to offer this world. We all deserve the right for freedom to express ourselves the way we choose, inside and outside of our religious lives, without men dictating to us how we are supposed to do that. Women are the

23

life givers, the nurturers, and the very backbone that holds cultures and traditions together. Most cultures and religions have a rich history of the important role that women have played in the development and growth of the religion. In most cultures, it was the women who passed these traditions down to the next generation, to keep the traditions alive.

In Judaism there are many feminine references to God. The Shekhinah (the spirit of God) which is feminine, is mentioned a lot in our texts. The ancient Israelites worshipped Asherah, the wife of El, up until the destruction of the Temple around 586 B.C.E. They also worshipped the "Queen of Heaven" and, in addition, King Solomon also worshipped Asherah, alongside Yaweh. There are several names for God that are feminine, like Shaddai (which means breast). Israel, and Zion are referred to as feminine. Somewhere along the way, the roles of women and the importance they played were suppressed and the ancient religion was totally replaced with patriarchal-run institutionalized religion. Misogyny and the demonization of women and the Divine Feminine took over. God became only a man.

In my Jewish faith we have a lot of feminists who have and who are now changing the face of Judaism, but we still have problems, and misogyny is still alive and well. I live in the dessert Southwest United States, and I am a member of and attend a Conservative synagogue. I attend this synagogue because I love, admire, and respect my Rabbi, and our rich Anusim/Sephardic community. I do wish though that our community was more progressive/liberal, and more accepting of the Divine Feminine/Hebrew Goddess. That has not stopped me however, from trying to introduce more feminine focused teachings and programs at my synagogue, and although my Rabbi is very supportive and encouraging, the community seems lukewarm, and only a few are interested.

My synagogue is what is called "egalitarian." According to the Stanford Encyclopedia of Philosophy, this means that all humans are equal in fundamental worth or social status. The definition of "egalitarian" in Conservative Judaism, means that women can be counted in the minyan (a quorum of ten Jewish adults required in Judaism for public worship) since 1973.

For example, the Torah cannot be taken out during services without a minyan. Egalitarian synagogues can also have ordained women Rabbis, Cantors, educators, and gay and lesbian Rabbis. But just because a synagogue is egalitarian, does not mean all the men or women accept that. That's where there is a problem.

In my congregation, if a man or a woman prays using the names of the Matriarchs (Sarah, Rivkah, Raquel, Leah), eyes will roll. The Torah's teachings are written mostly by men, about men. My Rabbi, who is super supportive of the women, allows me to deliver lessons on the Torah from a Feministic perspective. I've heard responses by men in my synagogue that we don't need to address the women, they are already assumed. What's that? If their roles are assumed, then why can't we talk about them? If you agree that God is both masculine and feminine, what's wrong with using feminine gender language when talking about God? I hear all the time that the masculine descriptions of God are gender neutral. What's wrong with including feminine descriptors for God as gender neutral then?

There are other traditions in Judaism that are considered for men only. Women are discouraged from participating in them, using the argument that women don't need these activities, because we are more spiritual than men – or that we are so busy at home that we are excused from these responsibilities. This is nothing more than men trying to keep us away, and we women have bought it.

Wearing tefilin (the black leather prayer boxes with leather straps, worn on the arm and head during weekday morning prayers) and tzit tzit are discouraged for women. I myself wear tefilin, use a prayer shawl, and have worn tzit tzit under my clothing. I am not concerned about the approval of others and I choose to express my faith in a way that makes me comfortable. I also caused a bit of a stir because I asked why women were not called upon during services to carry the Torah. So now I (and some other women) have been asked to carry the Torah. However, there are some men that will not touch and "kiss" the Torah if a woman is carrying it.

I recently started a women's Rosh Kodesh group to get more women into the synagogue for Rosh Kodesh morning services.

Rosh Kodesh celebrates the New Moon and marks the new Jewish month – which is and has been traditionally a women's holiday, celebrated by women. Since the moon is feminine, this is only natural, but a lot of Jewish women have very little knowledge of or desire to continue the practices of Jewish women in ancient times. I also wanted us as a group to learn about and discuss the divine feminine within our own religious texts and customs. What surprises me is the apprehension and lack of interest by women to learn about and embrace the Divine Feminine. But I am not going to quit... I will continue to get more women interested, even if it's just a few of us. I have started a hand drumming / healing circle for women only – to connect with our inner God/dess and tap into Her healing energy. I have had gatherings at my home, and I am now planning to host them at my synagogue.

Other branches of Judaism, like the Orthodox, Ultra-Orthodox, and Chasidic, are not egalitarian, and there is a great deal of inequality when it comes to women and their role within the religion. More and more women in Judaism are speaking out and demanding change. For example, in Israel, in certain neighborhoods and situations girls and women are spit on and harassed if they are not covered up enough (the rules on how girls and women are supposed to dress are enforced by men!) and have to sit in the back of some buses. A Jewish divorce in Israel cannot happen unless the man gives the woman a "get," and right now, only the man can initiate this. We still have much work ahead of us to bring about equality so that women are treated with the same respect as any other human being. But this is not going to happen if we women are not comfortable with our own Divine Feminine. We need to embrace Her ourselves *first,* and realize how important Her role is.

In Kabbalah (mystical Judaism) there is a concept called "Tikkun Olam" which alludes to *repairing the world.* It is my personal belief that true and complete Tikkun Olam cannot and will not occur until there is a balance of masculine and feminine energy in the world. Right now there seems to be a battle to destroy the Divine Feminine and all the beauty that is part of it. It should not be about one energy dominating over the other, both are necessary, and both have to work together, because both are equal halves of the One Whole. To hate and destroy the Divine Feminine, is to hate and destroy the One we all come from.

Our Jewish texts still have some feminine references to God. Some of the female prophetesses are mentioned – and the important roles the women had are still hinted at, as they could not suppress Her completely. She left a trail, and if you look deep enough, you will find Her. The Shekhinah is rising, and She will claim Her rightful place.

As a Muslim Feminist

Shehnaz Haqqani

I HAVE BEEN A FEMINIST ever since I began to engage with patriarchy as a conscious human being. That was also the same time when I realized that I was not the only woman struggling for space to breathe in a misogynistic world that strives to suck out every spirit of being from women, from people of color, from "minorities." This started in my late teenage years when I began noting gendered double standards in the way that the community I was being raised in dealt with issues of gender and sexuality. I grew tired of it to the point where I have wanted to scream ever since. And it's been over a decade. But the reasons are too multifaceted to be attributed to misogyny alone. And the only things that have kept me sane and given me reasons to be enthusiastic about this world and women's and gendered minorities' future are feminism and feminist initiatives.

Let me clarify here that I am a Muslim, and I identify specifically as an Islamic feminist. I'm a Muslim Islamic feminist. It is important that I emphasize my religion here because western feminism has traditionally tended to discredit other forms of feminism, particularly feminists of faith, feminists of color, feminists who are otherwise not privileged due to their socioeconomic status. My struggles as a feminist working toward gender equality and justice are similar to the struggles of other feminists, but my struggles also differ in that I have another current working against me alongside patriarchy: Islamophobia in the West.

As a Muslim feminist who is sincerely devoted to Islam, I am constantly combating two major forces – misogyny within Muslim communities and within patriarchal Islamic traditions that date back to the 7th century and before – *in addition to* non-Muslims and ex-Muslims whose shortsightedness prevents them from recognizing any beauty in any religion but, at the moment, specifically in Islam. And, frankly, as a Muslim feminist, I am tired of the mockery of Islam by non-Muslims and former Muslims whose bigotry and insincerity mislead them into thinking that the identity of "Islamic feminist" is an oxymoron. They seem to believe that no brain-possessing woman can and should be valuing Islam as her religion because Islam, and no other religion but Islam alone, is supposedly inherently misogynistic. This ignorance is rooted in today's unfortunate politics of Islam and Muslims' relations with the West, in the assumption that the identities of Muslim and Western are mutually exclusive, in the misguiding claim that Islam, and no other religion but Islam alone, is a stagnant religion and tradition that lacks room for fluidity and has no movements within it for re-interpretations, which all other religions apparently automatically come packed with. This fabricated image of Islam, and no other religion but Islam alone, as incapable of guiding its followers toward positive change needs to be countered with the reality of Islam and Muslims and specifically of Muslim feminists: We exist! We have always existed! And we will never stop existing! And we are constantly speaking out.

There is plenty of dialogue among Muslims themselves, and with Muslims' and Muslim feminists' allies, there is plenty of scholarship and literature from within Islam, there is a strong enough voice from Muslims and Muslim feminists themselves to promote positive change and gender justice in our societies and communities, and we therefore do not need the voice of those who consistently interrupt us and try to break our voices, who claim that we have no voice and that they need to "give voice" to us.

We have a voice; we simply lack the appropriate audience from time to time—and that audience includes all those who believe any of the following popular claims: "Islamic feminism is an oxymoron," or "Islam oppresses women (unlike all other patriarchal / misogynistic religions, obviously)," "Muslim women need a voice (sometimes better known politically as 'Muslim women need saving')," or "Women in Islam versus women in the West." If you believe any of these things, we the Muslim feminists need you to be silent and listen to us speak about ourselves instead of speaking for us.

As a Muslim feminist, I am tired of explaining that there is no contradiction between my feminist values and my religious beliefs because my religion is just as open to interpretations and re-interpretations as any other religion; it has always been that way, and it will always be that way because that is how religions work—their texts are intentionally ambiguous and speak to their audiences and followers in their own time and space, as any good text does. Hardly any Muslim will deny that Islam recognizes women's rights in theory, but few of us follow through with those rights. Feminism for me, and Islamic feminism specifically, is the bridge between the theory that Islam recognizes and values women's rights and the practice of working toward implementing those rights in Muslim communities.

As a Muslim feminist, I am done with popping all the bubbles blown for me, breaking all the categories created for me, transcending all the boundaries demarcated for me—because they do not fit me, they do not represent me, they do not speak to me, and they are not me. They are not large enough, not wide enough for me to fit into them. No, rather, let me rephrase: I do not want to fit into them because I am not one to be satisfied with anything created *for* me without my consent. I am dynamic like my faith is, and I fluctuate like my faith does. As a Muslim feminist, I have the full capacity and the full knowledge of myself and my faith to create my own space for myself. I do not work within lines and boundaries; I have never done so, and I will never do so. I do not thank anyone for trying to help when their understanding of "helping" me is a condescending, degrading enforcement of their own values on me, when their "help" is in effect a mockery of me, my faith, my beliefs, and of a people whose number exceeds a billion—the Muslims of the world.

As a Muslim feminist, I am tired of reminding those feminists who believe they know what's best for all other women all over the world that they have a right to speak only for their individual selves. No two experiences, no two individuals, let alone multiple groups of women or other genders and sexes on multiple continents, are alike. To pretend we understand each other just because we are all women is to dishonor our own core feminist values of justice, of equality, of inclusiveness, of recognizing all women's ability and power to represent their own struggles because they are capable of doing so. The only thing they need from us, the only thing that we all need from each other, is solidarity; we need love and support as we navigate through a world that has falsely been perceived as created *for* us and not *by* us.

As a Muslim feminist, I am tired, so tired, of asserting my being, proving my existence in a world that doesn't tire of attempting to silence me on every front, suppress my voice by claiming that I have none because I do not exist, because I am an oxymoron, that I'm a living, walking, talking contradiction. I am tired of saying I'm not. I'm a living, conscious, active being; I'm a feminist Muslim and a Muslim feminist who lives to fight misogyny, Islamophobia, and all other forms of bigotry no matter who I have to fight in the process. I call for other feminists and activists who believe in justice and peace for *all*, not just for those who share their experiences, beliefs, understanding of life, or even the struggles they face.

Just as well, as a Muslim feminist, I am incredibly grateful to all those feminists and allies who have stood by me and other Muslim feminists because they understand that feminism has no one meaning, that to limit feminism and its definitions is to tear it from the root and never see it grow again. This world is beautiful, and it can remain so only if we listen to each other's voices and appreciate each other's capacity and right to speak for ourselves instead of being spoken for. Feminism is a beautiful thing, and to acknowledge, support, and embrace each other is to allow feminism to remain beautiful and blossom with each feminist voice that differs from our own.

The Goddess Movement:
A Global Awakening

Priestess Bairavee Balasubramaniam, PhD

THIS IS A MASSIVE AWAKENING, with multiple geographic epicenters arising in tandem. Political changes in Africa and the rising of female leadership, the energizing of public discourse on sexual attitudes and the 'causal' attitudes of rape in India, women's voices emerging from the Middle East – point to this being something that is happening across the globe. Clearly, the awakening is spreading like wildfire in the West, and that is something to be cherished and celebrated in its own right – but that does not make the West its epicenter.

On more than one site, I have seen casual references to how this Re-Awakening is a 'Western' (read: Caucasian or North American / European) phenomenon and that women from those regions will lead the way for others. When I hear or read about how the West will re-ignite the Goddess movement, I feel dismayed and to me history begins to echo once more.

I immediately recall the patronizing discourse of 'educating the natives' that arose with the earliest proselytizing attempts in Africa and Asia. I recall how the modus operandi of repressive, colonial regimes (in India for example) was to alleviate the suffering of the oppressed women there, who needed freeing from the shackles of their own religions and customs. That led to the codification of a multiplicity of Indian traditions, and in one single blow outlawed certain controversial customs, but also de-legitimized the many practices of peoples of the so-called 'lower' castes who had far more fluid attitudes toward marriage and sexuality (a step backwards you could say). Many other examples from the history of colonialism and the ideological machine that legitimated it provide so many examples of the same.

When we look to history, we see that any teleological (different from theological) explanation or description given to mass movements has almost inevitably reflected entrenched power hierarchies. In the narrative that I see arising, the West is (once again) the center of the globe – this time with its women, rather than its men, bringing Enlightenment for the Globe. And I find this a mistake that we can avoid, with some circumspection, critical thought and consideration.

Many of the compassionate, awakening, men and women I have on my site are Caucasian, and some of the most evolved spiritual individuals and teachers I know are Caucasian. So I have no issues there, no reason to argue why Western men and women cannot or should not be a part of this movement. What I find problematic is when a particular racial and/or geographic group begins to be uncritically hailed as 'leaders' for others to follow.

When we make such categories, when we draw the spiritual geography of this Earth with a particular location of the globe as its center, we make the same kinds of boundaries, hierarchies and power relations which so many of us on the Goddess Path rejected so heavily when it appeared through the institution of patriarchy. Let us avoid making the same judgments when so many of us seek equality and a leveling of the playing field.

We are at a critical time now where our movement has begun to amass enough energy that it stands at the brink of divergence, fragmentation, consolidation – or some other process. We get to choose to avoid the errors of the past, we get to choose to not have to re-learn the lessons of history – just as so many of us are beginning to see the need for herstory or even, ourstory.

For some who might think this to be a 'trivial' point, it is important to bear in mind that discourse – the way we talk about things – reflects, very powerfully, the way we think about things. When we privilege any one race or region as being the focus, we (whether we do so consciously or unconsciously) relegate other centers to a peripheral focus. This was the thrust of the ideological machine used to justify colonialism and bringing 'God to the natives'. This is the reason why the World Map we all know makes Africa smaller than it is and exaggerates the size of the United Kingdom.

And on top of everything else – for those you who integrate an understanding of the Earth's Kundalini (The Serpent of Light) and its rising in December 2012 – the epicenter of that awakening took place in the Andean Mountains of Peru. Ironically, it is in 'the West', but not part of what most people mean when they use that term. Their teachings are sifting further and further into collective consciousness, but few ever consider this sacred site to be the 'center' of the awakening, and frankly, one does not have to!

This is a movement, as I understand it, for all. For men and women from North, South, East, West. It is a moment where we get to equalize. Where we get to right the wrongs of the past, or at the very least, to create a new balance that celebrates plural perspectives and provides multiple centers.

Unfortunately – and feel free to disagree with this if this is not your perspective – as a Priestess of Colour and a scholar of politics and history, I find that a lot of Western discourse and attitudes toward the spiritual traditions that have found center-stage in the 'New Age' movement are far too reminiscent of the ideology and attitudes of Orientalist scholars studying the 'exotic' other. So many traditions are being appropriated and given new life, which is a wonderful thing, but they are being done so in ways that do not always look at the reality of the people who live in the contemporary regions those spiritual teachings emanate from.

The spiritual teachings that so much of the New Age subscribes to very often co-exist paradoxically with oppressive, unequal realities for women in other parts of the globe. The beauty of Goddesses and the words that describe them in scripture fly across Facebook walls, but with few reflections on how a land that produced such prose can still kill its daughters and view them as burdens. Very often, these traditions become romanticized in themselves, and the critical question of – Why didn't it work before? Why didn't it empower the women of the land to rise? – is completely missed.

And to me, these are critical questions and provide a key opportunity for us to engage with traditions of the past and identify new pathways for change. We may need to revisit or revamp these traditions that have on the one hand elevated female metaphysical energies, but barred its daughters from real positions of power – be it in politics, or even in the right to hold spiritual office... or even to enter a temple during their menstrual period, if only to open their Heart to The Divine. Whilst honoring traditions are important, idealizing them to the point that the key questions – of what didn't work and what needs reworking? – needs to be equally addressed. And to this effect, the local knowledge and awakening that is happening concurrently in different global epicenters needs to be honored, integrated and seen as a valuable part of the Goddess Movement.

In the name of respecting 'ancient traditions of the East / South', let us not uncritically mouth the same ideology that somehow kept the women of those lands suppressed / oppressed.

Let me give you a concrete example: I have seen a rise in artistic and photographic imagery of the Goddess Kali / Durga as a Caucasian woman. (Nothing wrong with that). But as a movement, little consideration is given to the message that imparts to women (from India) who are considered to be too 'low' to ever think of themselves as Goddesses. Have you ever seen a Laxmi with Dark Skin? Or one that wasn't flawless? Ironically, at an anti-rape protest event that I participated in, I saw Indian women carrying placards that said that 'we don't need to be goddesses, just treat us as people'. Coming from the land of a million goddesses, this is a powerful statement.

What do we do with those messages? And why are they valued less, or sub-consciously perhaps, integrated less in the mainstream of this movement? We have so much to learn from the fierce self-assertion in the West (in this example) and the desire to assert oneself/be counted outside of the context of religion as expressed by Indian women. But until we see both 'ways of knowing' as equal, each side is bound to repeat the painful mistakes of the other... Food for thought...

In closing:

Daughters and Sons of the Mother, wherever you are, whatever the colour of your skin may be – now is the time to Rise. Together, we are all — at the Center.

With Respect,
Bairavee, Daughter of Kali

Seeking Sophia: How a Christian Girl Found Her Spiritual Home on a Yoga Mat

Monette Chilson

She is the light that shines forth from everlasting light,
the flawless mirror of the dynamism of God
and the perfect image of the Holy One's goodness.
Though alone of Her kind, She can do all things;
though unchanging, She renews all things;
generation after generation She enters into holy souls
and makes them friends of God and prophets,
for God loves the one
who finds a home in Wisdom [Sophia].
She is more beautiful than the sun
and more magnificent than all the stars in the sky.
When compared with daylight,
She excels in every way,
for the day always gives way to night,
but Wisdom [Sophia] never gives way to evil.
She stretches forth Her power
from one end of the earth to the other
and gently puts all things in their proper place.

(Wisdom of Solomon 7:26-8:1, The Inclusive Bible)

I WOULD HAVE STOPPED DOODLING MERMAIDS and fallen off the worn oak pew in awed wonder had someone read me these verses as a child growing up in a small town Southern Baptist Church. Especially if they had invoked the name of Sophia (Greek for Wisdom). Desperate to see myself reflected in my religion, I longed for someone to look beneath the patriarchal doctrine and dogma and show me that I was a part of the grand epic woven in the pages of the Bible. Someone to assure me that God wasn't the exclusively masculine being described from every pulpit I'd encountered in my young life.

I stumbled through my formative years, grasping at the good in my faith tradition, while grappling with the parts that didn't make sense to me. I couldn't shake the feeling that something was missing. I just didn't know where to find it. Often, I found myself going back to the same dry well, looking for water. I faithfully played Mary every year in the church Christmas pageant, joined Girls in Action (like Baptist Girl Scouts), memorized famous women missionaries and studied their lives, looking for clues to what inspired their faith. My freshman year in college, I frequented the Baptist Student Union. I know now that doing the same thing over and over again and expecting different results is the definition of insanity. It was the only way I knew to live back then. I was searching for the spiritual essence of my faith, but I kept coming up empty-handed—or worse, disillusioned and dejected.

Luckily, God's ways are always more expansive than mine. I was slowly drawn along a path that makes sense in retrospect, one that honored some inner wisdom regarding my physical and spiritual self. I was the oddball who asked for a juicer for Christmas one year in high school. Then I stopped eating meat after writing a paper on vegetarianism my sophomore year in college. I was always intrigued by yoga and finally began practicing a few years out of school. Through this progression, I learned to be true to myself—the person God was calling me to be—even when it went against the grain of my Southern upbringing.

I didn't know that my yoga practice would be the antidote to the unrest I felt with my religious life. I had no idea the missing piece of practical spiritual wisdom I'd been seeking would appear as I sat on a mat in an incense-filled room listening to unfamiliar words chanted in Eastern tongues. How strange it felt to have finally found my spiritual home while simultaneously fearing I was betraying my faith tradition.

On my mat I felt the part of God that had eluded me for years. God flowed into me on my breath, moved through my limbs and settled into my heart center at the end of my practice. Suddenly God was free to be God, or rather I was freed to experience God without the inferences of maleness. It took me a while to recognize God in this new guise. There were no robes, crosses or religious icons to tip me off. I could see myself reflected in this new divine vision.

While today I intuitively interpret that feeling as God at work in me, back then I didn't know what to make of it. I knew it felt spiritual, but I had no way to explain this newfound spirituality or to integrate it into my religious beliefs. For a while, it worked because I had put religion on hold during my post-college twenty-something years. I simply buried my fears about yoga being contrary to the Christianity of my youth. My yogic spirituality sustained me, while I pointedly avoided organized religion. When my husband and I became parents and decided to go back to church in our thirties, I began the process of reconciling the two.

First I tried making my yoga Christian. I thought it quite clever to find Bible verses to accompany my favorite poses. For example, I used Psalm 45:3-4, "Strap your sword to your side, warrior! Accept praise! Accept due honor! Ride majestically! Ride triumphantly! Ride on the side of truth! Ride for the righteous meek!" (The Message) to sanctify warrior pose. I had corresponding verses for bow pose, child's pose, mountain pose and others. I convinced myself that if I read Bible verses with my poses, they would be redeemed. That my faith and my practice would become one. I was bridging the chasm with holy words.

I developed and taught a class using this approach. We opened by meditating to a folksy version of the classic Christian hymn *Be Thou My Vision* and ended by listening to my good friend Robbie Seay's *Breathe Peace in Savasana* (still a favorite of mine). In between, we did yoga poses to a litany of Bible verses I had carefully chosen as the soundtrack to our practice. While this Christianized yoga was a valuable stepping stone for me, it ultimately felt contrived—like I was trying to make both yoga and Christianity something they weren't. I had yet to realize that the chasm I was attempting to bridge didn't exist. The two weren't as spiritually incompatible as I had been led to believe.

I knew that the sacred source I encountered on my yoga mat was not male. In fact, it felt distinctly feminine to me. Was it because I was finally seeing myself mirrored in God? Or was there, legitimately, a female side of God that existed in my faith tradition? How could this have been overlooked or ignored by so many? And why did I find her here in my yoga practice instead of in church? Did I dare to explore this unorthodox view I was beginning to espouse?

It was these questions that ultimately set in motion the research that culminated in this book. It was this quest that lead me to

Sophia and enabled me to practice both yoga and Christianity without internal conflict or angst. The answers I found made me whole again. It is my fervent hope that my experience will light the way for others out there looking for their own answers, seeking to integrate their yogic and religious lives.

Though we may be on similar trajectories, each of our paths is our own. Sophia was the key to my spiritual reconciliation. Her role in your journey may be significant or peripheral. In either case, you owe it to yourself to meet her.

Greek for wisdom, Sophia surfaces repeatedly in both the Christian and Hebrew[4] Scriptures, yet her identity remains unclear. Some see Sophia as a deity in her own right, others see her as representing the Bride of Christ (Revelation 19), others as a feminine aspect of God representing wisdom (Proverbs 8 and 9), and still others as a theological concept regarding the wisdom of God. Sophia, by her very nature, defies definition, allowing us to revel in the mystery that surrounds her.

She is there within each and every one of us—male and female—whether we choose to embrace or deny her existence. She is the Holy Spirit. She is the breath we breathe. She is God-given, not something women dreamed up to make us feel better about being left out of all the starring roles in the Bible. The truth is, we weren't left out. Sophia was there all along, beckoning to us—right along with Jesus. And it's not just women who were short-changed in the masculinization of God. Men, too, long to be able to experience God holistically, to acknowledge and rest in the feminine side of God.

Most of us will pay lip service to the fact that God transcends gender, but our experience—because of the stigma associated with the feminine divine in Western religions—does not include prayers, images or words that let us express this truth. Whether the aversion to referring to God in feminine terms stems from patriarchal roots, a desire by early Christians to separate themselves from Goddess worship or to differentiate themselves

---

4 The Jewish faith would, obviously, use the Hebrew translation of Wisdom rather than the Greek word Sophia. Because of its nuances, you might find Wisdom expressed as khokhma (wisdom) חכמה, bina (understanding) בינה, da'at (knowledge) דעת or tvuna (another word for understanding) הנובת.

from Gnostic communities, the result has been a severing of the sacred feminine that has silenced voices that would pray to God our Mother. Sophia embodies those missing pieces, giving us the prayers, images and words we need to complete our limited human perspective on who God is—and who God wants to be—in our lives.

Bringing that awareness of Sophia into focus is a function of being, rather than doing. It is passive, not active, and it requires us to back off and surrender to that voice that is whispering to us even when our internal dialog drowns it out. So how do we listen to a voice we can't hear? There are many ways to attune ourselves to divine utterances. The commonality of all these paths lies in the contemplative stance they require and deep spiritual connection they illicit. In psychological parlance, an introverted practice is needed to balance the extroverted world in which we live.

Yoga, in its fullness (not just the poses), can provide spiritual seekers with the tools they need to start hearing that sacred song they've been missing. By providing a space devoid of any pre-programmed liturgy, sermons or psalms, they allow us to sit with God. To move with God. Even to chant melodious syllables full of life force to God. Finally, to discover God.

When we sit in a church pew (regardless of the religion), we are surrounded by others' perceptions of God, both visual and spoken. When we sit on our yoga mat, we are carving out space for our own spiritual life to coalesce. Creating our inner sanctuaries and opening ourselves up to God's presence untainted and unfiltered by religious precepts. Yoga doesn't create the sacred. It merely reveals it in many beautiful ways.

Used with permission from Bright Sky Press.

We Should Look Within Ourselves

Rebecca Mott

I DO NOT BELIEVE – partly because I cannot believe – in any force or spirit that does little or nothing to give the prostituted freedom and a sense of justice. I cannot understand the concept of all-knowing god / goddess / non-gendered spirit that allows or ignores the pain, grief and screams for help from the prostituted class for well over 3,000 years.

This is my perspective as an exited prostitute: When it comes to whether that supernatural being is listening, we are not heard. Instead, the prayers, pleas, and tears of the prostituted turn to stone and the prostituted suffer endless mental, physical, and sexual torture. Every generation of the prostituted know that Hell is all around, for every prostitute carries the evil of man under their skin.

My parents divorced when I was around 5, and my families were split on religion. My father and step mum were Church of England, but never pushed anyone to go to church, so for most of my life, I rarely attended. My mother and stepfather were atheists. I attended the Church of England school, but only because it was a good school, not because it was religious.

In my life, faith and religion have very little meaning for me – so to be honest, I do not miss it. I look within myself for strength and courage, and the older I get, the more amazed I am at how much inner strength humans have.

Like all humans (especially atheists), I have thought deeply about why I cannot or will not believe that there is a god / goddess / spirit outside of my own self. I have explored many faiths, but always come home to atheism.

When I was a child, I kneeled next to my bed with hands folded on my bed – copying the Victorian pictures I faintly remembered – and I prayed. I prayed for my stepfather not to have sex with me, I prayed for my mother to care about me, I prayed to live with my father, I prayed for the pain to end. I prayed until all I heard were the echoes of my own desperation and the feeling that I was praying to *nothing* – or if there was some kind of supernatural spirit, it did not care or was refusing to listen.

I was about 6 or 7 when I told god to sod off.

I decided that if there were any gods or goddesses, they must be like the Greeks and Romans – a universe full of gods and goddesses who had no heart, played cruel games with humans, and created pain, natural disasters, wars, illnesses, and rapes – just because they were bored or restless.

I saw that the power of being fully human is to stand up against all gods and goddesses – or that which is unjust and an abuse of power. For even as a child, I saw that gods and goddesses were invented by humans as scapegoats for our negative emotions and actions. I saw clearly that humans can control whether they choose good or turn to evil – it is just harder to be good.

The less faith I had or have, the more I see with clarity that male violence is chosen and usually pre-planned. *It is no act of the devil nor is it a turning away from faith – it is a conscious choice to have power over another human.*

Let me take a quick detour here and explain another major reason I cannot or will not believe in goddesses. My opinion is based on my understanding of the history of prostitution, and my sense that there is very little solid proof that goddesses are not made for the benefit of males.

Many ancient goddesses were fertility symbols, so in modern terms, they were the typical women who were controlled by men who kept them pregnant. Some goddesses were symbols and carriers of all that was negative in man – such as war-loving, a fury that could and was made into madness, a carrier of all that was wrong with humans.

In addition, many goddesses are just sex symbols – goddesses of love, goddesses that spread the male seed, goddesses who are wives and queens but under male dominance.

Let me make it clear why I have a deep aversion to the concept of goddesses: As an exited women, I have lived inside an environment where goddesses were portrayed everywhere as porn, as so-called female empowerment, and as the founding-stone of the myth of the Happy Hooker.

Let me be frank. Punters (men who choose to buy the prostitute) loved the concept of the whore-goddess. I learned about goddesses from "intellectual" punters who told me that I should proud of being a whore, that I had some unique spiritual karmic connection with the source of sexuality.

But why was the whore-goddess invented? Well, it is simple: So men can rape and torture the prostituted class and make it into a non-event.

This practice probably began when the first brothels were invented and were later re-framed as homes of sex goddesses, vestal virgins, and other supernatural beings that men could use for endless sex and violence. These so-called goddesses were mostly slaves, prisoners-of-war, women, and girls with no rights and no voice.

These women and girls were raped on an industrial scale – but it was re-framed that the rapes were okay, because they were goddesses who had no human connection to pain. Painted as goddesses, it became truth that the prostituted were sex-crazed, did not know human pain, and of course were never unavailable to men.

The concept of the whore-goddess is the most damaging concept I know. Because of this, it has been determined that the prostituted can never be fully human, and so cannot be raped or even abused. Being non-human, the prostituted are not allowed to speak to their grief, know and speak out their pain, or have fury.

Instead, the prostituted are expected to be happy – or be gagged and prevented from speaking their truths.

Yes, faiths have grown and changed since the Greeks and Romans, but it still very rare that faiths make any room for the authentic voices of the prostituted. Instead, most faiths will control and take ownership of how and when the prostituted can speak. Most faiths will keep the prostituted in very specific roles

– the role of carrying the evils of men; the role of the victim who must be pitied; the role of the rebel; and the role of being consumed in secret.

All of these roles are just porn-dreams of men of many faiths, roles that many women of faith (unfortunately) hold tightly to.

There are no human aspects to these roles, there no strength to these roles, there is only a deep silence.

Where is the fury that is inside the prostituted? Where is the silent screaming that each and every prostitute knows? Where is the justice, where are human rights for the prostituted? Where is the empathy from those of faith? Where is the connection of down-trodden and the prostituted class spoken about by those of faith? Where is the rage that is the foundation of abolition?

To abolish the sex trade, it is vitally important that we listen and truly hear the multiple voices of the prostituted.

Remember, all of the history of prostitution is false for it was written primarily by men who consumed and profiteered from the sex trade. The voices of the prostituted have been stripped from history, and replaced by the story of the Happy Hooker and the Victim-Whore.

Here in this moment, we may be in a time of revolution, a time where the authentic voices of the prostituted are being heard, mainly through many courageous exited women (all cultures, ages, and backgrounds) from many realms of the sex trade.

This is a very vulnerable and dangerous time for the prostituted, for the more we are respected and heard, the more the sex trade lobby will want to destroy our voices and truths.

The sex trade lobby does not believe that prostitutes should have a life outside of the sex trade. It has invested a great deal in making the prostituted as sub-human goods—and has a deep fury that there are not only prostitutes who have exited, but now speak the powerful truth about the conditions of the prostituted.

We should be dead... Or so mentally ill we cannot speak out.

An exited prostitute – one who remembers what it was to be sub-human – is to be feared, for her voice will roar until all prostituted sisters and brothers are free.

Abolition is a very hard and long journey.

But listen… Hear the power of the prostituted, and it will push you forward.

Reclaiming the
Radical Feminism of the Qur'an

Sarah Ager

*"As a feminist, how could you willingly subject
yourself to such a misogynistic religion?"*

IT IS DISHEARTENING TO THINK how many times I've been
asked this question since I converted to Islam. However,
given my own misgiving toward the status of women in Islam
before I became one myself, I'm not completely surprised that
some people think calling myself a Muslim Feminist is akin to
being a meat-eating vegan. When the majority of media
representation shoehorns Muslim women into either victim or
terrorist categories, persuading people that my feminist
convictions are given wings by my Islamic faith, as opposed to
being clipped by it, is going to be tough.

Feminism and faith have always been closely linked to one
another in my mind. I was raised in a household where both of
my parents were Protestant ministers and considered equals in
their spiritual leadership roles as Salvation Army officers. I was
surrounded and greatly influenced by women leading prayers,
congregations, and even heading up the church on a national
and global scale. Women leading the way in faith has always
been my norm. So when I converted to Islam, I found myself at
the receiving end of the question: why would you give all that
up?

When I became a Muslim, I didn't shut out the voices of my
Christian friends but rather opened myself up to new voices
from the Muslim community, or *ummah*. Rather than losing
something, my network of friends and acquaintances has been
enriched by a multitude of gutsy Muslim women from around the
world whose activism covers a wide range of areas, from politics
to sport, as well as specific issues within the *ummah*, such as
appropriate mosque spaces for women, internal racism, and
discrimination against LGBT Muslims.

But when we strip away the cultural and theological differences
between Islam and Christianity, are the struggles women go

through really so different? Many of the obstacles I observed or experienced as a Christian woman are similar to those faced by Muslim women now, from lack of equal representation to shared frustration that women's voices are often dismissed. Naturally, these problems vary in degree and manifest themselves in different ways but women of faith in both traditions come up against negative attitudes toward women or Patriarchal structures that attempt to silence or, whether intentionally or as a side effect, inhibit spiritual growth.

Religious communities do not operate within an ideological or cultural vacuum. Therefore, interpretation of sacred texts at a specific point in history tends to reflect the prevailing views of that particular society. If a community, or the society at large, allows misogyny to roam around unchecked, then sadly it's going to find a way into our mosques, churches, or temples. Any negative or prejudiced attitudes that are present have the potential to influence theological interpretation and this can result in practises that engender the unequal treatment of women.

These attitudes need to be confronted head on. This is where Muslim Feminism comes in because although the essential problems that women of faith encounter are often similar, they need to be addressed within the specific context of that faith tradition. Muslims or Christians cannot simply copy and paste the other religion's unique brand of Feminist thought onto their historically, theologically, and culturally diverse traditions. Solutions have to grow organically from within. If we merely graft one community's solutions onto the other, we end up with a mismatch that won't take root or will be outright rejected because it bears no relation to the needs of that community.

Before we can talk about the broad topic of Muslim Feminism, we first have to address resistance to the word 'Feminism' itself among certain members of the Muslim community. As I mentioned before, I understand that many non-Muslims find it hard to come to grips with the concept of Muslim Feminism, but what really shocked me when I converted was the discovery that a significant number of Muslims themselves believe Feminism and Islam to be incompatible. For critics of Islam, it would be easy to assume this reluctance to even entertain the idea of Feminism is proof that Muslims conform to an inherently

47

sexist ideology; however, there are several layers to this issue which have yet to be unpacked.

When I speak out about the need to change negative attitudes toward women in certain Muslim communities, I inevitably come across responses along the lines of:

'Look, you don't need all this Feminism nonsense, sister' (and never has that word been more patronising than in this context) *'don't you know Islam gave women their rights over 1,400 years ago?'*

There's certainly a lot of truth in that final statement. The Qur'an and hadith, the sayings attributed to Prophet Muhammad (peace be upon him), contain striking instances of women receiving rights which were unprecedented at the time when the holy book was revealed. The Qur'an clearly states that women have the right to inherit[5], earn a living[6], choose a spouse,[7] retain their family name, own property before and after marriage[8], vote[9], divorce[10], and the right to obtain an education[11]. As for the latter, the Quran actually goes one step further and calls the acquisition of knowledge a duty for both men and women.

The wives of Muhammad (peace be upon him) are great examples of women leading the way for the tradition of Feminists in Islam. His first wife Khadijah was a successful business woman in trade and was actually the employer of her future husband. In fact, Muhammad (peace be upon him) was initially hesitant to ask for Khadijah's hand in marriage since he didn't have enough money to provide for a wife, but since she had the means to support herself, Khadijah agreed to marry him anyway.[12] His youngest wife, Aisha, was a highly praised

---

[5]Surah Nisa, Chapter 4, Verse 7

[6]Surah Nisa, Chapter 4, Verse 32

[7]Surah Nisa, Chapter 4, Verse 19

[8]Leila Badawi, "Islam", in Jean Holm and John Bowker, ed., Women in Religion (London: Pinter Publishers, 1994) p. 102.

[9]Surah Al-Mumtahinah, Chapter 60, Verse 12

[10]Surah Al-Baqarah, Chapter 2, Verses 229-230

[11]Surah Iqra and Surah Alaq Chapter 96, Verse 1-5

[12]Abdul Malik Mujahid, *Golden Stories of Sayyida Khadijah*, (Riyadh: Darussalem, 2012), p. 40

scholar who narrated over two thousand hadiths, delivered public speeches, and fought for social change.[13] Then there are prominent figures in later Islamic societies like Fatima Muhammad Al-Fihri who founded a mosque and madrasa in Fes in 859 and Jahanara Begum who took an active role in helping the poor and sponsoring the building of mosques.

I sometimes get the feeling however, that these examples of gender equality have, sadly, produced a sort of self-congratulatory attitude among certain scholars and lay Muslims (to borrow a helpful Christian term) in the here and now. Focusing on these milestones can result in complacency, a feeling that all the work for gender equality has already been done, which would render Muslim Feminists redundant. After all, if Islam already has women's rights covered, then it doesn't need, what is sometimes perceived to be, the Western influence of modern Feminism coming in and disrupting things. This view, however, completely misses the point of what most Muslim Feminists are trying to achieve.

Muslim Feminists recognise the rights given to women and seek to recapture the original vision of the Qur'an. This doesn't mean replicating the society of that time, but using the Qur'an as a template for a society which constantly evolves and strives for greater equality in the age in which we live.

To do this, we cannot be passive observers. Women's rights cannot magically jump out of the pages of the Qur'an and apply themselves to Muslim individuals, communities, and countries whose laws are influenced to various degrees by Islamic teaching. They have to be actively implemented in present day society otherwise they become meaningless. Likewise, the rights granted to women way back when cannot be used as a defense against sexism and misogyny now. Religious institutions, leaders, and believers have a responsibility to be active vehicles for social justice and to move with the times so that practises remain relevant to those who live out the faith in their daily lives. If they don't, they run the risk of alienating believers and even turning them off religion altogether.

---

[13]Aleem, Shamim. *Prophet Muhammad(s) and His Family: A Sociological Perspective.* (Bloomington: AuthorHouse, 2007) p. 130.

More young Muslims, especially women, have been turning away from traditional means of worship in mosques because either they do not feel welcome or they disagree with the messages being taught. This growing trend, in conjunction with the rise of the internet, has resulted in an increase of online faith communities where people can find support and inspiration within a global network.

Online faith communities have been a great source of inspiration and encouragement for me as a new Muslim living in Italy, where mosque scarcity and language barriers mean I am currently unmosqued. By searching online, I discovered and became part of an active and vocal community of Muslim women around the world. Not only are these Muslim women encouraging spiritual growth within their own tradition but also placing great value on interfaith friendships with women of diverse faiths, recognising our shared desire to grow closer to the divine and to one another as part of the same global body.

I am inspired by the boundless passion, strength, and striking honesty of the women of faith I encounter who are challenging the status quo within their respective traditions and adding their voices to public discourse, as well as amplifying the voices of others. By sharing together we can learn from each other's struggles and successes – and gain deeper understanding of diverse traditions. We know that real change takes a long time and there are huge hurdles to overcome along the way, but when we take into account past achievements and the inspiring work happening in the present, we can take heart that it is well within our power to create a fairer, more inclusive world.

REFERENCES

Abdul Malik Mujahid, *Golden Stories of Sayyida Khadijah*, (Riyadh: Darussalem, 2012)

Asma Society, Women in Islam, (accessed 16/09/14)
http://www.asmasociety.org/religion/women.html

Leila Badawi, "Islam", in Jean Holm and John Bowker, ed., Women in Religion (London: Pinter Publishers, 1994)

Shamim Aleem, *Prophet Muhammad(s) and His Family: A Sociological Perspective.* (Bloomington: AuthorHouse, 2007)

A feminist history of menstruation

Metis

O NCE UPON A TIME in primitive societies, menstruating women were made to walk through paddy fields because they were shedding "blood of life" from their bodies that was believed to help crops grow. This theory has only recently been proved to be correct when researchers and scientists have claimed that "cells coming out of menstrual blood are highly regenerative" and scientists have used stem cells from menstrual blood to save limbs[14].

Let us go back a few thousand years – primitive people believed that women were far more powerful than men and if a menstruating woman ran naked through a field in the night, the power of her menstrual blood would destroy all crop worms. It was this power that made ancient South American Indians maintain that humans were created from "moon blood" since fertility was attributed to the moon in early cultures. The gods of the moon, like Ishtar, Quilla, Dschan, Selene, and Luna were female and often linked to fertility.

Similarly, the Mesopotamian mother goddess, Ninhursag, was believed to have created humans out of her "blood of life" and Mesopotamian women made loam dolls for conception by painting them with their menstrual blood. This would be a perfect place to mention that the meaning of the name of the first man in many religions, Adam, means "*bloody loam*" and many ancient cultures believed that humans are created from "coagulated blood."

It was in ancient Egypt that taboo against menstruation can be first found. An inscription at the Hathor temple has a list of gods with their specific dislikes; one god disliked menstruating women because they were seen as extremely powerful and a likely threat to patriarchy. However, in general public sphere menstruation was considered to have a life-giving and healing effect and was used for producing medicines and ointments.

---

[14] http://www.newscientist.com/article/dn14559-stem-cells-from-menstrual-blood-save-limbs.html?DCMP=ILC-hmts&nsref=news8_head_dn14559#.VO4B_fmUeSo

Interestingly, menstrual blood was supposed to have a cleansing effect. For example, in ancient spells for mother and child menstrual blood was used as ointment to protect newborns from demons.

In a "Wisdom Text" from ancient Egypt there are hints about menstrual hygiene particularly the ancient use of tampons made from several types of material like flax, papyrus and cotton. It is believed that Isis was the inventor of the first tampon in the form of the "Isis knot[15]." We also now know that "sham menstruation"[16] and "sex-strike" was used by primitive women to *oppress men*.

Four hundred years before Jesus was born, Greeks firmly believed in the life-giving qualities of menstrual blood. Aristotle wrote in the 4th century BC that a fetus was born entirely out of menstrual blood and the role of the man was only to act as a 'catalyst.' Gradually Aristotelian view was displaced within 300 years by Greek myths that the woman's body merely provided a vessel for the child, which was in fact entirely created by semen. Thus, although up till the end of the 18th century and early 19th century it was the Aristotelian theory that was taught in medical schools throughout the world, major world religions took a deep interest in the patriarchal view presented by the later Greek myths. We, therefore, have Scriptures teaching both views: Aristotelian view that a fetus is made entirely of coagulated menstrual blood and the Greek myth that it is made entirely of semen. Both views, we know today, are wrong.

Slowly men began to fear powerful women and aimed to bring them down by firmly establishing patriarchy and teaching that menstruation was taboo:

The Talmud, ancient store of Jewish wisdom, states that if a woman at the beginning of her period passes between two men, she kills one of them. The Lebanese believe that the woman's shadow causes flowers to wither; a menstruating woman, they say, will kill the horse she rides. Pliny's "Natural History" states that the touch of a menstruous woman turns wine to vinegar, blights crops,

---

[15] http://en.wikipedia.org/wiki/Tyet

[16] http://www.amazon.com/From-Interaction-Symbol-communication-Literature/dp/9027243441

kills seedlings, blasts gardens, rusts iron (especially at the waning of the moon) kills bees and causes mares to miscarry. Frazer records that in Brunswick, Germany, there is a custom that if a menstruating woman assists at the killing of a pig the pork will putrefy[17].

A menstruating woman began to be seen as unclean[18], unsafe for others, in distress[19], and even mentally disturbed[20]. Men began keeping away from menstruating women and started to believe that having intercourse with their menstruating wives would harm the women (although today science has offered theories[21] that women feel sexiest and enjoy intercourse the most during their period which actually has **benefits** for their general health and well-being!). Unfortunately, in many cultures women on their period were put away in "menstrual huts[22]" and shunned completely.

Over time, menstruation became associated with male honour and hence odd traditional practices developed like the Jewish tradition (*note: it is not a religiously sanctioned tradition*) of slapping a daughter who starts her period. It is believed that the original purpose was to "slap sense" into a newly fertile girl, warning her not to disgrace the family by becoming pregnant out of wedlock; or to "awaken" her out of her childhood slumber and into her role as a Jewish *woman.*

In Hinduism a woman is banned from even approaching a temple[23]; in Judaism and early Christianity a woman had to purify herself after period by sacrificing two turtle doves in the temple. A Muslim woman must also 'purify' herself after menstruation by taking a ritual bath. She cannot touch the Quran, fast or pray while menstruating and according to at least one oral tradition of the Prophet Muhammad, menstruation of a

---

17 http://www.asphodel-long.com/html/menstrual_taboos.html

18 http://www.atruechurch.info/sexduringmenstruation.html

19 www.islamweb.net/emainpage/index.php?page=showfatwa&Option=Fatwald&Id=87273

20 http://peacetvpage.blogspot.com/2013/08/why-muslim-women-not-allowed-praying.html

21 http://pms.about.com/od/myths/a/menstrual_myths.htm

22 http://www.longmontacupuncture.net/hut.jpg

23 http://en.wikipedia.org/wiki/Culture_and_menstruation#Indic

woman leads to "deficiency in her religion[24]." Even today when science has constantly proved men (and women) wrong and cleared many myths associated with menstruation, men use menstruation as an excuse to oppress women by claiming that "women have less of these qualities than men[25]" especially when they are menstruating. There are communities that train their girls to believe that menstruation will make them sick.

Studies have now been conducted on the influence of religion on women's menstrual well-being that show that "women who were most likely to suffer from menstrual pain and problems were the ones whose religion told them they were unclean or that they had to be submissive to men.[26]"

Unfortunately women are not trained to capture the power of menstruation which was once widely feared in the ancient world. We are never taught as growing girls that "during the time of bleeding women's ability to dream, have visions and attain altered states of consciousness is strong.[27]" We are not taught that 4,000 years ago menstruation was neither shame nor taboo but was used as harnessed power making gods out of women. Instead of being taught that the fluctuations of our bodies make us more adaptable and resistant, we are taught by our societies that we have the "curse" – a result of our 'original sin', and that we are "unclean" and "in distress."

Truth is that "menstruation is an initiatory time when women can potentially open to a highly charged altered state, giving them access to a singular kind of power. The power of self-awareness, deep feeling, knowingness, intuition. A power that matures over time with each cycle" (Alexandra Pope).

Menstruation can be the best time for a powerful spiritual experience.

---

24 http://www.usc.edu/org/cmje/religious-texts/hadith/bukhari/006-sbt.php#001.006.301

25 http://islamqa.info/en/71338

26 *Luna Yoga: Vital Fertility and Sexuality* (1997) by Adelheid Ohlig. Published by Ash Tree Publishing. Also see http://www.apa.org/monitor/oct02/pmdd.aspx

27 http://www.apa.org/monitor/oct02/pmdd.aspx

Feminism and Spirituality:
Taking Back What Was Lost

Susan Mehegan

WHEN THE PATRIARCHAL RELIGIOUS LEADERS of the early centuries relegated the Feminine Divine to the realms of secrecy, intending to silence Her for all time, they didn't count on us keeping Her alive in our stories, myths, rituals, and everyday life. We have always rested assured that while the followers of organized patriarchal religions are still waiting for their God to return, ours never left.

Women first lost their position as spiritual leaders and teachers when Egyptian pagan Hypatia, a brilliant scientist, mathematician, and philosopher, was maligned by one of the first Christian zealots, Cyril (later sainted). Cyril opposed Hypatia, claiming she represented heretical teachings, including experimental science and Pagan religion. It was said she was a woman who didn't know her place.

Cyril's preaching against Hypatia instigated a mob of Christian monks who one day dragged her from her chariot and, according to accounts from that time, stripped her, killed her, stripped her flesh from her bones, scattered her body parts through the streets, and burned some remaining parts of her body in the library of Caesareum. Lost for all time was the written record of Hypatia's work that was a treasured part of the library.

From that point on, out of fear for their lives, women allowed themselves to be kept silent in the religious, academic, and political, spheres of society. Many remain there today, with Muslim women living under the heel of their fathers and husbands, denied free movement and an education. Catholic women are denied positions as bishops and popes. Some evangelical sects in America to this day allow women to teach only children, as it is forbidden for women to teach men.

Indoctrination in Patriarchal Religion

As a female growing up in the 1950s, I accepted what I was taught, that men held positions of importance politically and culturally, while women stayed at home and performed basic tasks for their husbands and children. I was taught that there is only one God, who is father, son, and spirit, a divine family completely devoid of a mother. When expected to join the church at age 10, I declined to do so, feeling that by joining a man's church I was denying everything that it meant to be female.

I must give credit to the internet for introducing me to women's spirituality and the Feminine Divine. After years of trying to find my niche in Christian religions, studying the Bible in depth and even becoming a lay preacher and liturgist, I still felt spiritually malnourished. Several vital components were missing. While I felt a powerful connection to Nature, organized religion taught only that man has dominion over it. I never felt above Nature, but rather an integral part of it. When I finally opened myself to the creative force of the universe that can only be described as Mother, I knew at last I was home.

Like most children of my era, I had a mother, but unfortunately had never bonded with her. I longed for the embrace of Goddess spirituality and found it in my Celtic ancestry. After being taught in institutionalized religion that it was forbidden to call upon ancestors or any other teachers/masters, I could no longer deny the truth. I know where I came from and to whom I shall return. It was finally time to recognize the beauty in being female, to rise above the attitude that we must bear the "curse," and to touch within us the animus and anima as balanced spirit.

Discovering Sisterhood

Growing up a tomboy in a family without sisters and having a distant relationship with my mother, I had never felt a true sisterhood in any of my friendships with other women. This is especially true for me as a victim of childhood sexual abuse by a female babysitter. But when I finally connected to the Feminine Divine, I discovered an incredible benefit – sisters; beautiful, wonderful, spiritual women, women seeking the same spirituality and feminine foundation I was. Within the Pagan community one finds a closeness with other women that makes friendships deeper with shared spirituality opening up a level of connectedness never before experienced. Even though distance prevents most of us from virtual meetings and gatherings, shared sisterhood brings with it a bond deeper than most virtual friendships. Distance does not lessen the relationships one bit.

The competitive attitude that separates women in today's society does not exist within the Pagan community. While intellectual differences occasionally surface, the animosity and competitiveness one finds between women in different fields of endeavor has been replaced by love, respect, and acceptance of one another. Pagan women have come to support one another whether they are in their maiden, mother, or crone years. Each stage of womanhood is celebrated and cherished. Women who choose to be stay-at-home mothers are supported by their spiritual sisters; and women who choose the corporate world are never viewed as enemies of motherhood. We work together. We play together. We cheer each other on.

Taking Back What is Ours

When men took over the business of delivering babies, they sought to have complete control over the birthing process and they succeeded, even to the point of discouraging new mothers from nursing their babies, encouraging them to give manufactured formula instead. In an effort to "clean up" childbirth, women had their pubic hair shaved and endured an enema to empty their bowels. They were then propped up in stirrups so they could not move and sterile cloths were draped over them. Sometimes, if it was a matter of convenience for the doctor, the baby was delivered by caesarian section.

In ancient times, giving birth was under the control of the women. When a woman gave birth, she was assisted by a midwife and other women in the clan. There are times when a hospital setting is necessary for the health and well-being of the woman and her child, but most routine births were and are less complicated and completely natural. We are learning... Because of the Pagan feminist movement, mothers are turning more and more to midwifery for pre-natal, natal, and post-natal care.

Looking to Nature

There is nothing more natural than our bodies, sex, and healthy appetites. Within religious sects who follow biblical tenets, nature has been deemed sinful and leads one to separation from deity. The Bible gives a lesser value to female babies and considers a woman "unclean" for several days following childbirth, and for a longer period of time when she gives birth to a female child. Looking to animals in nature, we find no such distinction, and new mothers are devoted to all offspring, regardless of gender.

It is no wonder we have come to hate our bodies and seek to alter them into an impossible form that we see presented in advertisements and the media. Pagan women have left those unnatural influences behind and are happier and healthier for it emotionally as well as physically. Our cycles are the Moon's cycles and we love our sagging breasts, broad hips, gray hair, and wrinkles. We have earned them.

In nature, all places are sacred places. You do not have to build opulent temples and churches in which to find God. Deity does not reside in buildings; She resides in everything, most assuredly in those who have searched and found her within. Our hymns are the songs of the birds, the rush of the sea, and the voices in the wind. Our Mother does not hold you to Her with threats of judgment and eternal punishment. She is the purest unconditional love you will ever know. While we still make mistakes, a Pagan takes full responsibility for all actions, good and bad, in the here and now. The soul returns untainted and uncorrupted to its source.

The Moon & Ancient Faith Reconstructed

Have you ever looked into the night sky and found the Moon has a strange power to stir something deep inside you? Does gazing at every phase leave you feeling a sense of awe and peace? Our ancestors saw the Moon as sacred and a reflection of the security we have in our seasons. We who have come back to our Pagan roots experience that same awe and peace, as we recognize the Moon as being the symbol of our Creator Mother and worship Her at its fullness and darkness equally.

Blessed are women today who have discovered the Goddess within. Unconditional love is ours. We are accepted as we are and given great power to use for our benefit and the benefit of others. With our sisters there is nothing we cannot face, nothing we cannot conquer. Let us journey forth together and claim all that we deserve.

Money and the Elephant in the Room

Trista Hendren

MONEY IS USUALLY THE REALM OF MEN. Churches (also typically the realm of men) have no problem suggesting a 10% tithe, but women who put their heart and soul into feminist work are often 1) broke, and 2) afraid to ask for money.

I've also heard numerous women criticize other "successful" feminists for "making money off feminism." This has to stop. Women in *all* professions, including those who work for the liberation of women and girls, deserve to earn at least a living wage.

I spent 13 years in the mortgage industry scrutinizing the finances of all sorts of people so the topic of money does not scare me. Money comes and goes. I know that all too well personally. I've been fairly well off and I've been dead broke. I've yet to get rich off feminism. I don't know anyone who has. Most of us volunteer our time (full-time, part-time, or all-the-time) to ensure the world changes for our daughters and granddaughters.

No movement can be successful without money. We live in a capitalist society. Capitalism and interest *are* evil. My years in the mortgage industry and as a single mother cemented that for me. No one in their right mind who understood an amortization schedule would ever refinance their home again—let alone even *think* of using a credit card unless their life depended on it.

That said, we still have to gain a basic understanding of how money works so that we can use it to our advantage.

We will always be considered inferior to men if we don't bind together and re-discover our power. Since we are behind in nearly every way economically, we must carefully consider the money we do have.

Marielena Zuniga wrote a brilliant paper that will stop anyone in their tracks who says feminism is not necessary. It's entitled "Women and Poverty". Here are some startling statistics:

- "It is estimated that the gender wage gap costs the average full-time U.S. woman worker between $700,000 and $2 million over the course of her work life."

- "The UN estimates that globally women's unpaid care is worth up to $11 trillion dollars annually. A woman's time spent as an unpaid caregiver restricts her ability to perform paid work or to migrate to higher paying jobs. Not having a paid job also makes her economically dependent on someone else."

- "The disparity in employment between single mothers and fathers, the gender wage gap that inevitably affects employed single mothers, and the fact that many single mothers do not receive child support contribute to the high rate of poverty amongst female-headed households. In 2010, 31.6% of American households headed by single women were poor. In Canada, 51.6% of single-mother families live below the poverty line."

- "More than 70% of all elderly persons living in poverty are women. The wage discrimination and care giving responsibilities inflicted upon women in their earlier years makes them more susceptible to poverty in their later years. This susceptibility is exaggerated in developing nations where women typically experience a lifetime of working in the informal economy or at home as an unpaid caregiver."[28]

When I set out on my new path after my divorce, I had to cut back my expenses more than 80%. Everything that was not essential had to go: my car, my smart phone and my personal upkeep. The fact is, I could not afford to live my dream while primping the way I had for most of my life.

---

[28] Zuniga, Marielena. "Women & Poverty". Revised September 2011.
http://www.soroptimist.org/whitepapers/whitepaperdocs/wpwomenpoverty.pdf

As Ruth Calder Murphy recently wrote, *I let myself go.*

"There's a phrase—an insulting, snide, sneering sort of a phrase—that tends to be preceded by the word "She":

"She's let herself go."

"She's let herself go" usually means that, as she's aged (whoever "she" might be) or as time has gone by, or since the last time we saw her and assessed her appearance, she's somehow become less attractive, less well-kempt, less physically acceptable, somehow, and that she really ought to have done more to fight the decline."[29]

In my case, the letting go was radical. I stopped shaving anything, quit dying and straightening the hair on my head, stopped wearing makeup most of the time and quit buying new clothes altogether. All those things are expensive—and are mostly "female" expenses that we are still expected to keep up despite the still-there and substantial gender pay gap that exists across the globe.

In my case, it was *freeing.* I never realized how much time, energy and money all this upkeep took. As Germaine Greer wrote, "...if a woman never lets herself go, how will she ever know how far she might have got? If she never takes off her high-heeled shoes, how will she ever know how far she could walk or how fast she could run?"

How true. I never would have finished *one* book. I would still be chained to my ideas of what I "needed to have" at the expense of working nonstop at a job that I hated in high-heeled shoes. I would be too drained to do anything creative or fulfilling.

As a mortgage broker I wore expensive suits to work paired with designer bags and shoes. I spent a great deal of time and money on my hair and makeup. I spent a lot of my financial gains on personal upkeep—I played the part and looked the part of a successful career woman. I made good money as a

---

[29] Murphy, Ruth Calder. "Letting Myself Go". *Elephant Journal*, March 2015. http://www.elephantjournal.com/2015/03/letting-myself-go/

mortgage broker. But I also spent it and my divorce drained anything that was left in my 401k.

These days, I wear comfortable hand-me-down jeans and sweaters from my best friend and rarely look in the mirror all day.

When we give up this idea of our primary importance being based on how we look, we stop buying into all the makeup, hair products, new clothes, etc that cost us thousands of dollars every year. We are talking about a **$7-billion-dollar-a-year industry in the United States alone that profits off of women feeling bad about themselves**.

I don't spend money on most of that any more. I spend any extra money I have on supporting women's projects, books and CD's—or reinvesting in my own projects.

It is critically important that we support each other spiritually, emotionally and economically. Just the simple task of buying a feminist book penned by a woman is an investment in yourself, your children and your grandchildren. It also supports a dream-project that empowers other women and enables the dreamer to continue her work.

It also gives women more ability to break apart from the systems that support the gender pay gap. When women open their *own* businesses, they have more flexibility and opportunities for growth and income. That said, I'd also like to look at how our giving to patriarchal religions drains time, money and resources from us as well.

When going through my divorce, I started taking my children back to the progressive church that my grandparents attended for more than 30 years. Initially, it was because my grandmother needed a ride to church every Sunday. It was important to her and I enjoyed spending this time with her near the end of her life. We made a day out of it, going for a long lunch together after the service and then helping wherever she most needed it. I made many friends there in the process, and we kept attending even after my grandmother passed in hopes of providing a strong community for my children to grow up in.

However, I fell into a trap of giving more of myself there than I could really afford to. My energy was already at one of its lowest points as a single mom to two young children and my finances were limited at best. I felt pressure to give money I didn't have. And I felt enormous constraints on my time as I became drafted to the Christian Education Committee, and then Moderator-Elect and the "Straw Boss" of a successful Strawberry Blues Festival.

While I was happy to do this work at that time, looking back it was enormously foolish of me and I resent these demands of my time. My unpaid labor could have been used to get a full-time job that would better support me and my kids. I was not in the position to be a full-time volunteer. It seems to me that the role of a church should be to support single mothers, not drain them further.

Later, when the male pastor would go on to verbally abuse several female members of that church—the same man who collected a hefty salary while many of us women slaved away for free as volunteers—few people batted an eye. I lost my respect for the entire organization and some of the people inside the church as well. This soon came to include the regional and national headquarters of that same church. No one in a position of power backed the abused women; and as a woman who had given so much of myself to this church, it *stung*.

Monica Sjoo & Barbara Mor posed a searing question near the end of *The Great Cosmic Mother:*

> "The burning question remains: Why do women continue to give our gifts—of spiritual devotion, of impassioned energy, of mental brightness, of profound social concern—to male-dominated and male-defined religious institutions which are based, structurally and ideologically, on a searing contempt and hatred for women? Why do women continue to give our physical endurance and biological endowment to patriarchal churches which exist, ontologically and practically, by attempting to dominate and control human female reproduction like a bunch of cattle breeders controlling the fertility of their cattle? What would happen, today, if all the millions of religiously active

women on earth just walked out of their patriarchal churches, just left them flat?"[30]

That's exactly what I did! I sent a searing resignation letter in to the entire church board and left. I began to devote my time and energy to *my* projects. I am proud of the results.

When you look at the financials of quite a few of the world's largest religions, they are in stark contrast to how most of the world lives. Almost half the world's population lives on less than $2 a day.[31] 70% of those people are women.[32] It's extraordinarily difficult to reconcile that with the stockpile of goods that many patriarchal religions are sitting on.

Recently Kristopher Morrison wrote in the National Post:

"It is impossible to calculate the wealth of the Roman Catholic Church. In truth, the church itself likely could not answer that question, even if it wished to. Its investments and spending are kept secret. Its real estate and art have not been properly evaluated, since the church would never sell them. There is no doubt, however, that between the church's priceless art, land, gold and investments across the globe, it is one of the wealthiest institutions on Earth."

A recent pew poll showed that almost two-thirds of the American public (64%) donated some money to a church, synagogue or other place of worship.[33] *And where is that money going?* According to a study from the Evangelical Christian Credit Union, most of it goes to personnel, buildings and administration expenses, while only 1% goes to local and national benevolence programs.[34]

---

[30] Sjoo, Monica and Mor, Barbara. *The Great Cosmic Mother*. (Harper & Row Publishers. 1987), p 349.

[31] "Almost half the world's population, 2.1 billion people, live on less than $2 a day. Of these people, 880 million live on less than $1 a day. " - World Development Report, World Bank, 2008.

[32] Zuniga, Marielena. "Women & Poverty". Revised September 2011.

http://www.soroptimist.org/whitepapers/whitepaperdocs/wpwomenpoverty.pdf

[33] "New Study Shows Trends in Tithing and Donating" The Barna Group, Ltd., 2009.

I spent a year looking at the budget of the progressive church I attended, and I'd say this was accurate there too. Progressive churches don't seem to fare as well economically, but the pastor's salary package was what I would consider generous.

This paper is by no means meant to be extensive, but if you look at the Muslim faith, you see similar red flags. Imams usually maintain their own job outside the mosque for their income, but the mosque itself is still a large expense. (I'll stick to the religions I have practiced personally in my critique, but I would guess there are similar trends in all patriarchal religions.) It appears that the conservative Wahhabi sect spends an enormous amount of money on promoting their particular brand of Islam.

> "As to how much money Saudi officials have spent since the early 1970s to promote Wahhabism worldwide, David D. Aufhauser, a former Treasury Department general counsel, told a Senate committee in June 2004 that estimates went **"north of $75 billion."** The money financed the construction of thousands of mosques, schools and Islamic centers, the employment of at least 9,000 proselytizers, and the printing of millions of books of religious instruction.

> Sheik estimated the Islamic affairs ministry's budget at **$530 million annually** and said it goes almost entirely to pay the salaries of the more than 50,000 people on the ministry payroll, Ottaway reported. That figure does not include the hundreds of millions of dollars in personal contributions made by King Fahd and other senior Saudi princes to the cause of propagating Islam at home and abroad, according to a Saudi analyst who insisted on anonymity because of the sensitivity of the issue. The real total spent annually spreading Islam is **between $2 billion and $2.5 billion."**[35]

I'd be curious to know exactly where this money comes from, but it goes against what I have always believed to be the purpose of Zakat in Islam. From what I understood, this form of tithing was only to go to help the poor and those in need. I've

---

[34] Schultz, Thom. 'The Shocking Truth of Church Budge. *Holy Soup.* August 6, 2013.
[35] "Al Qaeda, Other Terror Groups Swim in Global Sea of Saudi-Funded Wahhabi Institutions". The Center for Islamic Pluralism. August 22, 2007.

always appreciated what I considered to be the transparency of where your donations go within the Muslim faith. However, it's hard to reconcile these figures (even if they are not Zakat – which I don't believe they are) with my knowledge of how many women and children in the *here and now* live in absolute poverty.

We have nowhere near that budget to promote feminism— which *is* a doctrine that could uplift billions of people. I think that women are much better off lifting themselves and their children up than continuing to support patriarchal religions financially.

"In today's world, thousands of children starve to death every day; millions more suffer the kind of malnutrition that permanently damages the brain and the body. The priests of the world's major patriarchal religions—Christianity, Islam, Buddhism, Hinduism—do not consider this situation particularly "moral," but they do not consider it abnormal either. "The poor are always with us, "life is hell," etc.—the situation just seems to illustrate these priesthoods' biophobic case. In their ontological world-hatred and doctrinal nihilism, the "holy men" try to persuade us, and no doubt themselves, that suffering is the eternal and definitive human condition— and the daily starvation of children is just one more sad but inescapable example of our "mortal condition," of "fleshly sin and corruption," of samsara (the sorrow and impurity of the world), of "life on the wheel" of Buddhistic illusion. Male priesthoods of patriarchal religions—all of whom life in the maximum comfort and even luxury their cultures can afford— have been rationalizing the suffering of others for so long, throughout four thousand years of unctuous droning, no doubt they've come to believe their own words—for want of hearing anything else." – Monica Sjoo & Barbara Mor[36]

My point is that I believe women need to radically reconsider every single dollar they spend. My hope is that feminists will begin to really think about money; as strange or foreign as it may feel to us.

---

[36] Sjoo, Monica and Mor, Barbara. *The Great Cosmic Mother*. (Harper & Row Publishers. 1987), p 371.

If we want our message to really spread and take root, we don't have another option.

Last fall, it seemed likely that one of the few remaining feminist bookstores in the U.S. was going to have to close its doors. Several hours before their Kickstarter campaign was due to wrap up, I lamented about it on my Facebook wall. I was told by numerous people that I should, basically, just *wish it weren't so.*

The fact is that woman-owned businesses, writers and artists need money to survive. No amount of *wishing* is going to change our fate as women. We have to wake up and take action before our women-sacred spaces and businesses are gone. We have to reallocate the often limited funds we have as women if we truly want to see changes in women's lives globally. We have to take political action before we lose more of our Goddess-given rights. As Roseanne Barr said, "The thing women have yet to learn is nobody gives you power. You just take it."

Our systematic economic oppression underlies all other oppressions. We must begin to take an honest closer look at how religion and money work *together* to oppress women. Sister Joan Chittister wrote:

> "Women have been locked out of full humanity and full participation in religious institutions and society at large. This marginalization of women masquerades as 'protecting' them and even 'exalting' them. Instead, these attitudes serve to deny the human race the fullness of female gifts and a female perspective on life. As a result, women make up two-thirds of the hungry of this world. And women are two-thirds of the illiterate of this world. And women are two-thirds of the poorest of the poor, because they lack access to the resources and recognition men take for granted. **That's not an accident. That is a policy**—one supported by religious institutions that call such discrimination 'women's place' and 'God's will.'"[37]

---

[37] Chittister, Sister Joan. "Are Women Devalued in Religions?" *The Shriver Report: A Woman's Nation Pushes Back From The Brink.* January 12, 2014.

Our homes mirror the patriarchal reality we learn in our churches, mosques, temples and synagogues. Therefore, it is no surprise that when women are able to leave destructive relationships with abusive men, they are punished financially, and there are few laws to protect them. We need to find a way to ensure that ALL women and children receive the child support payments they are entitled to.

We have to find a way to make our cultures acknowledge, value and reward care-giving. Riane Eisler has spent years of her life work studying just how to do this. If you only take one thing from this essay, read *The Real Wealth of Nations*.

We must demand that there is no more wage gap. According to *A Woman's Nation Pushes Back from the Brink: Facts and Figures*, "Closing the wage gap between men and women would cut the poverty rate in half for working women and their families and would add nearly half a trillion dollars to the national economy."[38]

We must ensure that **no woman,** anywhere in the world, enters her crone years in poverty. These are the years where we should be reaping her years of knowledge and wisdom. The crone should be relaxing and reflecting on her glorious life—not slaving away at McDonalds worrying about how she is going to pay the rent!

We cannot accomplish any of these goals if we do not understand how money functions—and most importantly, if we don't work together. Our individualistic lives are killing us. We need to fight back—*hard.*

We can't change everything *today,* but we can find creative solutions to make our individual and collective lives easier. We can live communally, share resources and refuse to spend one-penny on anything that does not empower us as females.

Until we have economic equality, I urge you to consider how you spend your money. If you go out to eat, go to a woman-owned restaurant. If you buy a book or a CD or a piece of art, make

---

[38] "A Woman's Nation Pushes Back from the Brink: Facts and Figures" *The Shriver Report: A Woman's Nation Pushes Back From The Brink.* January 12, 2014.

sure it's been created by a woman. Every-single-place we spend our money has the potential to change our world.

No one sums this up better than Arundhati Roy:

> "Our strategy should be not only to confront empire, but to lay siege to it. To deprive it of oxygen. To shame it. To mock it. With our art, our music, our literature, our stubbornness, our joy, our brilliance, our sheer relentlessness—and our ability to tell our own stories. Stories that are different from the ones we're being brainwashed to believe."

We *can* refuse to participate in our own economic subordination. If we work collectively, we can also reallocate the money that runs the world in a way that works for *everyone*.

Here, She Is

Jacqueline Hope Derby

MY FRIEND CALEY is walking his mother through the dying process right now. Old hurts surface, begging for a balm of forgiveness or grace. The puss of regret seeps out, and madness wrecks many a sleepless night as the cancer eats away at his mother's mind and wellbeing. There are midnight confessions, spontaneous "I love you's!" whispered in the dark, and screaming fears in the light of day. Everything is upside down, topsy-turvy, and backwards.

Caley took his mother back to his own home to give his sister a respite over Thanksgiving. His mother, deeply afraid, asked him to walk with her through the dark house to make sure that there were no thieves in the night. Caley held onto her, as they made their rounds in the shadows. Bumbling. Bumping. Almost falling once, Caley begged his mother to let him turn on the lights, but she would not have it.

Caley's mother is dying to be healed, so Caley and his family minister to her where she is. They tend her body, and see it in ways they never had before. They stand with her in her confusion and rage, and wonder where their mother went. They hear her vitriol, and cringe—for they only want the final blessing of, *"My darling child, you are enough. You are good. You are loved. You have made me proud every day of my life."*

Caley is dying for his mother to be healed as well. The healing he desires is the one that touches both of them here in this place where the cancer ravages, the fears persist, and old familial wounds beg for gentle tinctures.

True healing requires the deepest of resolve to stand in the most horrific of places and answer the call to deepen, even if the thing we want the most is denied to us. Caley's mother is not going gently into the good night. She is kicking and screaming. She is biting and hitting. She is stumbling around in the dark of her past choices and clutching to her children in the hope that they can lead her to the light of grace and forgiveness and unconditional love before it is too late.

This healing is not cheap. It does not come like a wish granted by a fairy godmother or a genie in a bottle. Make me rich. Make me beautiful. Make the prince fall in love with me. These are cheap and without substance, and all-too-often what we think healing looks like. We believe that healing happens in a place where God puts right what once went wrong. The blind see. The deaf hear. The lame walk.

We desire this god—this male god—because the hard work of healing overwhelms us. We set ourselves up to believe that cheap healing and cheap peace are enough. We will and beg and beseech this god to come in and punish those who hurt us, wipe out those who are different from us, smite those who are evil (in our eyes), and take away all our afflictions. We believe all-too-often the lie that these actions will make things right, when in fact, they just add to the destruction of our very souls and the wellbeing of our precious planet and her children.

What we want is vengeance, not healing. Or at best we just want the bad to disappear from our lives and from our memories.

True healing is much more difficult to attain because it costs us our own cherished image of ourselves as better or above those around us. True healing invites us into the center of our being where we must confront our places of shadow, fear, regret, rage, love, hope, and light. True healing is a completely different force than vengeance. True healing is transformation. This healing is not holding our breath for something better to come along; this healing is breathing deeply even as it does not. True healing is not death, but instead birth, and birth, and birth. We are continually reborn into more compassionate, more giving, more loving, more accepting, more trusting, more wise, more awake human beings.

And being fully awake is the central invitation and gift of Mother God.

Awaken my child. Awaken. See with your open heart.
Hear with your own experiences of loss that taught you
compassion. Walk with your love of justice and your
longing for all of my creation to be whole.

Mother God ushers us through our darkest, most frightening nights. She does not turn on the lights. She does not protect us from all the bumps and bumbling and bruises. Why not? She is too wise and good to protect us from our learning. She does not set right what once went wrong because that would destroy our soul's opportunity to glean what it must for us to awaken further. She bears witness. She screams at us to grow the fuck up and stop hurting our siblings and ourselves. She whispers. She cajoles. She calls to our deepest truest root and reminds us that we are Her child and must act accordingly.

But She does not stop us. She does not make it so the boogeyman never enters the darkened house. She never prevents the horrible choices that lead to even more horrible consequences. The laws of physics are Her wisdom at play, so She never suspends them. To do so would be to abandon Her creation, Her boundaries, Her brilliance.

The child in me can never be unmolested. It always happened. I was always betrayed. I was always brokenhearted. I was always afraid of being killed by my stepfather. This God. This Mother. She does not make it not happen, and She does not rescue me. She only holds me and sustains me in it. There is seven year-old me being assaulted for the first time, but I am not alone there. She is with me. She is weeping with me. She is cooing me.

When I am dragged by my hair through the house after threatening to expose him, She is with me. She is telling me my name. She is calling me daughter. She is loving me. I am not alone, but it still happens. Shit still happens. She cannot fix it. She cannot make me forget it because even if my mind blocks it my body remembers for my mind. She cannot and will not abandon me, just as She will not stop it.

It will never be as if it never happened. Life just does not work that way. We are not Her puppets. We are Her *children*, and like Her we create with reckless abandon. We create good. We create love. We create connection. And we destroy that which we create. We destroy one another. We destroy ourselves. We destroy that which we loved the most. We destroy that which we hate. Destruction is not Her way or Her will, but too often it is ours.

So *here*, right here in the shit of it all and in the glory of it all, She is. *Here* where we are crushed by the weight of our dying mother on our arm in her terror of the middle of the night. *Here* where we are wrecked body and soul by the horrific actions of those who should be trustworthy and kind. *Here* where we destroy our gifts, our garden, our neighbor, ourselves. *Here* where we are uncertain, frightened, broken, and bad. Here, She is.

Here, right here in the stunning glorious beauty of it all, She is. *Here* where we get to whisper sweet nothings to one whose body we know better than our own. *Here* where we get to forgive the unforgivable and restore relationships. *Here* where we hold our newborn child in our arms. *Here* where we paint, dance, sing, jump, love, live, and celebrate. *Here* where we are confident, good, hopeful, whole, and enough. *Here*, She is.

Keep your petty, vengeful boy god. Your boy god is a child who yells and kicks and screams when he doesn't get his way. He is full of smite and smut. He hates things that go bump in the night. He casts away those most precious for childish reasons, like saying his name wrong, being the wrong gender, or the wrong color. He is petty and mean. He looks for quick fixes and wants a blood payment to prove your loyalty. He wants right answers to pop quizzes. He thrives on "us versus them." He is muddy and obscured by our own filth and fear to the point of being irrelevant.

Keep. Him. Away.

Instead, come to the darkness. Come to the unknowing. Come to the questions. Come to the liminal light between night and day and day and night. Come to possibility. Come to the here and now. Come to the broken pieces. Come to the truth—even the truths that pierce your heart or your side or your vagina.

Come here.

Come here where She is. Come to the place of mosaics built of broken pieces. Come to the place of the gilded phoenix being refined by the fire and then rising. Come to the sacred ground of the pupa where you are transformed. Come to the land of peace where we are all brother, sister, planet, creation, equal before

74

our Mother. Come to the here where your life is imperfect, messy, hurt, broken, and awkward.

Come here and listen to Her tell you again about the true healing She offers each of us:

> *Awaken my child. Awaken. See with your open heart. Hear with your own experiences of loss that taught you compassion. Walk with your love of justice and desire for all of my creation to be whole.*

For it is here that She is. And however much you may try to deny it, it is here where you are.

Faith in Action

Jen Raffensperger

WHEN I WAS A YOUNG GIRL, maybe seven or eight, my mother took me to the Right to Life march a couple of times. This annual demonstration is held by self-proclaimed pro-life activists on the anniversary of the Roe vs. Wade decision, January 22. It is a huge march that fills up much of the National Mall.

Reflecting back now, it doesn't seem much like her style, but I believe that my Mother was attending this event with one of the women's groups at our Catholic church. I also believe she made the decision to bring me along, more as an educational outing than anything directly political. My parents were never very politically active, and I of course was far too young to have any real grasp of the political or personal issues involved.

It was definitely a good educational experience. Growing up in the DC area affords a unique opportunity to see many parts of the democratic process in action, and large (mostly) peaceable assembly is decidedly an important part of our American heritage. We only went a few times, as it frustrated my Mother to see the news coverage only giving time to the "lunatic fringe" as she and my father called them. Still, it made a definite impression on me. So many people! It was usually very cold, and we would carry a Thermos of cocoa, and some sandwiches and granola bars. I learned that I hated Porta-Johns and that my fingers got very cold carrying around signs. I much preferred to hold a cup of warm cocoa. I liked stickers and pins and the marches afforded ample opportunity to pick up plenty of both.

My understanding of what we were doing, of what the issues were, was simplistic and shaky at best. I saw all the big pictures of dead babies and thought, "Well of course THAT'S no good!" My best understanding of "pro-choice" was probably "a choice between piles of dead babies or NO piles of dead babies," which was to my 8-year-old-self something of a no-brainer. I was solidly on the side of no piles of dead babies. Just like every time I went to the National Zoo, I would go look at the playful seals, and then I would look at the disturbing pictures of dead seals with their stomachs cut open to show the coins inside. The pictures were there as a visceral – and, one supposes, effective – reminder not to throw coins into the seal habitat. To me, at age eight, being against piles of dead babies was exactly the same as being against cut up dead seals with coins in their stomachs.

Eventually, I grew up. I learned about the issues involved in the Roe v. Wade case. I learned there was a lot more going on than could actually be assessed in the oversimplified sign-carrying and shouting that was happening on both sides of the Right to Life march. And in time I became pro-choice. I learned about how my body worked as a growing woman, and what being pregnant meant, and could mean, and how it could impact the rest of my life.

Still, I did not (and do not) resent my mother for taking me to those marches. It was educational and interesting. It was important to her as a woman of faith. It was easy to see, both as a girl and as a growing woman, how faith came in on the Right-to-Life marchers' side.

Learning how faith came to bear on the other side took much more time and questioning on my part. As many young Catholics do, I spotted something that bothered me. Specifically, the church's restrictions on birth control made very little sense to me. If abortion is a bad thing, I thought, shouldn't we do everything we can to avoid needing to have them? It was quite simple as a preadolescent to say, haughtily, "Well, just don't have so much sex!" (I will hasten to add that for most of my preadolescence I barely understood what that even meant.) It was even relatively simple to utter that same haughty statement as an overly-hormonal adolescent who was so hamstrung by the idea of talking to a boy she had a crush on that she never expected sex to be a thing she, personally, would have to deal with.

Many other questions and struggles compounded, I continued to grow, and eventually, I left the Catholic faith. I spent time with no sense of faith at all, a time I ultimately came to see as damaging.

When I joined the Unitarian Universalist church, my sense of faith and my relationship with God had changed a great deal since the days when I'd gone to those marches. I had been pro-choice for a long time. And I still had never thought of that particular political leaning from a faithful perspective. My sense of the idea of "liberal religion" was very new.

In the fall of 2013, my congregation had a service on Reproductive Justice. It was my first real exposure to that term, which arose out of a conscientious movement put forth by women of color, to raise awareness of the way inequalities regarding reproductive health and choice have deep and broad effects on many aspects of life. The best short definition I have heard for Reproductive Justice is "The right to have the number of children that you want when you want, the right not to have children if you so choose, and the right to raise your children in a healthy, safe environment." I wrote a blog post on reproductive privilege as my eyes were opened to that concept in a powerful, personal way. I learned that the Unitarian Universalist Association has a strong moral position on the importance of reproductive justice for the health and well-being of all women and men. Reproductive justice aligns strongly with Unitarian Universalism's first, second, and sixth guiding principles. The First Principle respects and holds sacred "The inherent worth and dignity of every person." The Second Principle respects and holds sacred "Justice, equity, and compassion in human relations." And the Sixth Principle respects and holds sacred "the goal of world community with peace, liberty, and justice for all." It is as right and sacred, I realized, to respect the lives of those faced with pregnancy, and how their lives will be forever altered by that state no matter what their decision.

I was humbled, and shocked, to realize how long I had been pro-choice without necessarily thinking of it as a right and moral choice. How long I had left that part out, because of the way my ideas were still colored by experiences from my youth. To realize I could stand up, raise my own voice as a woman of faith on the side of conscientious family planning and reproductive health for all.

From the perspective of recognizing my own privilege it was not much of a leap to arrive at a sense of my own responsibility. That is why in late March of 2014, I took a day off work and went into DC accompanied by several amazing women from my church to exercise our own right to peaceably assemble. We attended a faith rally at a Lutheran church and a demonstration at the steps of the Supreme Court to take a stand on the side of a full range of coverage for safe, legal contraception.

I had a number of conversations that day with people on both sides of the issue. All were civil, and all were thoughtful. I do not mean to impugn the faith of others and especially not their right to take peaceful action as their conscience dictates. I was pleased to be afforded the same respect interpersonally. But most important of all I was blessed (and, yes, privileged!) to be able to stand up as a woman of faith and be counted.

Does the Divine Feminine
Need Your Help?

DeAnna L'am

THE DIVINE FEMININE IS AWAKENING – how often have you heard this phrase? It became a truism, something we may take for granted, something we support in our minds, but how do our actions reflect this awakening? And more to the point: does the Divine Feminine need our help?

We women have been personally awakening for years. We became aware of our social inequity and fought to level the playing field (which is not quite level yet). We became aware of our needs and worked to become assertive in asking for their fulfillment. We found Goddesses in all indigenous cultures of the world, and embraced them as our role models and inspiration. We reclaimed the Feminine face of God. But are we hearing the Divine Mother's call for help?

It isn't enough to empower ourselves on a personal level, though it is a *necessary* first step! Once that step is taken, we need to widen our attention to include the whole. We talk about the emerging new era as The Age of the Feminine, of forging Feminine leadership models, of the Dalai Lama's reclamation of women as bringers of change to the world, yet in all this celebration of empowerment, are we listening to the Divine Mother's needs?

Let's continue, indeed, to empower ourselves and each other, but let us listen deeply as well... Let's close our eyes and go inward... Calm our breath and delve into the depths of the Earth, into the Womb of our Mother, and ask Her how can we serve her awakening...?

How can we help wake up the Divine Feminine in the hearts of all people?

We act as if we know a lot, and we probably do... But when we are in *service* to something greater than ourselves – we need to ask for guidance. In serving the Divine Feminine we can't come from a place of knowing, but from a place of inquiry... **The**

Divine Mother has been bearing the spite of a patriarchal world for millenniums. She has been humiliated, abandoned, degraded... Forgotten by a collective that once revered and honored her...

Our personal empowerment is a *facet* of Her healing, it is an expression of Her rising, an instance of Her awakening, but let's not forget that in the larger picture we are serving Her, not a separate self... Our personal rise is an aspect of Her awakening, not the other way around... It is not our personal empowerment that awakens Her. It is Her awakening that is expressed through our personal and collective empowerment as women!

We have been busy breaking our own shackles, which is a powerful and worthy cause. However, **this is not an end in itself.** It is a feature of Her rising! And as such, we need to become fully aware of the need to work collectively in Her service, attuned to Her needs.

Working personally in the service of empowering ourselves and women in the larger culture — is the vehicle in which the Divine Feminine can rise again in human consciousness. When we *collectively* engage in throwing off the shackles of the Divine Feminine, we are serving Her, not ourselves, and so we need to deeply listen... to yearn to discover what She *needs* from us at this time.

Liberation is a collaborative task, and service, when offered, is always to something greater than ourselves. When moving from 'Me' to 'We' it is essential to remember that 'We' are all facets of the whole that we aim to serve. And this Whole, the Divine Feminine, needs each of us!

Listen inwardly: **What is She asking of You?** How can you, with your unparalleled gifts, serve Her awakening in the hearts of all? In what ways can you dedicate your own journey of empowerment to serving a new dawn? How can you bring your unique hue to the wave of Her rising?

Our Struggles Are Not the Same: Inspired Solidarity with Turtle Island First Nations Women

Pegi Eyers

AS MEMBERS OF THE DOMINANT European cultural group who created racial, gender and class inequality in the Americas in the first place, many of us have come to the same conclusion (!), that to take responsibility for our unearned social power means demanding full human rights for all women. As we take on the work of social justice to right the wrongs of history, and act in solidarity with indigenous women who have been oppressed by Empire, we enter a liminal zone. In our time, the interface between oppressor and oppressed is a shifting ground of assumptions, protocol and intercultural sharing, a borderland of hearts and minds offering both joy and sorrow. And at the same time that white women are reclaiming our own earth-based spiritualities that value reciprocity with nature and the Ancestors, we must ensure that our work as Allies does not replicate colonialism, or impact indigenous women in the Americas with more negativity, such as white perspectivism, knowledge domination or cultural appropriation.

Once lost in the hegemonic agenda to destroy women's spirituality and indigenous knowledge (IK) all over the world, white women in the Americas are waking up in unprecedented numbers from the patriarchal mass delusion that dominates women, the Earth and tribal peoples that live in connection to Her. It has taken us a couple of millennia to finally rebel against the horrors and inequalities of white male supremacy (!) and our liberation is well underway. We are working hard within a vast coalition of women and men to shift our society to the feminine values that embody cooperation and inclusion instead of hierarchy and control. There is evidence everywhere of a collective movement toward the "Divine Feminine" paradigm promoting biophilia,[1] personal and planetary healing, community cohesiveness, earth-connected sustainability and peaceful co-existence. We are also being asked at this monumental time to choose between collaborating with, or resisting, racial injustice.

Any kind of racism perpetuates the division between women, and sabotages the potential for us to work together as allies and "Sisters in Spirit." Unfortunately there is not much common ground in feminist ideology, as white feminism has failed to acknowledge the historic differences between white identity and that of indigenous women, and white feminists have incorrectly assumed that non-native and native women are working through the same liberation process.

Yet, our oppressions are not interchangeable, as white women seek to reject or overthrow the patriarchy, while indigenous women are primarily working toward the recovery of their traditional culture, sovereignty and self-determination. It does not seem to occur to white feminists that the struggle in the dominant society for women's rights has no equivalent in indigenous resistance efforts that seek decolonization, as Poesia explains. *"There is a difference between fighting for 'rights' and fighting against ending occupation, imperialism, and femicide. When we seek 'rights,' we are asking to be integrated into a system that aims to destroy our entire existence."*[2]

Our trajectories are completely different, but if there is one thing that both native and non-native women have in common, it must be the countless years of enforced silence whereby our voices were denied, suppressed, criminalized, and unwelcome at the table. For the entire Christian era, white women were expected to be silent, obedient and invisible. The legend is passed down that when first learning of the status of white women at the time of European contact, First Nations often wondered – what kind of demented people would marginalize, enslave, denounce and abuse their own women?

To make things even more complicated, patriarchal oppression did not exist in indigenous societies, and is a colonial overlay, the racist agenda being to devalue both genders and set up false hierarchies where none existed before. Traditional indigenous societies were egalitarian and based on the model of the consensus circle, with the emphasis being more on gender harmony than gender equality. *"The Indigenous Circle of Life philosophy more appropriately embodies Aboriginal women's conceptions of human nature, their political philosophy and their strategy for social change and liberation."*[3] Also, the majority of Turtle Island indigenous women continue to deny the universalist notion of a *Global Sisterhood*, and reject the principles of modern feminism by situating it as a movement directed entirely by white privilege.

Indigenous women may also object to the idea that we share identity or experience simply by virtue of being women, and by possessing the same nurturing and reproductive female anatomy. But many would agree that the IK-based tenets of Celtic Reconstructionist Paganism (CR), Druidry or Goddess Spirituality are comparable to their own IK. Recovery from colonialism has no timeline, but it may be possible to embody at some point the heart-knowing that all women, both native and non-native, are the frequency holders for the global recovery of IK and a paradigm shift to earth-wise feminine values.

Ancient matriarchal cultures in Europe provide models for us today, and many indigenous societies have never relinquished their traditional matriarchal, matrifocal or matrilineal structures. In the pre-colonial Haudenosaunee world, as earthkeepers and life-givers, the Clan Mothers held the highest authority and were highly skilled at making decisions affecting the well-being of the whole tribe. As a point of mutual liberation, there is much evidence that the empowerment of women in our time and the resurgence of women in governance and spiritual life is either culturally inclusive or transcends ethnicity altogether. The prominence of women in key leadership roles continues to rise in Turtle Island First Nations community, and in cultural and ethnic groups worldwide, as well as in the dominant society. Meanwhile, our job as white women is to become re-rooted in our own IK and recover the sacred essence that perpetually spirals us back to our own deep connection with the land. Call me a dreamer, but could our love for Mother Earth be the force that unites us all?

To use the patriarchy as a lens through which to view history, and to describe our liberated and recently-reclaimed history as white women in broad strokes, we lost our best European wise women, keepers of the Old Ways, "waeccan," "wycces" or wicca practitioners and healers in the 1450–1700 genocide of the Burning Times (otherwise known as the "Women's Holocaust"). In the total supremacy of a "man's world," white women have long been the passive and suffering victims of Empire, or the supporting cast and game players who internalized the values of the patriarchy and were complicit with the colonial directive. Until the flowering of first-wave feminism with the suffragettes in the late 19th century, European women were owned, dominated, controlled and victimized by the patriarchy for millennia.

And as much as we have achieved emancipation and empowerment today, we need to realize that the benefits and privileges we experience as white women are the result of Euro-supremacy. The gifts and amenities we take for granted in the Americas today have come at the high cost of human suffering, and the near-annihilation of both indigenous cultures and the land.

> "There needs to be struggle in order to lay out a path to co-existence, and that the process of being uncomfortable is essential for non-indigenous people to move from being enemy to adversary to Ally."[4] (Taiaiake Alfred)

As we come to understand colonization over millennia and the historical impact it has had on all people, including us as Europeans, we become aware of how and when our eco-values were stolen from us, and how many of our own people lost their lives as a result of the structural violence endemic to establishing Empire. As we were forced to assimilate into the monocultural white mainstream in the Americas we had to leave behind our own IK – our traditional European languages, foods, music, games, rituals and spiritual expressions. Military invasion, war, the socio-economic class system, food shortages and poverty (as a result of hegemonic policies and patriarchal greed) drove us to abandon our deep-rooted traditions in the frenzy of expulsion and relocation. During the collective dementia of economic, religious and forced immigration, we sacrificed our European histories and spirituality, our love of place, our deep connections to our Ancestors, and our most important cultural keystones. In exile, our survival mechanism kicked in, our IK was traded away and our cultural loss forgotten in the promise of a new land and a new life.

> "The Settler Society were **all** displaced – they **all** left something behind, and that must be why they are attracted to Native Spirituality."[5] (Lee Maracle)

Today, as the descendants of the Settler Society, we need to examine how this immense cultural soul loss has led to our collective and personal dysfunction, and how the stories of our disconnect must be at the root of our ongoing spiritual hunger and yearning for holistic earth-connected community. Clearly the exile from our own IK is the contributing factor to our romanticization and appropriation from the vibrancy of other cultures. Today, the majority of Turtle Island First Nations knowledge keepers have had enough of non-native inroads into their spirituality, and we are being told to cease and desist from cultural theft.

Elements of cultural and spiritual property that have been lifted from Turtle Island First Nations are found in pseudo-rituals for creating sacred space, four directions petitioning, smudging, talking stick circles, drumming, "featherwork," vision quests, sweat lodge recreations, sacred fire gatherings, initiation rites, and the delights of indigenous material culture such as wardrobe, headdresses, jewelry and decor. To ignore the directives coming from Indian Country, and to continue the appropriation of any element of First Nations material or spiritual culture just because it appeals to us, is an act of arrogance and cultural imperialism. White women need to stop their highly offensive appropriation and romanticization of native cultures and become accountable for their white privilege in a realistic way. Through "allyship" we now have an appropriate model that allows white people to draw close and give back to First Nations community, as activists in the struggle for racial justice.

As stripped of our ancestral myths and knowledge as we Settlers seem to be, we defy the position of patriarchal dominance and undermine the notion of cultural superiority when we reclaim the roots of our own authentic indigenity. It is our birthright as human beings to declare our true status as people of the Earth (as it is for all cultural groups), and if we collectively reject the delusional separation from nature that Empire has forced upon us, we move back into right relationship with the earth and all beings.

Anchoring ourselves deeply into our earth-connected heritage will create a true coming-together of hearts and minds in equality, right relationship and emotional integrity. In building a bridge between cultures, white feminists need to remain aware of the legacy of colonialism (which is our own history), and to value First Nations counter-narratives as fully equal to our own. There is no level ground in this coming together, no "automatic harmony," and to expect otherwise is to dismiss native identity and impose yet another form of assimilation. *"There is a reductionism inherent in liberalist conceptions of unity, and from the Aboriginal perspective, the best laid plans for native/non-native partnership may always have the feel of homogenization."*[6] We need to be aware that in all sectors of culture and society (Pagan, Wicca, Goddess and New Age spirituality included), neo-liberalism claims a universalist, humanist approach while having an effect on the oppressed that is the exact opposite.

Those in the dominant society have a way of forgetting that the genocide of millions of indigenous peoples and the theft of their lands made the rise of our modern American and Canadian nation-states possible. Yet, for the First Nations of Turtle Island, it is only since the late 1980's that a renaissance of healing, collaborating, rebuilding, and re-visioning has occurred, and the future looks very positive for the continued resurgence and reclamation of their self-determination and traditional IK. Through decolonization, the bond to the land and the holistic aspects of traditional teachings that are evoked in IK hold the key to restoring the hearts and minds of the individual and the community, and Turtle Island First Nations have much to celebrate as they take renewed pride in their spiritual worldviews and traditional values such as balance and interconnection. A benefit of the healing process for all those affected by intersectional oppressions is that one can slowly reawaken the heart, optimally recovering the lost parts of the soul, and restore the ability to feel empathy for one's self and others again.

> *"Perhaps it is time to make our way back through our oral traditions, written words and deeper sorrows. Then, indigenous people can collectively create new understandings and go willingly through the painful memories once again, in order to resolve and release the historic trauma and free ourselves from its tyranny."*[7]
> (Aboriginal Healing Foundation)

In reconciliation work of all kinds, it is recognized that forgiveness can be an expansive practice that often has nothing to do with the abuser, yet can free and heal the self. Native people are in charge of their own recovery and I do not presume to speak for them, but based on my own warm friendships with First Nations women I envision a multitude of safe spaces where encounters can take place between native and non-native community members, and social relationships can be healed. This aspect of the reconciliation continuum would require an expansion of intimate heart-knowing for all participants, and we could be encouraged to acknowledge the residual pain of historic and contemporary injustice. *"One can forgive but one should never forget."* Modeled after the Truth and Reconciliation (TRC) process in Canada to hear First Nations testimony, create awareness, make recommendations, and work toward justice, these gatherings or small groups could continue to take place in diverse communities. If it is something we truly want, perhaps we can navigate the emotional waters together, seeking an opportunity to have "risky conversations," while edging toward shared acceptance and reconciliation. I think that together we can become agents of unconditional love by mutually recognizing the devastation of the past, mapping out an understanding of our common future, and working toward the goal of peaceful co-existence. It could be that the directive to re-indigenize ourselves and reclaim our own IK is a parallel objective, and that our mutual responsibility, as native or non-native, is to coexist as green seers, wisewomen and Keepers of the Earth. It's a jump I know, to go from colonization to mutual co-arising, but considering the Seven Generations code, [8] where else can we be going?

NOTES

1. The term "biophilia" describes our innate affinity for all living things, as popularized by biologist E.O. Wilson's famous essay of the same name. "Biophilia" refers to the organizing principles that guide people into closer connection with the systems of Earth, as well as our primeval roots that can be re-awakened at any time. In opposition to "biophilia," Wilson identified a "selfish gene" which stresses individual gain over collaboration, and the competition for wealth and power that is linked to resource extraction and environmental destruction.

2. Poesia, "Death of Empire: Decolonizing Feminism(s)," Shades of Silence (SOS) Colors of Revolt, June 5, 2013 (http://shadesofsilence.org/2013/06/05/death-of-empire-decolonizing-feminisms)

3. Grace J.M.W. Ouellette, The Fourth World: An Indigenous Perspective on Feminism and Aboriginal Women's Activism, Fernwood Publishing, 2004

4. Taiaiake Alfred (Kahnawake Mohawk), Introduction, Unsettling the Settler Within: Indian Residential Schools, Truth Telling and Reconciliation in Canada by Paulette Regan, UBC Press, 2010

5. Lee Maracle, "Idle No More: Looking Back, Moving Ahead," panel discussion, Lakefield Literary Festival, 2013

6. Sam Grey, "Decolonising Feminism," Enweyin, Vol. VIII, 2003-2004 (www.academia.edu/1330316)

7. Aboriginal Healing Foundation, "Report on Historic Trauma and Aboriginal Healing," Aboriginal Healing Foundation, 2004

8. It is an important teaching of both the Algonquin Anishnaabe and Haudenosaunee to consider the well-being of the Seven Generations yet to come in all endeavors, and this responsibility requires the ethics of sustainability and care. Ultimately, the tribal landbase, well-being, cultural traditions and collective identity in the past, present and future are all enhanced and protected by this directive.

Jesus and Sophia

Liz Hall Magill

WHAT WORKS FOR ME ABOUT CHRISTIANITY – what has always worked, though my church-going has always been sporadic – is Jesus. I love his humanity, his passion—turning over tables in the temple because he's sick of hypocrisy, crying out in a moment of doubt on the cross. I love his divinity, his miracles of healing and grace—walking on water and turning water into wine and casting out sickness and bringing back a lost son to his grieving mother. And oh, how I love the combination of his humanity and his divinity—his embodied compassion, poured out for those around him, feeding them spiritually and physically even when he was exhausted. Of course, Christians cannot truly separate Jesus' humanity from his divinity. This means that every moment I love about Jesus—his anger at hypocrisy, his doubt on the cross, his compassion poured out for those around him—are God's moments, enacted through a human being, a man.

It is because of this man-who-fully-embodied-God that I name myself Christian, despite my sometimes conflicted relationship with Christianity. Although I've considered myself Christian since I was a teen, I've often felt uncomfortable in church. I went through a confirmation period in a Presbyterian church at 16, yet didn't fully grasp many church traditions, such as Pentecost. As an adult, I have sometimes felt like an outsider at church, someone who didn't really get what was going on or why it was important.

As a young married woman, I was recruited to be on far more church committees than my husband was, expected to comfortably plan Sunday school classes or make decisions about church activities. In the churches we attended (there were a few, as we moved around a bit), I chipped in to help gladly, but still felt at a loss to understand how I fit in to the grand scheme of things—how church and God and Jesus and I were all working together to do whatever it was we were doing. And in the back of my mind, I was annoyed that my husband was rarely, if ever, asked to chip in.

And then there are my opinions and my friends' opinions—I don't think Jesus is the only path to God, and I think God is fine with all people living their authentic selves in ways that don't harm others—sexually, spiritually, and otherwise. My friendships reflect my approach to life and to spirituality. That means I hear a lot of perspectives, and I want to be open to them all. I think God is open to them all. Although there are many Christians who feel this way, their voices don't get much airtime in our culture, and the voices of intolerance often made me feel as though I wasn't a "real" Christian.

This is where I was—attending a new church, this one Episcopal and much more open and accepting than any I'd previously attended—when a woman leading a spiritual group introduced me to the book *She Who Is*, by Elizabeth A. Johnson. As I was in the midst of a political feminist awakening, this book fit right in with my work, and opened my eyes to what I'd always felt was missing in my faith but hadn't consciously named.

I was missing the feminine divine, a female God working through people, bringing compassionate action to a world that needs it. I was missing Sophia.

Sophia is often referred to in the Bible as Wisdom, as Compassion. Ms. Johnson describes Sophia as "…a female personification of God's own being in creative and saving involvement with the world."[1]

Conceiving of God as female as well as male is not an either/or proposition—not a betrayal of Christian belief, but rather a way to settle more fully into it: "The mystery of God is properly understood as neither male nor female, but transcends both in an unimaginable way. But insofar as God creates both male and female in the divine image and is the source of the perfections of both, either can equally well be used as metaphor to point to the divine mystery."[2]

As humans, how we conceive of God matters a great deal. To believe that divinity is always and only male requires us to shut down the truth and wisdom that Sophia brings—creation, compassion, and engagement in the here and now of this world's pain and struggle. And that is what I have always loved most about Jesus—his ability to engage, as God, in the here and now of human experience.

Bringing Sophia to my faith has shed new light on the stories from Jesus' life, all those stories of Jesus treating women with radical equality for the time—speaking to the woman at the well, stopping a crowd from stoning a woman who had committed adultery, allowing a prostitute to wash his feet, connecting to women as his apostles, his emissaries, his sisters. This Jesus, too, I had loved, and not seen fully. Now I see him, just as I see Sophia in him—helping us reclaim that which we have lost, so that we might learn how to move as God moves, fully aware of our own powers, and with compassionate action as our guide.

NOTES

1. Johnson, Elizabeth A. *She Who Is: The Mystery of God in Feminist Theological Discourse*. Tenth Anniversary Edition. (New York: The Crossroad Publishing Company, 2012.), p. 91.

2. Johnson, Elizabeth A. *She Who Is: The Mystery of God in Feminist Theological Discourse*. Tenth Anniversary Edition. (New York: The Crossroad Publishing Company, 2012.), p. 55.

Mothering as Spiritual and Political Resistance to Patriarchal Structures of Oppression

Liona Rowan

VALUING WOMEN AND WOMEN IN THEIR ROLES AS MOTHER will not occur until there is a return to a consciousness of a Divine Female or Divine Mother. We have invested our male gods with the power to create life without the involvement of female gods or women. As a result, women have been denigrated, objectified and seen as required only for raising "men's sons" and providing future breeders / helpers. In many cases, this role of helper is little more than glorified house keeper and sex slave. While that may seem shocking at first, it is the reality that we live with – under the guise of marriage, commitment, diamonds and promises of equality that never seem to materialize.

The Abrahamic religions (Judaism, Christianity and Islam) and other patriarchal religions have subordinated women, a misogyny that has persisted to this day, under a veneer of glorification of mother as selfless, self-sacrificing, all forgiving and nurturing to their children and men. Greek and Roman history is full of examples where women are used as prizes or spoils of war. Stories of men giving their daughters to other men or sacrificing their daughters to the Gods are retold to our children as examples of honor. Mothers taken from their children or having their children killed in front of them (for whatever reasons the men in these histories deemed necessary) are then expected to be good wives to the men who killed their children. How is any of that honorable – and for whom?

Using an autoethnographical (Stevenson 1) approach – combined with a feminist viewpoint and feminist spirituality based in a deep and abiding belief in a Divine Female that is imminent and transcendent, omniscient, omnipotent and omnipresent – I will examine my mothering as a spiritual and political act of resistance to patriarchal structures of oppression. Through a lens of a feminist spiritual standpoint I have critically analyzed the texts in the bibliography and incorporated many ideas into my world view and approach to mothering. I am a middle-class, middle aged married white American woman. I have four children, three girls and one boy ranging from 43 to twelve years old, and one of my children is adopted. I am deeply committed to raising feminist daughters and now a feminist son.

I became a mother at the age of 21. My pregnancy was a surprise and I chose not to abort. In hindsight this seems like a very ill advised decision, as I was single, underemployed and, what many would have called, *out of control*. While I do not advocate the decision I made for others, my decision to have my child saved my life. I was reeling from a childhood filled with the results of patriarchal oppressive structure. I had stepfather who was a child molester, a mother who was powerless in her relationship with her husband, but all powerful and violent with her children.

A father who saw his children as the mother's emotional and physical responsibility and a stepmother who was powerless in her relationship with my father and was submissive due to her Christian religious beliefs. My way of coping with these family dynamics was to move across the country as soon as I graduated high school and experiment extensively. My daughter was perfect in my eyes. She had red hair and blue eyes and I loved her fiercely. At the moment of her birth I decided that my child would never have to suffer the things that I suffered. I knew that the only way to make sure of that was to change the course of *my* life. So I did, although not without difficulty. I went to, and graduated from, nursing school so that I would always be able to provide a home and food for her without depending on anyone else.

Many changes in our lives have occurred since her birth – many of them good, some of them not so good. Recently I asked my now adult daughter if she thought I was a feminist mother. She said, "No, you were just mom. You always took care of us, and you always worked." I then asked her, through my disappointment, if any of my feminist teachings had sunk in. She replied, "You were always a strong woman. You took care of stuff. Because of you I am a strong woman. I feel like I can see things differently than other people, that I have a larger perspective because of talking about how different things on T.V. or books that affected you or might affect me." I heaved a heavy sigh of relief. She simply laughed and said, "You worry too much." Perhaps she is right.

I spent so much of my time trying to be the 'perfect mother' when my girls were small that I thought I would lose my mind. I was working full time nights (I lived with the girls' father at that time), volunteered two days a week at school, made some of their clothes, sewed Halloween costumes, made cookies, dinners, always had a vegetable garden, and tried to have a social life so that they could see that you don't stop being a person simply because you become a mother. And, as if that wasn't enough, I was going to school part-time. Their father did "help" me in this, but it was understood that it was my job and he helped. My biggest demand was that I didn't do dishes. After ten years of this unrelenting schedule I had a nervous breakdown. There was, and is, no such thing as a perfect mother, so there is no way to achieve this goal—no matter how hard I (and many, many others) tried.

In their book, Susan J. Douglas and Meredith W. Michaels explore the portrayal of mothers in the media during the exact time period I was raising my children in the early 1980's. In *The Idealization of Motherhood and How it Has Undermined All Women: the Mommy Myth,* Douglas and Michaels analyzed 30 years of media, print, television and radio. They looked at how women and mothers were portrayed, as well as the political climate surrounding women and mothers. Since the Reagan years, there has been a war against women, specifically in their role as mothers. Childcare, healthcare and education have all been deemed by the media, and consequently, the government, to be the responsibility of *mothers; not* the community, not the government, not *fathers.* "Experts" on child rearing, nearly all male, placed the emotional, psychological, physical and educational well-being of children directly on the shoulders of *mothers* and provided nearly no resources with which to do so. I was trying to be the perfect mother, and the society around me, through various sources of media, expected me to be the perfect mother. The pressure was internal, due to a traumatic childhood and the external forces that drive institutionalized misogyny and promote unrealistic expectations of mothers.

According to Douglas and Michaels' extensive documentation, there has been a concerted effort to undermine the safety and well-being of children through the destruction of AFDC (Aid to

Families with Dependent Children) programs, preschool programs, and childcare in general – in an attempt to get all mothers back in the home and out of the workforce. Support for this decimation of public programs has been elicited through blatant racism; by inventing "welfare queens" who are, of course, always African American even though most women and children on welfare are white. The impression is given that welfare mothers are black, lazy and don't deserve to have shelter, food and healthcare for *their* children. Meanwhile, women's magazines started profiling "celebrity mothers" who were white, well groomed, thin, smiling and talking about how "motherhood fulfills them." Never mind that they worked long hours away from home for months at a time earning a salary that most of us will not see in a lifetime of work, fulfilled or not. (Douglas, Michaels 173-202). The conservative right counted on the racism in the U.S. to do the rest, and they were rewarded for their confidence.

During the same time as "the war on welfare" in the 1980's, there was an increase in the reporting of often untrue stories of child molestation rings in daycare centers, alien abductions, and human abductions of children into the sex trade (Douglas, Michaels 85-110). There are enough true stories of sexual molestation, child abductions and physical abuse to send any caring human into night terrors, but this was a time of hyper-reporting and fear mongering. Women were warned about "having it all" at the cost of their child's innocence. Isn't it odd how fathers were never included in the "having it all" nightmare? It was all moms' fault for wanting a job, for wanting to be autonomous, for wanting to show her daughters and sons that women are people and deserve more than to be a servant to the needs of others. This was the reality of the social/political climate when my girls were small.

Despite all of the negative reporting trying to scare women into giving up their dreams and their jobs, I found great childcare for my children during the day so I could sleep after work. Our local public school was a "California Distinguished School" with a bilingual program from first to fifth grades. Not one alien took my children (although I did worry about it quite a bit) and they were not molested to the best of my knowledge, although I did worry about that even more.

Childcare remains an issue in the United States. In 2006, my son was three and was enrolled in an excellent day care at our local community college while I attended school full time as a PhD student. The fee was $545 a month for full time child care. This was a great price and the center provided excellent care. However, even at this reduced cost (the average cost for full time childcare in this county is anywhere from $800 per month to $2000+ per month) our family had to do without some luxuries. We were lucky that it is only luxuries that we had to give up. Many families (including mine twenty years ago), struggled to make ends meet and make sure the necessities were covered.

The pressure of trying to be a perfect mother with significantly less sleep than is recommended caught up with me. Through therapy, it occurred to me that life wasn't fair, life wasn't logical, life wasn't reasonable – so why do I have to be? So I stopped trying to be perfect according to others' expectations and started trying to be *good enough*. The internal relief was palpable for me. I quit my job at the hospital and started sleeping at least seven hours a night. Sometimes I even took naps. I continued in school full-time and worked part time. I also decided to leave my kids father because his "help" wasn't helpful.

The idea of 'the perfect mother' was created and extensively promoted during the 1980's and 1990's and continues into the present as a trap – an endless loop to keep women from resisting the oppression placed on them by the institution of motherhood. This loop starts by manipulating the love we have for our children and warps into a control mechanism to keep mothers "in line." The manipulation always starts with, "We know you love your children, you want the best for them. If you *really* loved them, you wouldn't *want* a job. You would want to stay home and wait on your child hand and foot, intuiting what they may or may not want." This manipulation continues into the "right" products to buy, the "right" exhibits, videos, shoes, clothes, toys, games etc. – so your child will be the smartest, best, and most loved. If you were a *good mother*, you would find a way to make it happen. Oh, you're poor? So sorry, the poor need not apply. For *you* to be a *good mother* you must sacrifice your time with your child and work at a crappy job while placing them in good childcare that simply doesn't exist. We are so busy chasing the unobtainable, whether we are poor or not, that we don't have time to say *wait a minute!* What about fathers?

What about childcare? What about healthcare? What about community? Where are the alternatives?

In her book, *Of Woman Born: Motherhood as Experience and Institution,* Adrienne Rich explores this very concept. Originally published in 1976, the ideas of the oppressive nature of intensive and solitary motherhood are still relevant today, nearly 40 years later. Rich explores the nature of the institution of motherhood; and how mothers somehow stopped being women when they became mothers. Their love for their children is supposed to be, "...continuous and unconditional." Love and anger cannot coexist. Female anger threatens the institution of motherhood" (Rich, 46). So if you love your children you can never show anger. How is one supposed to stage any kind of revolutionary act if one is not allowed to show anger?! Where is that anger supposed to go? Away? To where? The very idea that a woman is not happy in her role as mother as assigned by the institution of motherhood implies that she does not love her children and, again, is inferior.

Rich examines the nature of mother anger and where it goes in her chapter entitled, "Violence: The Heart of Maternal Darkness." In this chapter, she explores the powerlessness and desperation of the isolation and dependency of traditional motherhood:

> "...the invisible violence of the institution of motherhood, the guilt, the guilt, the guilt. So much of the heart of darkness is an undramatic, undramatized suffering: the woman who serves her family their food but cannot sit down with them, the woman who cannot get out of bed in the morning, the woman polishing the same place on the table over and over, reading labels in the supermarket as if they were in a foreign language, looking into a drawer where there is a butcher knife. The scapegoat is also the escape valve: through her the passions and the blind raging waters of a suppressed knowledge are permitted to churn their way so that they need not emerge in less extreme situations as lucid rebellion" (Rich 277-278).

She continues a few pages later:

> "...we would see the embodiment of rage, of tragedy, of the

overcharged energy of love, of inventive desperation; we
would see the machinery of institutional violence wrenching
at the experience of motherhood" (Rich 280).

While I find these descriptions to be moving and heartbreaking,
they presuppose a woman who is required, and financially able,
to stay home with her children. Both the stay at home mothers
and mothers with paid positions experience the "institutional
violence wrenching at the experience of motherhood." Their guilt
for their anger, for their absence, for their continual presence,
for their ambivalence toward mothering is fostered – not only
through organized Abrahamic religions, but through theories of
pre-history that see the ancient past as a less mechanized and
a more violent male as dominant version of the present.

Anywhere a woman might look for spiritual or intellectual help in
seeing depictions of herself in traditional religious or educational
systems there was none to be found. No heroes, no women
resisting, no women anywhere except in submission. There
seemed to be no way out. Women were, apparently, not
relevant in the past, they did nothing but marry and have babies
if they were good women – or if they were bad women, they
were prostitutes, but mostly they were simply non-existent. In
the Old Testament, man is created from the dust by God. There
are two versions of this creation story – one has Eve created at
the same time as Adam (Genesis 1:27) and one does not
(Genesis 2:21-22). For my purposes it does not matter which
version you prefer. What is apparent is that God did not need a
female counterpart to create life. No women need apply... God
did it all by Himself. This is directly counter to everything we
know about procreation on this earth.

In *Lesbian Nonbiological Mothering: Negotiating an (Un)Familiar
Existence* by Dawn Comeau and in *Mother Outlaws* edited by
Andrea O'Reilly, I found what seems like a plausible explanation
for the gradual expansion of man's ownership over the pro-
creative abilities of women and the expansion of patriarchal
structure as a result. In this article, the role and feelings of the
non-biological lesbian mother are explored. When reading the
feelings of the role of the non-biological mother, I wondered, "Is
this how men feel? Is this how men have always felt?" Granted,
fathers have a recognized role within society that is honored
and in many cases, revered; but the non-biological mother has

no *recognized* role, even though she is co-parent in every way. The experiences of being outsider-ed in the birth of their own child was very alienating. One woman described it, "…[I] don't' think you realize how much attention is focused on the pregnant woman (Comeau 161)." Another described it, "…I kinda felt like behind the scenes I was working my butt off to do this and do that and the stuff you don't see. You don't see my stomach growing [but I'm working just as hard at being a parent]" (Comeau 160).

Perhaps it is this feeling of alienation that originally led men to want more of a place in the birth process. Clearly, that desire for involvement got completely out of control and turned into a successful attempt to own – not only the process, but the child and the woman who mothered the child. It is this feeling of ownership that we are still trying to free ourselves from.

The God of the Old Testament is punitive. As a "tween" I saw so many good people, honest and loving people, chastising themselves for not being good enough Christians. I wondered what could they possibly do to improve? If these good people were not good enough, then what about me? How could I ever measure up? I often wished death upon my molester. I couldn't stop myself from talking back to my mother when she was clearly not telling the truth about my life. I wasn't excelling in school. It seemed I was breaking at least one of the Ten Commandments before I even got out of bed. So I decided if God wasn't going to protect me, or to believe in me, I wasn't going to believe in God. So I stopped. I stopped going to church. I stopped trying to be good according to those rules. I couldn't believe in a God that was just so mean.

I remained atheist/agnostic from the age of eleven until I was well into my 20's. While a dedicated feminist since nearly the same age, the idea of spirituality or religion just wasn't a part of my life. The introduction of the *possibility* of a divine female, Goddess, was life altering for me. The very concept, was at first, shocking. It just had simply never occurred to me; the idea that God could be female. In my primary education I was taught ancient myths and I was also taught that they were not truths. I was certainly not taught that these myths were ancient religions that were practiced with as much devotion as the ones practiced by Christians and Jews in my own community. Christianity was by far, the dominant religion; little consideration was given to the few Jewish kids among us. Certainly no one ever mentioned the possibility that God could be female. I decided I must find out who, exactly, this female deity was.

What I found was both exhilarating and heart-breaking. I found immense amounts of information about Goddess in many different forms in many different cultures: Evidence that our first deity was female through the works of Marija Gimbutas, Riane Eisler, Merlin Stone, Monica Sjoo and Barbara Mor, even Joseph Campbell speaks of Goddess; translations of a priestess in the Middle East, named Enheduanna, who wrote poems for and worshiped Inanna; and beautiful and heart breaking creation stories from Africa, India, Asia, Europe, and the Americas, both north and south.

These Goddesses were powerful and autonomous and everywhere. I felt so lied to by the educational system of this country! Why was I not told of these Goddesses, these priestesses?! Why was the evidence demeaned, denigrated, negated and hidden? What were clearly religious icons used to keep the divine close were turned into fertility fetishes, or worse, pre-historical porn. Not only blaspheming other, older religions, but mocking and denigrating ancient practitioners of those religions by turning them into self-pleasuring maniacs. The very idea of a female creator mocked at every turn.

These Goddesses were mothers! Our mothers. Instead of the judgmental and punitive father God, we had a mother Goddess who showered Her children with abundance. Goddess, loved all Her children, not just the ones who looked like her. Her daughters and sons and all of the plants on the earth – which was/is Her body. I believe that there must be a reintroduction or resurrection if you will, of the Divine Mother, of Goddess.

This resurrection of a Divine Mother would be in cooperation and *partnership* with a Divine Father. A heavenly couple, *equal* in power and authority, who model loving *all* of their children. When I say *all* I mean *all*, not just able-bodied white males, but all colors, races and ethnicities – all women, all children, all abilities, all genders (not just the two recognized in the west), all sexual orientations, and any and all combinations of the above. It is difficult to imagine a world where we are all equally valued as humans and how that would change mothering and fathering, but I believe this world is possible.

Martha C. Nussbaum, a classically trained philosopher and lawyer has developed, along with Amartya Sen, in her book, *Women and Human Development: The Capabilities Approach*, what I believe to be a very useful model in advancing an equalitarian form of parenting. Nussbaum does not posit this approach as a parenting solution but as a social justice solution to gross inequalities between sexes. I believe that this approach, when applied to one's own life and applied toward mothering and fathering, would be helpful in creating the space for the acceptance of a Divine Mother and change, or perhaps eliminate, the *institution* of motherhood. This will allow mothering and fathering to be more fluid and equitably shared. The basics of Nussbaum's Capabilities Approach are as follows:

1. **Life.** Being able to live to the end of a human life of normal length; not dying prematurely, or before one's life is so reduced as to be not worth living.

2. **Bodily Health.** Being able to have good health, including reproductive health; to be adequately nourished; to have adequate shelter.

3. **Bodily Integrity**. Being able to move freely from place to place; having one's bodily boundaries treated as sovereign, i.e. being able to be secure against assault, including sexual assault, child sexual abuse, and domestic violence; having opportunities for sexual satisfaction and for choice in matters of reproduction.

4. **Senses, Imagination, and Thoughts**. Being able to use the senses, to imagine, think, and reason – and to do these things in a "truly human" way, a way informed and cultivated by an adequate education, including, but by no means limited to, literacy and basic mathematical and scientific training. Being able to use imagination and thought in connection with experiencing and producing self-expressive works and events of one's own choice, religious, literacy, musical and so forth. Being able to use one's mind in ways protected by guarantees of freedom of expression with respect to both political and artistic speech, and freedom of religious exercise. Being able to search for the ultimate meaning of life in one's own way. Being able to have pleasurable experiences, and to avoid non-necessary pain.

5. **Emotions**. Being able to have attachments to things and people outside ourselves; to love those who love and care for us, to grieve at their absence; in general, to love, to grieve, to experience longing, gratitude, and justified anger. Not having one's emotional development blighted by overwhelming fear and anxiety or by traumatic events of abuse or neglect. (Supporting this capability means supporting forms of human association that can be shown to be crucial in their development.)

6. **Practical Reason**. Being able to form a conception of the good and to engage in critical reflection about the planning of one's life. (This entails protection for the liberty of conscience.)

7. **Affiliation A**: Being able to live with and toward others, to recognize and show concern for other human beings, to engage in various forms of social interaction; to be able to imagine the situation of another and to have compassion for that situation; to have the capability for both justice and friendship. (Protecting this capability means protecting institutions that constitute and nourish such forms of affiliation, and also protecting the freedom of assembly and political speech.) **B**: Having the social bases of self-respect and non-humiliation; being able to be treated as a dignified being whose worth is equal to that of others. This entails, at a minimum, protections against discrimination on the basis of race, sex, sexual orientation, religion, caste, ethnicity, or national origin. In work, being able to work as a human being, exercising practical reason and entering into meaningful relationships of mutual recognition with other workers.

8. **Other Species**. Being able to live with concern for and in relation to animals, plants and the world of nature.

9. **Play**. Being able to laugh, to play, to enjoy recreational activities.

10. **Control Over One's Environment. A. Political**. Being able to participate effectively in political choices that govern one's life; having the right of political participation, protections of free speech and association. **B. Material**. Being able to hold property (both land and moveable goods), not just formally but in terms of real opportunity; and having property rights on equal basis with others; having the right to seek

employment on an equal basis with others; having the freedom from unwarranted search and seizure (Nussbaum 78–80).

This approach is not exhaustive, but the changes would be forever life altering for all if we were allowed to pursue our capabilities instead of being forced to fit some unobtainable, and I believe, damaging, role of feminine or masculine behavior. Even before I knew this approach existed, I have lived my life and sought to create a family that is a site of resistance using many, but not all, of the strategies proposed in Nussbaum's Capabilities Approach. At the same time, I have pulled from the knowledge that powerful women in history have always existed. I have discussed these powerful women from the past with my daughters. The only deity they have known is female.

I asked my youngest daughter if she thought I was a feminist mother and if that changed or affected her in any way. She said: *"Yes I do think you are a feminist mother. I think if it did change me, it would be for the better. Perhaps in the way that thinking that women are not only supposed to do one thing or have one job or stay at home and cook, that they have a choice whether they want to do those things or not. I try to see things more equally and not so one sided. And to stand up for myself, if I don't like how I'm being treated or what is going on in a certain situation to stand up for myself and say what I'm thinking. I don't know if I would have acquired these aspects of me if you weren't a feminist. I wouldn't say it changed me in a bad way because feminism doesn't mean man hating, if anything it taught me that I deserve to be respected and heard too, but not to hate. I just like to be able to do what I do and say what I like to say and if something gets in the way of that I'm going to have something to say about it."*

As a mother, I am proud of all my daughters and my son. I am also proud of myself for being able to instill feminist values in my children while still struggling with issues of equality and emancipation myself.

REFERENCES

Chodorow, Nancy J. *The Reproduction of Mothering*. Berkeley: University of California Press, 1999.

Comeau, Dawn. "Lesbian Nonbiological Mothering: Negotiating an (Un)Familiar Existence." *Mother Outlaws: Theories and Practices of Empowered Mothering.* Toronto: Women's Press, 2004.

De Shong Meador, Betty. *Inanna Lady of the Largest Heart: Poems of the Sumerian High Priestess Enheduanna.* Austin: University of Texas Press, 2000.

Douglas, Susan J. and Meredith W. Michaels. *The Mommy Myth: The Idealization of Motherhood and How It Has Undermined All Women.* New York: Free Press, 2004.

Eisler, Riane. *The Chalice and the Blade: Our History, Our Future.* San Francisco: HarperSanFrancisco, 1995.

Gimutas, Marija. *The Goddesses and Gods of Old Europe 6500-3500 BC : Myths and Cult Images.* Berkeley: University of California Press, 1982.

Gimbutas, Marija. *The Living Goddesses.* Ed. Miriam Robbins Dexter. Berkeley: University of California Press, 2001.

Nussbaum, Martha C. *Women and Human Development: The Capabilities Approach.* Cambridge: Cambridge University Press, 2000.

O'Reilly, Andrea, ed. *Mother Outlaws: Theories and Practices of Empowered Mothering.* Toronto: Women's Press, 2004.

O'Reilly, Andrea. *Rocking the Cradle: Thoughts on Motherhood, Feminism and the Possibility of Empowered Mothering.* Toronto: Demeter Press, 2006.

Rich, Adrienne. *Of Woman Born: Motherhood as an Experience and Institution. New York: W.W. Norton & Company, 1986.*

Ruddick, Sara. *Maternal Thinking: Towards a Politics of Peace.* New York: Ballentine Books, 1989.

Stevenson, Laura. *Taking an Autoethnographic Perspective: On Becoming a Member of a Tertiary Community.* 1 Dec. 2005. www.aare.edu.au/05pap/ste05594.pdf

Wolkestein, Diane and Samuel Noah Kramer. *Inanna Queen of Heaven and Earth: Her Stories and Hymns from Sumer.* San Francisco: Harper & Row, 1983.

The leaving of calm waters

Metis

*"I hate to hear you talk about all women as if they were
fine ladies instead of rational creatures.
None of us want to be in calm waters all our lives."*
— Jane Austen, Persuasion

I DO NOT KNOW when exactly I decided that I didn't want to be a 'fine lady' and left the calm waters, but I think I can estimate a time when the process began. It may also have to do with the fact that I began to appreciate the most common definition of feminism.

The Merriam-Webster dictionary describes feminism as "the theory of the political, economic, and social equality of the sexes." Feminism within 'faiths' becomes trickier because women of faith want to remain within their particular faith while *desiring* equality with men in the political, economic, and social areas. However, most faiths are patriarchal because they were started by men before the rise of what we call 'feminism' or the *desire* to be equal to men. Many of such religious systems do not believe in the political, economic, and social equality of the sexes. These systems promote gender roles and a gender hierarchy that is often very strict and sometimes even harsh.

I was born and raised in quite a traditional Sunni Muslim family. Around the time I was growing up my father found a rekindled interest in Islam and made sure that all his daughters were raised 'strictly' as Muslim. My mother, a free-spirited and independent woman, took her independent nature for granted until she fell in love with, and married my father. Thereupon she grew increasingly frustrated with her "wings being constantly clipped." That frustration set off a chain reaction that resulted in my decision to finally label myself a feminist.

Feminism, in my view, is not an irrational desire to be equal to men. A woman becomes, or realises that she already is, a feminist when she notices how she is constantly pulled down, degraded, or even humiliated for being the *wrong sex*. It happened to me around the time I turned eight and learned (ironically, through my mother) that she never wanted a daughter and consequently the day of my birth had become "the

106

saddest day" of her life. It took me more than three decades and a Facebook comment from a stranger to finally understand her predicament – the dilemma of a 'God-fearing woman.' Her understanding of God is that *He* is male and chose to speak only to men. For her, the male sex is already empowered, wise and in control. She wanted to do things in life but fell in love and willingly entered into a marriage that had a definite male head. She prayed to a male God, that male God told her that she must be faithful to one man, and she had to seek permission from that man to do what she wanted – sometimes he permitted her, but mostly she was too 'wild' for him to assent to her requests. Growing up without a father and in a family full of independent women (due to their fatherless situation), this became her dilemma. A son she desired but never had would have provided an escape from this cycle of suppression. She would have raised him in a way that she would be in control; he'd be her little knight, her caregiver in old age, her provider – just the way she wanted, without having to ask him for permission to do anything. Or at least that is what she thought.

I work with feminism within faiths because I have not known a world without faith. Although I often choose to separate feminist activism from spirituality, I fully value the emotions of feminists who want to operate within their faiths. These women need a lot of support, especially those who belong to patriarchal organized religious systems. I work with such feminists and have recently begun to understand that while the respective religious systems support women's causes, they do not necessarily empower them in the modern sense because these systems were established in another space and time. For example, while my parents' faith supported my mother as a wife and a mother and gave her some rights, she was never *equal* in the marriage. The Quran never once tells the believers that the two sexes are *equal* or *same* in terms of gender rights on earth. There is, however, 'equity' (2:228) and 'justice' (4:34) and 'similarity' (2:228).

Nevertheless, both sexes are completely equal in terms of spirituality and both are promised equal recompense in the Hereafter if they stay on the Right Path, and serve their time on this earth within the gender roles chalked up for them.

There are numerous women within Islam, and other religions as well, who are completely satisfied with this gender role arrangement. Many find such arrangements convenient; some even consider them empowering. But there are also women who desire equality between sexes on this earth to reflect the equality promised in the Hereafter. For many feminists who are Muslim, the main role model is Khadijah (first wife of the Islamic Prophet, Muhammad) who married Muhammad before his prophethood and spent 15 years of her total 25 years of marriage to him in pre-Islamic period of Arabia. Khadijah symbolizes not only female empowerment but also complete equality with men. She proposed marriage to Muhammad who was her employee and did not have the means to get married. Therefore, she paid for the wedding and Muhammad moved in with her. She was a woman whom "the apostle never opposed" (Ibn Ishaq's Sirat Rasul Allah, p. 313). Most Muslim feminists refer to Khadijah's example to show that it is possible to demand equality between the sexes within Islam.

But such arguments are not that simple since most of Quranic law regarding gender roles was revealed and written down in Medina after Khadijah's death. There are numerous Islamic feminist scholars who make arguments in favour of gender equality (in this world) by reinterpreting the Quranic law. One of the pioneers is Dr. Amina Wadud for whom I have deep respect. I acknowledge that neo Islamic/Muslim Feminism would have never even properly started if Dr. Wadud had not attempted to 'reread the Sacred Text from a woman's perspective.' The book gave many Islamic feminists the hope and encouragement to reinterpret the Quran from a Muslim woman's perspective. Thousands of Muslim and Islamic feminists use these feminist interpretations to claim that "Islam elevates the status of women." These feminists compare the exploited status of women in Arabia before Islam with the "elevated" status post-Islam in Medina. Ironically though, they ignore to note that Khadijah grew up and lived fifty five years of her life in pre-Islamic Arabia. I want to use this example to point out that Arabia of that time was not anymore monolithic than it is today. The 'status of women' varied from city to city and from one tribe to another.

There were patriarchal tribes and matriarchal tribes. There were patrilineal lineages and there were matrilineal lineages. There were tribes that killed their baby daughters and there were tribes that trusted their daughters with the Keys to the Kaaba. There were fathers who sold off their daughters and then there were women who proposed to men they wanted to marry. There were fathers who left nothing for their daughters and then there were daughters who received generous inheritance from their fathers, like Khadijah. There were women who were not allowed to divorce and there were women who divorced their husbands at will and arbitrarily. Some tribes had polygynous men, while in others women married multiple times. Islam brought one law. It tried to strike a balance through 'equity' by creating gender roles. This Law gave many women rights they had never experienced before in their tribes, but it also took away some rights that other women had enjoyed. Fourteen hundred years later, feminists are asking for rights that were done away with initially like equality in divorce, inheritance, scholarship, profession, and marriage to name a few.

Many other feminists who are Muslim generally separate spirituality from social activism. Such feminists believe that Quran "contains sufficient seeds for those committed to human rights and gender justice to live in fidelity to its underlying ethos" – however, it "far from the human rights or gender equality document that Muslim apologists make it out to be" (Farid Esack). I believe that Esack could have appreciated that human or gender rights are socially constructed and hence are always time-bound. Many apologists and critics alike fail to either notice or acknowledge this.

I want to end this piece by sharing a question I was recently asked on Facebook. Someone asked if "Islam oppresses women." This is a very complicated question. First of all, what is Islam? Islam is neither monolithic nor an ideology that can be defined simply. Every Muslim has their own Islam. Some Muslim men do oppress women but that does not mean that Islam, as a supposed monolithic religion, oppresses women or that even these men's Islam teaches oppression of women. Second, times have changed and some of the 7th Century laws laid down about women are many times not applicable today. For example, in a world where many women work and support their parents in old age it is hardly fair to allot a lesser share in inheritance to them. Or for instance we cannot stop a Muslim female astronaut from going into space without a mahram (male)!

Similarly in the modern world it is simply not suitable to require the witnesses of two women to equal that of one man. And most modern women would not accept disciplining of any form from their husbands. These laws were perfectly fine 1,400 years ago, but they may seem oppressive today. Muslims who are feminists utilize different methods to make feminism work within their practice of Islam from reinterpreting Islamic texts to subscribing to secular feminism. What works for me personally is acknowledging that we don't live in the Arabia of the 7th Century, separating 'social law' from 'religious law', and separating spirituality from feminism. It is the only way I have found to make my feminism compatible with my faith.

My Heart, My Spirit, My Faith

Patty Kay

IN THE BEGINNING WAS THE ONE. Existence was brought forth from nonexistence. A Kabbalist might say that creation manifested with the sole intent to create a creature and fill it with delight (Kosinec, 2014). A truly joyful notion for a Cradle Catholic who was taught a lot of hellfire and damnation!

Regardless of the how or why of existence, we are here now. I pray for all creatures who share this reality with me to ask the One to help humanity find the point in our hearts that meets the point in our souls where a human level of understanding resides. I seek a truer purpose for mankind, one that doesn't involve money or prestige or power. I pray for humans to live as Earth Warriors. May the understanding I seek be purposefully aimed at restoring the world to a place of clean air and water.

Physician and author of several books espousing the role of religion and spirituality in health care, Dr. Larry Dossey has noted the importance of spirituality not only in wellness for humans, but for the environment as well. In a review of Matthew Fox's book, *Meister Eckhart*, Dr. Dossey wrote, "Whether our species has a future on Earth does not depend on more of the gee-whiz technologies, but on whether we are willing to move into a psycho-spiritual dimension... time is not on our side."

There was a time when our world was seemingly new and pristine. We could smell trees instead of exhaust fumes. We could drink our water and had no fear that the toxins in it might burn our skin or be absorbed by our bodies and cause cancer. We could trust the ground we stood on not to form into a sink hole due to all the fracking going on. I pray for the Creator to send out the Spirit and renew the face of the Earth (Ps. 104). Literally.

Practically since I was born, prayers from my tradition have urged me to "Look Beyond" the main-line teachings of my faith. "As it was in the beginning is now, and ever shall be, world without end." The creed I recite says, in part, "I believe in one God... Maker of heaven and earth, and of all things visible and invisible... God of God, Light of Light, true God of true God... by whom all things were made."

The consensus of scientific evidence indicates that time and space and all that is visible and invisible began from a numinous singularity that swelled into an inchoate soup. The creative stew then morphed countless billions of times as the universe unfolded. Indications are that the expansion continues still (Swimme, 1992). I take this as the universe following the divine command to increase and multiply (Gen. 1:22).

I think no point-in-time inside eternity exists as distinct from any other point-in-time. It could be that everything is still in the formation stage of creation. All I know is that I believe in God and I believe in the universe. And for all I know, it's all the same. We and "it" are one.

Some images of Jesus portray Him on the cross with no hands or feet. To me, that particular rendition serves as an invitation to join in the creative process. I see the Creator bidding us to move into eternity and learn new ways. Then we may return to this finite place as co-creators where we become the action part of further emergence. We are expected to move forward and create a new peace, a new beginning, a new everything. It is not privilege, it is a mandate. I believe that is the true message of the Paschal Mystery.

We need to stop believing that commerce is the answer to all our woes. My wish is for all of us to re-learn the value of our senses. Seeing beauty could be a universal desire worth more than gold. Smelling the freshness and vitality of our plant sisters and brothers will be expected. And the right to delight in olfactory sensations will be fought for with the same ferocity we currently express when fighting over carbon. We will want to hear the chirping and tweeting, roaring and snorting, and all the sounds that emanate from our animal relations. It will be music to our ears. Food will taste better as we move closer to an appreciation for it, and for the miracle that brought it to us. And finally, we will all long to touch one another spiritually.

History has shown us that the way we are going does not work. Ever since we stood up on two legs, we have exploited the planet that sustains us. We have soiled our God-given gifts of water, air and earth. Convenience and financial gains have won out over survival and compassion. We need to call on wisdom (rather than just knowledge) to take us forward now.

Wisdom has long been embodied as feminine. The ancients had Athena, Minerva, Isis or Eve to personify it. St. Teresa of Calcutta, Sister Simone Campbell, Malala Yousafzai, and numerous other brave women fighting for justice have carried forth the wisdom tradition in my own lifetime.

So I call forth that feminine spirit in all of us to honor the Earth we wish to save. Roman Catholic priest and world-renowned environmentalist, Thomas Berry, called ecology a "functional cosmology." Gaia, Our Mother Earth, is a living creature. She needs our love and protection as we move into a new thinking that involves conservation and sustainability in a wiser way of living that I call Praxecology (Segall, 2009).

REFERENCES

Ducote, Darryl. "Look Beyond." The best of the Dameans. GIA, n.d. Vinyl.

Kosinec, Anthony. ""Kabbalah Revealed" Episode 2: Perception of Reality." Transcript. kabbalah.info. Kabbalah, Bnei Baruch - Kabbalah Education & Research Institute.

"NEW ADVENT." NEW ADVENT: Home. Ed. Kevin Knight. Baronius Press Ltd, 8 Jan. 2012. Web. Spring 2014. http://www.newadvent.org.

Segall, Matthew. "Logos of a Living Earth: Towards a Gaian Praxecology." Footnotes 2 Plato. N.p., 21 Nov. 2009. Web. Summer 2014. http://footnotes2plato.com/2009/11/21/logos-of-a-living-earth-towards-a-gaian-praxecology.

Swimme, Brian, and Thomas Berry. The Universe Story: From the Primordial Flaring Forth to the Ecozoic Era--a Celebration of the Unfolding of the Cosmos. San Francisco, CA: HarperSan Francisco, 1992. Print.

Letters from the Mother

Zoe Nicholson

N 1995, MY CLOSE FRIEND, LAURA WAS DIAGNOSED with stage four ovarian cancer. For the next 18 months, she tried everything within her reach to get back to ease, to leave dis-ease, to stall leaving her life. It was unshakable. It was inevitable and the time arrived that all we could do was search for peace with this early and permanent parting.

There was so much I wanted to tell her. There were things that I knew were true but had no authority to tell her in my own voice. So I took a leap, a risk and wrote 12 letters to her from the voice that comforts me, that speaks to me, that lives in you and me. I spoke in her voice, The Divine Mother's Voice.

Here are two of the letters:

~ REUNION ~

My Dearest, Darling Daughter,

Before you were born, before you took on your current body, before you entered into the world of thought, we made plans. We met and talked, as we do before all of your incarnations. Together we surveyed your progress, your path, your soul's code and together we set in place the course of your next lifetime.

Though your life may feel complex, together we chose two or three lessons for you to learn. These lessons repeat many times, in many ways in one lifetime. They remain the essence of a single lifetime. Families are chosen, relationships are formed, circumstances are unveiled to lead you through your lessons and bring you eternal wisdom. Even the body you have chosen is part of our plan.

All the time I am watching, I am guiding, I am waiting. Many times you ask for help and I always hear you. I answer in the only way I can; I reveal myself in your heart. Many times you do not hear me and it is because you do not stop your

114

thoughts and look to your heart. You do not put your words aside and feel me within your heart. I am there, I am always there.

As you journey through your life, you must know that all of the attractions you form, the aversions you feel, are at your own request. When you cross paths with people in need, you must give. When you are in need, you are meant to receive.

When the world begins to overwhelm you, it is because you are looking too far from your own path. Do not grieve for those you do not know. Do not suffer for those you cannot help. Do not take into your heart the millions around the world. Compassion is learned in the context of your individual life. Respond fully and openly to those who present themselves to you. They are the guardians and guideposts of your unique lessons.

As you find your life unfolding, you are at the service of your neighbors. And they are at your service. You must not waste your energy on imagined suffering. If you find yourself in great joy, it is yours. If you find yourself in great loneliness, it is yours. If you find yourself in great chaos, it is yours. If you find yourself in great peace, it is yours. Together, we designed your plan, your path, your particular way. The world is one grand and holy plan to bring you to the light.

When the time comes for us to meet again, you will find your body is ready to rest. This may come without notice. This may come through disease. This may come in your sleep. This may come in your youth or your old age. This may be a surprise or the result of a long illness. Either way, anyway, it is the time for us to meet again.

In the inversion of your world, death has become deeply misunderstood. It is a time of great importance. It is not a time to fear. It is not a time to avoid or hide. You have built thousands of hospitals and isolating institutions to shroud this great transition. Science has tried to forestall our appointment, extending lives beyond their service. Souls are sitting in bodies that I am ready to meet. Do not avoid our reunion. Stop your thought and you will not be afraid, you will know when the time is right, and we will keep to our plan.

Death is part of life. You are meant to witness it. You are meant to watch, hold hands, wish others well. Death is a wonderful celebration that a soul has completed its journey. Death is a moment of joy, when a soul lets go of the body, steps out of the world of thought and rests in my arms. Do not hide it from the children. Do not hide it from each other. Do not hide it from yourself. Death is a completion of a cycle and the entrance to my world, the light.

When you arrive, we will rest, we will plan, we will laugh, we will love each other. There will be no judgment. There will be no guilt. There will only be joyous reunion. You will recognize me instantly because you are me and I am you.

~ CONTINUITY~

My Dearest, Darling Daughter,

Imagine that your soul, your essence, your discrete divinity is a delicate, intricate and radiant lattice. Within this lattice is everything you are. It is not the people you know or the places you've been. It is the on-going record of everything you have collected and will collect on the way to Enlightenment.

This divine tapestry is unique to you. It is what never dies and is never born. It is infinity itself. It takes on a name, learns a language, and thinks thoughts. Eventually, as an incarnation progresses, it even believes it has an identity. Looking to parents, to the tribe, to the world, it learns to believe. More importantly, it learns to forget.

All of this is not necessary. All of this is not my intention. According to my plan, you may know the truth. You may know who you are. You may remain in constant communication with me. You may be fully conscious of my presence in your many lives.

I am the energy which radiates through your soul. I am called light, prana, shakti. I am the life which radiates through your world. I am the source of vibration. I am the source of radiance. I am always present. I am always with you.

Stop your thoughts and you will find me. Turn your attention away from the obvious, for I can never be obvious. Turn your attention away from the immediate, for I am infinite. Turn your attention away from this particular incarnation and you will remember our relationship.

Before the formation of words, I am present. Outside of the torrent of thoughts, I am present. Waiting for you to create openings, I am present. Waiting to flood your world with light, I am present.

I will bring with me fresh air, clean water, rich forests, and most importantly peace. I will take the entire planet through the darkness and violence you accept as part of everyday living, and restore peace. The grace and mindfulness you practice will make room for me to infuse the world with peace.

Printed with permission
© Lune Soleil Press

Finding My Inner Goddess

Erin McKelle

FEMINISM WAS DEFINITELY NOT a part of my faith tradition, or my family's values, during my childhood. I was raised in a Christian household as a Lutheran. I went to Church every Sunday, attended Lutheran school, and my Mom was even my Sunday school teacher for a few years. Even when my parents divorced, it was always important to my Mom that faith be a central part of my life, and she made it a point to take me to Church and Sunday school, even on the weekends when I stayed with my Dad.

Through this, I learned that I should never, ever sin, always have faith in Jesus, and repent in order to get into heaven. I also was taught (both implicitly and directly) that sexuality was shameful, that women's roles were to primarily be wives and mothers, and that those who indulged in the pleasures of the Earth would be damned in hell for eternity.

Because I went to a religious school every day, all of this was very much a part of my thinking and my life. I knew nearly all of my friends through some sort of a religious means and I wasn't involved socially with anyone who wasn't Christian.

Fast forward to when I was 13 with my dad's family on vacation in Myrtle Beach. I had brought along a book called *Conversations with God for Teens* (an adaptation of the original based on teen's questions) to read while I was there. As I cracked open the book by the pool one day, the whole world opened up right before my eyes. As I was reading that God wasn't angry with me for using his name 'in vain,' or wanting to have sex and explore my body, or even questioning God, I started to question *everything* I'd ever been taught about my faith.

Soon, I began reading more books and expanding my field of vision as much as possible. I wanted to learn everything there was to know about religion and theology. I realized that there were so many different religions to explore and faith traditions to learn about. Since I was taught that questioning God or my

Lutheran faith was wrong, I had never learned about other types of belief. I now knew I had been missing out. I read books about Taoism, Hinduism, Islam, Buddhism, Jainism... anything I could find!

As I was reading and learning, I saw my faith in Christianity crumble before my eyes. I didn't understand how one religion could declare itself to be the truth and deny the obvious beauties and truths present in others.

I also began to see the ridiculousness of a lot of the supernatural aspects of the Bible, especially in regards to the Devil and Hell. I couldn't see how any logical, rational human being could take these things seriously. It was so obviously created to scare and I didn't understand how no one else could see that. If God was love, why would they ever damn anyone to Hell? If there was a God, I knew that the Christians were wrong about who they were.

This all happened during the summer before I started eighth grade, my last year at my parochial, religious school. I wished I could never go back, but I knew I didn't have a choice. If I told my Mom about my change of heart regarding religion, I knew she would be upset with me. If I told my Church, teachers, or peers at my school, I knew they would judge me. I felt trapped, with no way out. I had to keep the truth inside of my heart and force myself to not shout it at the top of my lungs.

This time in my life really inspired my feminist work that was to come. I felt called to live wholly and to love everyone, and I saw the hypocrisy many in my faith lived (by claiming that Jesus accepted all, but actually judging anyone who they deemed imperfect). I knew that wasn't who I was and I didn't want *anyone* to feel that they could lead a life of judgment and scorn or have to fear that God was judging them. This really sparked my love for all people and my strong sense of justice. I wasn't willing to let anyone be discriminated against or shunned for who they were.

I also began to see the ways in which women in my school were treated, which was nothing short of sexist. They weren't allowed to be Pastors or leaders in the Church and were policed to almost no end, it seemed. I remember how the boys in my class

119

would get away with cursing and talking about sex, but when *I* would do it, I would be punished. Most of the other girls didn't curse or talk sex at all, I'm guessing because they knew what the consequences would be. I started to become really angry as I noticed these things and my inner feminist Goddess started to become awakened!

Because of my anger, I started to veer spiritually toward agnosticism. As I read books written by people who all assumed to know all of the answers, I became frustrated. I knew I couldn't claim to have that kind of truth about the universe or the divine, and I felt that those who did were either full of themselves or buying into indoctrinated ideology. As Socrates once said, *the wise know that they are ignorant.*

My agnosticism led me to care more about the planet and its inhabitant's well-being though. I realized that everyone on Earth had to work together to sustain it, since we could not assume there was a God or Goddess who could do so. It was our job to make life beautiful. We had to take ownership.

Taking charge of my life is exactly what I did. As time went on, I realized I was living in a very toxic way. I was battling an eating disorder, abusive relationships, and felt like I could never truly be happy. I was walking self-destruction and I was destroying every beautiful thing in my path. While I was starting to work for others justice and humanity, I couldn't even acknowledge my own.

This caused me to spiral downward personally, but as an activist I began to thrive. I pushed myself to the limit, taking on as many projects as possible, to fill the gap in my heart. I felt like I had nothing to give other than my work, which I was good at. While it took me very far professionally, personally it was more than I could take.

When I went away to college, I reached a breaking point. My eating disorder got out of control and emotionally, I was a wreck. I was working myself out of an emotionally abusive relationship, which took a lot of strength and energy. I was soon burnt out and felt more hopeless than ever.

I was lucky to find the strength within to keep going. I knew that there was something better at the end of the tunnel and I kept going, no matter how much I wanted to throw it all away. Self-sabotage has long been a friend of mine and I knew that if I wanted to get anywhere, I had to cut her off.

It was then that I started recovery, in every sense of the word. I found my soul again, which had been buried in a year's worth of shame and self-deprivation. I put my all into therapy and healing and although I made some mistakes, I saw myself doing better than ever. I was truly thriving.

I started to feel like there was an inner-Goddess inside of me who was guiding me toward the truth I was meant to live. It wasn't like a person, but more like an emotion, a state of being. It represented balance and truth, compassion and love. The more I listened, the better things got. One day I was walking home from school and I remember thinking, "*If there's a God, this is what it must feel like.*" Then I realized maybe that *was* God.

While my faith has been all across the board, one thing has stayed the same: my inner-Goddess. Even though I haven't fully discovered her yet, she's always been there. When I started to question my faith in middle school is when I really started to feel her. The voice sounds like my own, but what's underneath is something exquisite, divine, and perfectly imperfect. In essence, it's me, but it's the enlightened version of me. I believe every one of us has this within, but until we turn within instead of outside to seek truth, we will not find her.

Being a Goddess has allowed me to become a fearless feminist and live my life without remorse. The power she holds inspires and motivates me every day to do better.

Now the question is, what will finding your inner Goddess do for *you?*

A Female Rabbi is Like an
Orange on the Passover Plate
Women and the Rabbinate: Challenges and Horizons[39]

Rabbi Dalia Marx (Ph.D.)

I wonder what it's like to be a Jew.
I have been close to Jews all my life;
I've eaten with them, eaten and even cooked
their kosher food.
I've drunk their kosher wine
and said 'amen' to their blessings.
I've dressed up and gone to their synagogues on Sabbaths
and holydays.
I've even fasted on their fast days.
I've given money that I have earned to their charities.
I've read their books and learned to read,
from right to left, their holy tongue.
I've watched them at their prayers, their Bible chanting, their
Torah carrying.
I'm beginning to wonder why I'm here,
Because I'm only Jewish....and
Jewish is to Jew as greenish is to green.
Almost, but not quite.
A Jewish Woman [40]

---

[39] This article is based on: Dalia Marx, "A Female Rabbi is like an Orange on the Seder's Plate: Women in the Rabbinate, Challenges and Horizons", Walter Homolka and Hainz-Guenther Schoelter (eds.), *Rabbi – Pastor – Priest: Their Roles and Profiles Through the Ages*, Berlin: DeGruyter, 2013, 219-240.

[40] Yocheved (Eunice) Scheinbok Welber published this poem in 1973 in the newsletter she herself edited for her synagogue, Kehillat Bet Torah of Mount Kisco, NY, after her daughter was denied an egalitarian ceremony to celebrate her forthcoming marriage. I thank her for allowing me to cite her poem and for her many editorial and other helpful suggestions for this article. I also thank her granddaughter, my friend Rabbi Chaya Rowen Baker, for bringing the poem to my attention. Thanks also to Taffy Sassoon for additional editing.

A LTHOUGH THE FOLLOWING STORY IS RELATIVELY
new, its variations are many. The most common variation
speaks of a rabbi (a male rabbi, of course) who rebuked a
woman when she asked whether women can serve as rabbis.
He dismissed her question by saying that women had as much
place on the pulpit as an orange had on the Passover *Seder*
plate. As an act of defiance, many liberal families now add an
orange to the ritual *Seder* plate on their Passover table.[41]

This paper is dedicated to an examination of the topic of
women in the rabbinate. After a short history of the subject, I
shall discuss some of the unique aspects of women rabbis:
What they bring to the rabbinate, what special challenges they
face, and how they have changed the profession. I will address
the special case of women rabbis in Israel and will conclude
with a consideration of the immediate and far-reaching
consequences of increasing numbers of women in the pulpit.

1. A Brief History of Women in the Rabbinate

There are a few salient examples of women who served as
leaders in ancient Israel (such as the prophetesses Deborah
and Huldah); in the Middle Ages (such as Asenath Barzani,
1590–1670, in Iraq); and in the Chassidic communities of
Eastern Europe from the 18th century onward (such as Edel,
daughter of the founder of Chassidism, HaBaal Shem Tov).[42]
In recent times, women have become active members of their
synagogues, engaged in cooking, serving, cleaning, fund-
raising, committee work, etc. These functions have been done
on a voluntary basis, usually without any formal recognition.
This paper, however, deals specifically with women who strove
to become rabbis and with others who actually succeeded in
achieving an institutional or private ordination.

According to Pamela Nadell, author of *Women Who Would Be
Rabbis*,[43] the question of whether women can serve in the

---

[41] Susannah Heschel, considered to be the source of this story, later explained that it
was not accurately told, and that the reason for including an orange was to express
solidarity with Jewish gays and lesbians as well as with other marginalized groups in
the Jewish community (http://www.jweekly.com/article/full/17548/orange-on-
seder-plate-tale-is-flawed-feminist-says).

[42] Renee Goldberg, *Hasidic Women Rebbes from 1749-1933*, rabbinical thesis, HUC-
JIR, 1997.

rabbinate was first asked more than 120 years ago. She cites a short story written in 1899 by the journalist Mary M. Cohen, a member of the traditional Philadelphia synagogue Mikveh Israel. Entitled "A Problem for Purim," the story was prominently published on the front page of *The Jewish Exponent*. The issue posed by the story is whether women could help American Judaism thrive by becoming rabbis. The story's protagonist is a promising young man, Lionel Martinez, who is preparing for the rabbinate. A few days before Purim, he invites a group of friends to discuss Jewish affairs. The topic for discussion is "Ministers and their work" and initially the talk revolves around sermons and the possibility of exchanging pulpits in the hope that this might offer "some vitalizing influence". Then a young woman, Dora Ulman, superintendent of a local sewing school, speaks up, warning that her words "will shock you considerably."

She blushed a little, then made a desperate plunge into her subject. "Could not – our women – be – ministers?" All but Lionel were struck dumb. Even Jack's boasted calmness had taken flight; he sate *[sic]* in open eyed surprise. Martinez said quickly: "Will you explain your idea or plan, Miss Dora?" He was, however, secretly a little astonished: he had not expected anything from her until later on, and then, "views" on sewing schools. "It seems to me," said Dora in response, "that there are trials in the lives of women that men do not and cannot understand. About these our sex could probably preach and teach better than men could. At present men minister to both sexes and why should women not do the same? Of course I do not mean that women should supersede men in the pulpit [...] but the profession should be opened to women too."

Dora continues by explaining her idea to the astonished gathering. Questions are asked to which she gives clear and forceful answers. The men's objections are important for our purposes (and are still familiar to us).

No fewer than six arguments are raised against Dora's appeal: 1. There are few if any women suitable for the pulpit; 2. Doubt that women can see sufficiently beyond their "circumstances

---

[43] Pamela Nadell, *Women Who Would Be Rabbis: A History of Women's Ordination 1889-1985* (Boston: Beacon Press, 1998).

and horizons" to become engaged; 3. Fear that "our people" are not ready for this; 4. It "constituted too severe a break with the past"[44]; 5. Fear that women's ambitions to become rabbis will meet with ridicule, people "would laugh openly to see a woman at the pulpit"; 6. Fear of what we would today call the feminization of the profession, a phenomenon that would diminish the profession's status.

Interestingly, these arguments would be heard again and again with regard to the ordination of women, all the way up to the present time. Cohen responds to these objections through Dora's mouth and concludes by citing an anonymous Christian clergyman who wrote that "the pulpit will never reach its sublimest power until Woman takes her place in it as a free and equal interpreter of God".[45]

It may not be coincidental that Cohen chose to publish her story just before Purim, the feast of masquerade and light-headedness, when in traditional *yeshivas* (houses of study) a special role-reversal game takes place. One of the students, typically a bright and independent-minded one, is elected to serve as "Purim Rabbi" for the day, in order to embody the Purim concept of *venahafokh hu* (let us turn it upside down). The Purim Rabbi's task is to create a humorous mood in an institution that is usually dedicated to very serious study. By her choice of the story's title and date of publication, Cohen may have been alluding to Queen Esther, the orphan who saved the Jewish people from extermination. While couching her revolutionary idea in a topsy-turvy Purim context, Cohen may not only have been warning people not to take her too seriously but she may also have been using parody as a safe way of expressing unconventional truths that otherwise could not be tolerated.[46]

Indeed, Cohen's arguments reveal a climate of rising expectations for changing female roles in American Judaism. This was the time of what the historian Jonathan Sarna calls

---

[44] Nadell, *Women*, op. cit., 4.

[45] *Ibid.*, 3.

[46] With regard to the social and psychological function of organized subversion in the context of carnival, see the classical work of Mikhail Bakhtin, *Rabelais and His World*, trans. Helene Iswolsky (Cambridge, Mass.: M.I.T. Press, 1968).

the "great awakening" in North America in general, and in Jewish America in particular.[47] Many of the changes affecting women's roles and place (literally and symbolically) occurred "from the bottom up" and were accomplished by young people, some of them women. Rabbis praised women's sincere religiosity, encouraging them to attend the synagogue; mixed choirs were founded in many communities; and girls participated in confirmation classes and were confirmed together with boys.[48] The confirmation ceremony itself was a novelty in Judaism, enabling both boys and girls to ascend the *bimah* (pulpit) and address the congregation. But for girls it was a once-in-a-lifetime experience, whereas for boys it could be merely the first step toward public Jewish careers.

Some Jewish women did get public recognition as community leaders and preachers. Before the 1930s there were several in the US who received the title "first female rabbi." Although none of them was actually ordained, they paved the way for women's ordination. I will mention a few.

Ray Frank (1861-1948), "girl rabbi of the Golden West",[49] was a Sabbath school principal. In 1890 she agreed to preach in Spokane, Washington, after learning that there was no rabbi in the congregation. These were the first sermons she delivered and the first religious services she led. At that time a few Protestant women pastors were in office; Elisabeth Blackwell is considered to be the first of them. Frank studied for some time at Hebrew Union College (HUC), the Reform rabbinical seminary in Cincinnati. She wrote about what she would do if she were a rabbi but she explicitly declared that she did not desire to become one or even to seek a formal theological education.[50] Frank is considered by many to be the first Jewish

---

[47] Jonathan Sarna, *A Great Awakening: The Transformation that Shaped Twentieth-Century American Judaism and Its Implications for Today* (New York: Council for Initiatives in Jewish Education, 1995).

[48] K. Herrmann, "Jewish Confirmation Sermons in 19th-Century Germany," Alexander Deeg, Walter Homolka and Heinz-Gunther Schottler, eds., *Preaching in Judaism and Christianity: Encounters and Developments from Biblical Times to Modernity* (Berlin: Walter Degruyter, 2008), 91–112.

[49] Reva Clar and William M. Kramer, "The Girl Rabbi of the Golden West," *Western States Jewish History*, 18 (1986), 91–111, 223–236.

[50] Nadell, *Women*, op. cit., 41.

woman functioning without formal ordination as a rabbi. She was followed by a number of other women, most of them from the liberal branches of American Judaism, who fulfilled rabbinic roles without having been ordained.[51]

Henrietta Szold was the first woman to be admitted, after a long struggle, to the Jewish Theological Seminary, the rabbinical seminary of the Conservative Movement in New York, where she studied from 1903-1906.[52] A scholar and Zionist leader, she was ambivalent about the issue of women's ordination and occasionally expressed negative attitudes toward it.[53]

The issue seemed to wane but it regained vitality within the debate about modernizing Judaism in the 1920s. Five women studied in rabbinical schools long enough to become eligible to receive ordination. Apparently none of them was aware that women's ordination had been a contentious issue thirty years before their admission to seminaries.[54] Martha Neumark, daughter of an HUC professor, began her studies there in 1922. The HUC faculty and the Central Conference of American Rabbis (CCAR) proclaimed in that year, in response to Neumark's application to the school: "Women cannot justly be denied the privilege of ordination." Despite this historic declaration, it took 50 more years before the first woman was ordained at HUC.[55] Neumark's admission was described by Jacob Z. Lauterbach, a prominent HUC professor, as "a very bad investment" since women are expected to get married and she would probably decide to answer her calling of "mother and home maker," thus causing the college to train and support her "eight years for nothing."[56] Neumark was the only woman in her class of 100 students. In fact, she did not complete her studies but left after seven and a half years to get married. But she was the first woman to receive the degree of "religious school superintendent".[57]

---

[51] *Ibid.*, 30-117.
[52] *Ibid.*, 53-59.
[53] *Ibid.*, 54, 57-58.
[54] *Ibid.*, 61.
[55] *Ibid.*, 62.
[56] *Ibid.*, 65.
[57] *Ibid.*, 72.

Neumark and a handful of other women who wanted to become rabbis sought, as Martha Neumark's daughter Rey Montor stated, "to be taken seriously as an intellect and at the same time to be taken seriously as a woman."[58] Some of them were daughters of rabbis or scholars, or married to rabbis, but most of them were isolated individuals encountering powerful forces of resistance by those in power, all of them men: seminary faculty members, boards of governors, and classmates. Even some of the most openly supportive rabbis and leaders of women's quest for equality showed a great deal of ambivalence and hesitation when it came to actually ordaining women. For example, Rabbi Isaac Meir Wise, founder of HUC and the Central Conference of American Rabbis, expressed enthusiasm for and genuine appreciation of the female students at his institution, and at the same time hesitated to grant them rabbinic ordination.

Some faculty members believed that only an exceptionally outstanding candidate could compel such a radical departure from tradition. However, Nadell shows that these gatekeepers revealed their hesitation by bestowing honor grades on female students for their work while simultaneously claiming that they were "average" or even "poor" students. (It should be noted that these women were not entitled to scholarships or any kind of institutional help.)[59]

The Great Depression further hindered the possibility of women's entrance into the rabbinate, as well as into other professions. Furthermore, the 1930s brought to the U.S. a large number of rabbis fleeing Germany and women did not want "to take the place of a young rabbinical graduate, or perhaps a refugee, anxiously awaiting a call".[60]
Meanwhile, on the other side of the ocean, Regina Jonas was ordained in Germany in 1935. This historic event took place without the knowledge of her contemporaries in North

---

[58] *Ibid.*, 92. The quotation is ascribed to R. Montor, *Origins: How I Got Here and What's in My Baggage*, 7.

[59] *Ibid.*, 96.

[60] *Ibid.*, 99. These words are ascribed to Helen Levinthal, a leading candidate for ordination, after she received a Masters degree in 1939 from the Jewish Institute of Religion in New York.

America, and in fact, unbeknown to the general Jewish public until very recently.[61] Born in 1902 to a traditional family, Regina Jonas studied in the *Hochschule für die Wissenschaft des Judentums,* the rabbinical seminary in her native Berlin. The topic of her thesis, which would have been a requirement for ordination, was "Can a Woman Be a Rabbi According to *Halakhic* [Jewish legal] Sources?" She answered her own question in the positive, based on a thorough examination of Biblical, Talmudic and rabbinical sources.[62] Her request to pursue ordination was rejected by the Talmud professor of the institute. She then turned to Rabbi Leo Baeck, the leader of German Jewry, who also refused her request, arguing that the ordination of a female rabbi would cause massive intra-Jewish problems with the Orthodox rabbinate in Germany. Eventually, Jonas received a private ordination from Rabbi Max Dieneman, a Reform rabbi in Offenbach.

Jonas served as a preacher and chaplain in various Jewish social institutions and communities but never had her own congregation. As mentioned previously, many rabbis were emigrating at the time from Nazi Germany and many communities, especially small ones, were left without a rabbi. Ironically, while the emigration of German rabbis to the US hindered the entrance of women to the rabbinate there, it may explain the relative ease with which Jonas was accepted into rabbinic positions, albeit without a pulpit of her own.

In November 1942, she was deported with her mother to Theresienstadt Concentration Camp, where she continued her work. One of her tasks was to receive Jews who were transported to the camp and help them adjust to the difficult reality awaiting them. She was sent to Auschwitz in October 1944, where she was murdered two months later at the age of 42. Although many of the people who knew her and her work survived the Holocaust, including some of her colleagues, Regina Jonas was all but forgotten for more than six decades.

---

[61] Regina Jonas has recently received a significant amount of public attention thanks to a biography written about her by Elisa Klapheck, *Fräulein Rabbiner Jonas: The Story of the First Woman Rabbi,* trans. Toby Axelrod (San Francisco: Jossey-Bass, 2004). Information about Jonas became available after the re-unification of Germany in 1990 and the subsequent opening of the East German archives.

[62] Elisa Klapheck, ed., *Fräulein Rabbiner Jonas: Kann die Frau das Rabbinische Amt Bekleiden?* (Teetz: Hentrich & Hentrich, 1999).

This case of "communal amnesia"[63] deserves a separate discussion.[64] It is *sui generis* in that it took place against the background of the extreme situation in Nazi Germany and therefore does not reflect the normal course of events that gradually brought about the ordination of women.

It took another 37 years for Sally Priesand to receive rabbinic ordination from Hebrew Union College-Jewish Institute of Religion (HUC-JIR) in Cincinnati in 1972. She became the first ordained woman rabbi in North America and the first woman to be ordained by a rabbinical seminary. Her dean, Rabbi Kentor Roseman, described her as a "good B student and a leader in our student body" but admitted that she was not accepted as "one of the boys" and she was not invited to join "when they go out for a beer."[65]

The new wave of American feminism continued to surge and, one after the other, all the liberal rabbinical seminaries began to ordain women. Sandy Eisenberg Sasso was the first woman to be ordained, in 1974, in the Reconstructionist Movement.[66] The Reconstructionist Rabbinic Association had begun accepting women into the rabbinical program from its establishment in 1968. One year after Sasso's ordination, the first woman rabbi was ordained in Leo Baeck College in London in 1975. It took another decade and a fierce debate that threatened to split the Conservative Movement before the Jewish Theological Seminary in New York ordained Amy Eilberg, the first Conservative woman rabbi, in 1985.

In Israel progress has been slower. The first woman rabbi there, Naama Kelman, who had applied to HUC-JIR in 1981, was ordained in HUC's Jerusalem seminary in 1992. The following year, Valerie Stessin was the first Masorti (Conservative) rabbi ordained in Israel. Last but not least

---

[63] This phrase was coined by Sybil Sheridan in her article "History of Women in the Rabbinate: A Case of Communal Amnesia," 1999 (*http://www.bet-debora.de/jewish-women/history.htm*).

[64] Sheridan's article (see previous note) offers some possible answers.

[65] George Vecey, "Her Ambition Is to Become a Rabbi - and a Housewife," New York Times, March 1972. I thank Rabbi Mindy Avra Portnoy for sending me this article along with many important documents regarding women in the rabbinate.

[66] The Reconstructionist Movement, then the liberal wing of the Conservative Movement, which later became an independent movement of its own.

among the "first" liberal female rabbis is Alina Treyher, who was ordained in Germany in 2010 at the Abraham Geiger College. As the first post-war female rabbi in the cradle of Reform Judaism, her ordination received much media attention.

The focus is now on Orthodox women. While there is no longer any significant formal public discussion of the right of women to receive rabbinic ordination in the non-Orthodox movements, a heated debate is raging in modern Orthodoxy on this issue. Rabbi Avraham Weiss, head of Hebrew Institute of Riverdale and founder and dean of Yeshivat Chovevei Torah, both in New York, ordained Sara Hurwitz in 2009 with the new title of *MaHaRaT* (*Morat Halakha Rabbanit Toranit*, a female rabbinic law instructor),[67] thus making her the first woman to be an Orthodox rabbi.[68]

As these lines are written, ever growing numbers of Orthodox women prepare themselves for rabbinic ordination, both in the United States and Israel. Time will tell how these courageous women, who face challenging obstacles from within and from without, will change the rabbinate and the Jewish world.

Let us now concentrate on women in the non-Orthodox rabbinate, where the phenomenon is more established.

---

[67] Before Hurvitz, another woman, Haviva Ner-David, was privately ordained in Israel, but she decided to forgo her ordination when she realized that she did not identify with Orthodox Judaism anymore. Haviva Ner-David, *Life on the Fringes: A Feminist Journey toward Traditional Rabbinic Ordination* (Needham: JFL Books, 2000).

[68] See: Sara Hurwitz, "Orthodox Women in Rabbinic Roles," Elyse Goldstein, ed., *New Jewish Feminism* (Woodstock: Jewish Lights, 2009), 133-143.

The following table presents the proportion of female to male rabbis in the Central Conference of American Rabbis (Reform):

	Total	Male rabbis	Female rabbis
Members of the CCAR[69]	2042	1453 (72%)	589 (28%)
Ordination classes 2010-11	72	20 (28%)	52 (72%)

This table shows a dramatic reversal from the relatively low number of women rabbis to their becoming an overwhelming majority among those most recently ordained. According to Tanya Sperling, Assistant to the Director of Rabbinic Placement in the CCAR, 42 of the 52 women rabbis ordained in 2010-11 are currently working in congregations while ten are doing non-congregational work such as Hillel director on university campuses, military chaplain, or other leadership positions.

2. How Have Women Changed the Rabbinate?

Women rabbis, like their male counterparts, are not a monolithic group. Some are fiery feminists while others don't define themselves as feminist at all; some are very traditional, even conservative (with a lower-case "c"); some are social-justice warriors while others are fervent spiritual leaders. Nevertheless, it is hard to take issue with Rabbi Laura Geller's statement: "Women rabbis have changed the face of Judaism."[70]

When the topic of women rabbis is discussed, one often hears statements (meant positively or negatively) such as "what a novelty, a woman rabbi after thousands of years of exclusively male rabbis!" One must remember, however, that the rabbinate as a profession is a relatively new phenomenon in the Jewish world. Before the 19th century, rabbis served as

---

[69] The information is updated to 16 September 2011. I thank Tanya Sperling, Assistant to the Director of Rabbinic Placement of the CCAR, for it.

[70] Laura Geller, "From Equality to Transformation: The Challenge of Women Rabbinic Leadership," T.M. Rudavsky, ed., *Gender and Judaism: The Transformation of Tradition* (New York & London: New York University Press, 1995), 244.

communal leaders, teachers and *halakhic* (religious legal) authorities, but often they had another occupation as well. Today's profession of congregational rabbi did not exist. This by no means belittles the revolution inherent in women's ordination; on the contrary, the mere concept of women as leaders of congregations, let alone as formally ordained rabbis, is a revolutionary one.

However, the understanding that women bring something essentially different to the profession spread rather slowly. The first women rabbis tried to do everything their male predecessors did; they were not looking to be revolutionaries.[71] They did not have role models to inspire them and many of them wanted to maintain a low profile with regard to gender matters or to work together with men to raise awareness for women's issues. For example, with regard to maternity leave, Rabbi Laura Geller reveals that back in the early years of female ordination, women rabbis were advised "to handle the situation as individuals" and to postpone raising the subject until they had "a solid and sure relationship with the congregation or community."[72] It took almost two decades after the first women were ordained in the US before they began celebrating the unique aspects they bring to the pulpit.

2a. Balance, Intimacy and Empowerment

Rabbi Janet Marder, who later became the first female president of the CCAR (2003-2005), wrote in 1991 that women rabbis share a commitment to three fundamental values with regard to their rabbinate: balance, intimacy and empowerment.[73]

By "balance" she means greater equality between professional and personal life. The rabbi is no longer in his/her office from morning until late at night, being "on call" for congregants all day, every day (and night). Many women rabbis choose to work part-time in order to tend to their families, while others find a *modus vivendi* by working in small or medium-size congregations. (I will return to the question of community size

---

[71] *Ibid.*, 244-245.

[72] *Ibid.*, 248.

[73] Janet Marder, "How Women Are Changing the Rabbinate," *Reform Judaism*, 19:4 (1991), 5.

later.) Seeking jobs that would allow them to strike a balance between their career and their personal life, women were willing to take jobs considered less prestigious, like hospital chaplains, Hillel directors and teachers. In this way, they contributed to a broadening of the rabbinate as a profession.

Awareness of the need for flexible work hours, as well as frequent in-depth conversations about leadership and work style, benefit a wider circle than women rabbis alone. In many cases, women rabbis have become role models for their congregants, both male and female, of how to lead healthy, balanced lives. Their example also gives legitimization and encouragement to men rabbis and other professionals to reconsider their own priorities and to create work environments that allow them to dedicate significant time to personal and family life.

Unlike more traditional rabbinical models, in which the rabbi depends on his *rebbetzin* (rabbi's wife) to cook, bake and play hostess while he teaches and converses with congregants, most female rabbis (and some modern male rabbis as well) have to bake and serve their own cookies while engaging in profound learned discussions with their guests.

By "intimacy" Marder is referring to women rabbis' efforts to develop close relationships with congregants and their commitment to creating a warm sense of community. According to a 1995 study by Rita J. Simon and Pamela S. Nadell, women rabbis understand themselves to be:

[L]ess formal, more approachable, more egalitarian, more likely to reach out to touch and hug, less likely to intrude their egos, and less likely to seek center stage. They asserted that they perform rites of passage differently.[74]

While women rabbis have an easier time establishing intimacy and a sense of community, at least in theory, they sometimes have difficulty establishing intimate relations with life partners. In 1995, Sylvia Barack Fishman asked rabbis ten years after their ordination about spousal relationships: 33% of the women had never married, compared with only 2% of the men;

---

[74] David J. Zucker, "Women Rabbis: A Novel Idea," *Judaism*, 55 (2006), 112.

and 46% of the women had no children at that point while only 8% of the men were childless.[75]

By "empowerment" Marder means the stress on greater "shared responsibilities, privileges and power" with their colleagues and congregants. Women rabbis have less of a need than do men for hierarchical structures, both in their professional staff and with their congregants.[76] The very presence of women in the rabbinate forces congregants to approach the Divine in different ways. Geller maintains that for some Jews there is "an unconscious transference that they make between their rabbi and God."[77] Having a female rabbi on the pulpit or in the chaplain's office prevents them from making this unconscious identification and transference, and forces them to experience Divinity and holiness in creative and personal ways. Approaching this issue from a different angle, the American Orthodox feminist leader Blu Greenberg said that women have helped "demystify the rabbinate." Greenberg, herself married to a rabbi, explained that women rabbis "have assumed more 'earthy' roles than men. They do not put on airs. They are not as apart from their congregants as previous rabbis – male rabbis – have been."[78]

2b. Liturgy and Ritual Innovations

Women rabbis have had a profound impact on Jewish liturgy and ritual on at least four levels.[79] In this context there are differences among the various liberal religious movements: while many Reform, Reconstructionist and Jewish Renewal

---

[75] *Ibid.*, 111. See also: Emily H. Feigenson, "Female Rabbis and Delayed Childbearing," *CCAR Journal* (1997), 74-76.

[76] Jacqueline Koch Ellenson, "From the Personal to the Communal," Elyse Goldstein, ed., *New Jewish Feminism, op. cit.,* 125-132.

[77] Geller, "From Equality to Transformation," op. cit., 245.

[78] Arthur J. Magida, "How Are Women Changing the Rabbinate," *Baltimore Jewish Times,* 8 August 1986, 57.

[79] Many of the early feminist liturgists suggesting an entirely innovative liturgical language based on gender inclusiveness were lay women, such as Marcia Falk. See: Marcia Falk, *The Book of Blessings: New Jewish Prayers for Daily Life, the Sabbath and the New Moon Festival* (San Francisco: Harper Collins, 1996); *idem,* "Notes on Composing New Blessings: Toward a Feminist-Jewish Reconstruction of Prayer," *Journal of Feminist Studies in Religion* (1987), 3, 39-53. However, it was women rabbis who eventually encouraged the incorporation of such changes into the liturgy.

rabbis are apt to make liturgical and ritual innovations and changes, Conservative rabbis are generally more reluctant to do so. The following is a short description of the four levels of female innovation in this field:[80]

1. They have introduced more inclusive language, e.g., a choice between male and female pronouns and verbs. For example, in the early-morning prayer "I thankfully acknowledge," the feminine form "modah ani" is added next to the male form "modeh ani."

2. They have added representative female figures to the male ones found in the liturgy. For example, the matriarchs (Sarah, Rebecca, Leah and Rachel) are now mentioned along with the patriarchs (Abraham, Isaac and Jacob) in the Amidah, the central prayer of every formal service.

3. Women rabbis have reclaimed and adapted old rituals, like those for Rosh Hodesh (the New Moon) or weaning a baby. They have also created new rituals and ceremonies, e.g., for baby-girl naming, healing from loss or illness, miscarriage, divorce and, in Israel, the beginning of military service.

4. Women rabbis, especially from the Reform, Reconstructionist and Jewish Renewal movements, are engaged in creating gender-balanced, gender-inclusive and gender-diverse metaphors for God, addressing the Divine in new and creative ways. In addition to the traditional barukh ata Adonai (praised are You, O Lord), they have proposed a variety of addresses, such as "Fountain of Life," "Spirit of the Universe" and others. Arguably, the greatest challenge is altering the pronounced gender specification of the Hebrew language.

Women are very active in creating new liturgies, prayer books and commentaries. Some of the monumental creative works of liberal Judaism have been written and edited by women. The new American siddur (prayer book) Mishkan T'filah (New York: CCAR Press, 2007) was edited by Rabbi Elyse Frishman[81];

---

[80] For a detailed discussion of this topic, see: Dalia Marx, "Gender in the Israeli Liberal Liturgy," Elyse Goldstein, ed., New Jewish Feminism, op. cit., 206-217; idem, "Influences of the Feminist Movement on Jewish Liturgy: The Case of Israeli Reform Prayer," Sociological Papers, 14 (2009), 67-79.

The Torah: A Women's Commentary was edited by Rabbi Andrea Weiss and Dr. Tamara Ashkenazi (New York: Union of Reform Judaism, 2008)[82]; and four Israeli Reform rabbis edited *Parashat Hamayim: Immersion in Water as an Opportunity of Renewal and Spiritual Growth* (Tel Aviv: Hakibbutz Hameuhad, 2011, in Hebrew). All these projects were team efforts which incorporated many contributions, especially those of women rabbis.

2c. Challenges to Overcome

Many of the problems confronting women in the rabbinate are not essentially different from those encountered by other professional women but, given the nature of the task, some of the problems are unique. The difficulty of balancing work and family is especially intense for them because the busiest times for a rabbi are precisely those that other people devote to family and personal affairs: evenings (committees, meetings, visiting), Shabbat and holidays. In her novel *A Place of Light,* Rhonda Shapiro-Rieser describes the fictional Rabbi Lynda Klein's struggle, saying:

[T]here was no time. The congregation waited, a jealous lover. Hundreds of people wanted her to inspire them, to lead them to God, or prayer, or to their own souls.[83]

The desire for balance leads many women rabbis to seek part-time jobs, to work in smaller congregations and to shy away from serving as senior rabbis in larger congregations. Marder refers to it as a cognizant choice of an "alternative" path to that of their male colleagues.[84] But it is a choice which leads to salary discrepancies, less public exposure and fewer opportunities for influence.

---

[81] See: Elyse Frishman, "Entering Mishkan T'filah," *CCAR Journal* (Fall 2004), 56-67.

[82] See also: Elyse Goldstein, ed., *The Women's Torah Commentary: New Insights from Women Rabbis* (Woodstock: Jewish Lights, 2000); idem, *The Women's Haftarah Commentary: New Insights from Women Rabbis on the 54 Weekly Haftarah Portions, the Five Megillot & Special Shabbatot* (Woodstock: Jewish Lights, 2004).

[83] Rhonda Shapiro-Rieser, *A Place of Light* (New York: Poseidon Press, 1983), 242-243. Cited in: David J. Zucker, "Women Rabbis: A Novel Idea," op. cit., 110.

[84] Marder, "How Women Are Changing the Rabbinate," op. cit., 5.

Laura Geller challenges Marder's approach, asking whether women rabbis are indeed *freely* choosing the "different voice".[85] She refers to the glass ceiling impeding women, not only due to discrimination against them in the rabbinate but also because women are having "difficulty imagining being a senior rabbi because there are no models of women senior rabbis".[86] Many women believe, says Geller, that the reason they are hired as assistant rabbis more readily than men is that male senior rabbis assume that women are "more docile and easier to manage".[87] Geller herself has been the senior rabbi at Temple Emanuel in Beverly Hills, California, since 1994, which makes her the first woman ever to lead a major metropolitan synagogue. Today, six of the 51 largest American Reform congregations (defined as 1,000 or more families) have a woman as their senior rabbi.[88]

It is increasingly apparent that women have been changing the professional language of the rabbinate. Some 650 women now serve as Reform rabbis in the United States, out of a total of 1,800. Rabbi Jackie Koch Ellenson, head of the American Reform "Women's Rabbinic Network"(WRN), notes that women rabbis are inevitably having an influence on their male counterparts. She argues that many male rabbis, "bolstered by their women colleagues' ability to conceptualize and combine work and family / personal life in a humane way... have happily adopted some of the alternative rabbinic models that women created".[89]

At the same time, many women rabbis report that people often interact with them "in vastly different ways" than they do with male rabbis.[90] In and of itself, this is not a negative thing (as noted above) but informality sometimes contains or leads to inappropriate remarks, many relating to physical appearance.

---

[85] Geller refers to Carol Gilligan's book *In a Different Voice* (Cambridge: Harvard University Press, 1982).

[86] Geller, "From Equality to Transformation," op. cit., 246-250.

[87] *Ibid.*, 149.

[88] Information provided by Tanya Sperling, Assistant to the Director of Rabbinic Placement of the CCAR.

[89] Jacqueline Koch Ellenson, "From the Personal to the Communal," Elyse Goldstein, ed., *New Jewish Feminism*, op. cit., 131.

[90] Irit Printz, "Women in the Conservative Synagogue," Elyse Goldstein, ed., *New Jewish Feminism*, op. cit., 188.

("Look what a cute rabbi I found for you," said a father to his *bar-mitzvah* son when I met the family for the first time.) Some people wrongly interpret women's accessibility and lack of formality. ("Is it okay to kiss a rabbi?") While I don't have firm data, I believe that women rabbis are much more often touched, kissed, patted, etc., by congregants and colleagues than male rabbis are.[91]

The question of women rabbis' dress code falls within this area of uncertainty. Many female rabbis complain about the elusive professional dress code expected of them. They are expected to be elegant and feminine without being over-dressed or sexy. Questions of fashion (suit or dress on the pulpit? academic robe or traditional *kittel*? can I wear trousers? what are proper colors? how short can a skirt be?) are often discussed among female rabbis and may reflect a broader lack of clarity with regard to women in the rabbinate.

Last but not least of the challenges is what is sometimes referred to as "male flight".[92] The increase in the number of women seeking the pulpit and the relative normalization of the phenomenon has been accompanied by a decrease in the number of men who want to become rabbis or be active in Jewish affairs in other ways. As early as 1978, HUC-JIR sociology professor Norman Mirsky said that "the actual existence of a woman rabbi may serve once and for all to confirm the adage that being a rabbi is no job for a Jewish boy".[93] A few years later he added that women may not have driven men out of the profession "but they panicked the men who were already in doubt about their own masculinity".[94]

Mirsky's assessment in 1986 has become a very present reality in our times. Men shy away from the liberal synagogues because of what one male congregant called "the feminine vibe" in the temple. Another said that in the synagogue he feels that "mom's in charge". Liberal Jewish men withdraw not

---

[91] Geller, "From Equality to Transformation," op.cit., 150.

[92] Sylvia Barack Fishman and Daniel Parmer, *Matrilineal Ascent/Patrilineal Descent: The Gender Imbalance in American Jewish Life* (Waltham: Brandeis University, 2008); Magida, "How Are Women Changing the Rabbinate?" op.cit.

[93] Magida, "How Are Women Changing the Rabbinate?" op. cit., 61.

[94] *Ibid.*, 61.

only from the synagogue but also from Jewish youth movements and summer camps, causing anxiety among Jewish leaders.[95] Women are often blamed for this situation, implicitly or even explicitly. (Recall the young men's responses to Dora in Mary Cohen's 1899 Purim story.) A separate discussion is required to deal with this challenge and its possible solutions. Here I will only mention Rabbi Joseph Meszler's article, "Where Are the Jewish Men," in which he suggests that the re-engagement of men "requires the help of Jewish Women."[96] He proposes separate men's study groups where men would feel free to discuss spiritual and emotional issues with other men. Lately, in its conventions and conclaves, the Reform Movement has held separate prayer services for men, many of whom have felt (as many women still feel) that they need "a room of their own" to express their religiosity and spirituality.

3. Women Rabbis in the Holy Land[97]

Many of the challenges that women rabbis in Israel face are not essentially different from those confronting their colleagues in North America. One would also expect that due to the traditionalist and even macho nature of their society, Israeli women rabbis would encounter more discrimination and suspicion. It's been said that the best Israelis can do is allow women to be ordained, but even then they cannot truly accept them as rabbis. However, often this is just part of the larger picture: the immediate problems that non-Orthodox Jews encounter in Israel have to do first and foremost with their liberal, modern and inclusive values and practices, not directly with gender issues.

Non-Orthodox rabbis of both sexes have to close ranks because they are all members of the same *salon des refusés*, laboring

---

[95] See for example: Joseph B. Meszler, "Where Are the Jewish Men? The Absence of Men from Liberal Synagogue Life," Elyse Goldstein, ed., *New Jewish Feminism*, op. cit., 165-174.

[96] B. Meszler, "Where Are the Jewish Men," op. cit., 170-171. Interestingly, he cites Nelson Mandela in this context (p.174): "The oppressor must be liberated just as surely as the oppressed."

[97] I thank my colleagues Rabbis Judith Edelman-Green, Rabbi David Ariel-Joel, Rabbi Ilana Bird, Rabbi Naama Kelman, Rabbi Alona Lisitsa, Rabbi Mira Raz, Rabbi Galia Sadan and Rabbi Diana Villa for sharing their insights with me.

under constant challenges to their legitimacy by the Orthodox establishment and denied funding and recognition not only by the (Orthodox or ultra-Orthodox) Chief Rabbinate, but also by the Israel Ministry of the Interior. Israeli Reform and Conservative rabbis are not authorized to officiate at weddings or burials, nor do their synagogues receive government funding as Orthodox synagogues do. The gap between male and female liberal rabbis, especially with regard to officiating in life-cycle events, is much smaller than the gap between both of them and Orthodox or ultra-Orthodox rabbis.

Rabbi Alona Lisitsa, when she served as the Israeli representative to WRN (Women of Reform Judaism), said in her 2009 address to her colleagues in North America: "We are proud to be equally discriminated against with our male colleagues by the Israeli establishment. The de-legitimization campaign against all of us is manifested in the outrageous statement by Rabbi Eliyahu, former Chief Rabbi of Israel, blaming Reform Jews for the Holocaust."

Perhaps because both men and women liberal rabbis are marginalized in Israel, there is more equality between them there. In fact, women rabbis in Israel seem to get to be in leadership positions somewhat more easily than their colleagues in the US. Women rabbis lead some of the larger congregations in the country, and many women serve in leadership and executive roles. For example, Rabbi Maya Leibovich heads the Reform Rabbis Council (MaRaM); Rabbi Naama Kelman is dean of the Jerusalem campus of HUC-JIR; and Rabbi Tamar Elad-Appelbaum serves as vice-dean of Schechter Rabbinical School, the Conservative rabbinical seminary in Jerusalem.

In practice, the Israeli Reform Movement (IMPJ) is at present significantly more egalitarian than the Israeli Conservative (Masorti) Movement, with 14 male and 14 female rabbis serving Reform congregations, whereas only five out of the 18 female Conservative rabbis are presently functioning as congregational rabbis:

The Reform Movement in Israel[98]

	Total	Male rabbis	Female rabbis
Members of MaRaM, the Israeli Council of Reform Rabbis (2012)	86	51 (60%)	35 (40%)
Rabbis officiating in congregations (2012)	28	14 (50%)	14 (50%)
Ordination class of 2010-2011	7	3 (43%)	4 (57%)

The Masorti (Conservative) Movement in Israel99

	Total	Male rabbis	Female rabbis
Members of the Rabbinical Assembly (2012)	150	132 (88%)	18 (12%)
Rabbis officiating in congregations (2012)	18	13 (72%)	5 (18%)
Ordination class of 2010-2011	5	3 (60%)	2 (40%)

Israeli society is very oriented around family life. Although childcare centers are far from optimal, women in Israel can rely on them and on a long day at kindergartens. Paid maternity leave is mandatory (albeit relatively short) and is protected by law. Short distances, tight relationships and mutual informal social support facilitate dependence on grandparents and friends for help with young children. For this reason (and due to economic necessity), in most Israeli families both spouses work outside the home. Since juggling between work and family is relatively natural for Israeli women, female rabbis are among the beneficiaries.

Liberal congregations in Israel tend to be rather small and therefore, in most cases, present their rabbis with a bearable work load. Moreover, their low budgets enable many

[98] I thank Rabbi Galia Sadan for this information. The numbers include both part-time and full-time rabbis, as well as some rabbinical students.

[99] I thank Shira Marx-Sapunar for this information.

congregations to employ only a part-time rabbi (whether male or female).[100] The fact that many synagogues do not have full office and maintenance support does not discourage women rabbis, who are willing, as one of them said, "to get their hands dirty" by sweeping floors, arranging chairs, making phone calls, sending letters, etc. It seems that women rabbis often respond more positively to these extra chores than do their male colleagues.

4. Can Overt Sexism Be an Advantage?

Sexism and machismo can be found in every society, regardless of how progressive it may be. In Israeli society it is overt and explicit and disturbing. Still, it can be argued that a direct and blunt style, which is typical to many Israelis, may sometimes be an advantage: It is easier to detect, less subtle, and therefore easier to respond to. On the other hand, when discrimination is covert and expressed through a veil of political correctness and propriety, it is harder to identify and it is certainly harder to respond to.

I and my female colleagues constantly confront excluding and doubting remarks made by bar mitzvah parents, board members, and school principals, as well as taxi drivers and service providers. We respond to statements like "separation between men and women always existed in the synagogue" by explaining about the history of the women's section in the Temple in Jerusalem and in the ancient synagogues. We readily tell those who claim that "when a woman is standing on the bimah, congregants will look at her as a woman, not as a rabbi," that our femininity does not contradict our professionalism; on the contrary, it shapes it and enhances it. When young couples tell us that they would really love it if we officiated in their wedding but they "just cannot do it" because their old aunt would freak out to see an officiating female rabbi, and they need a male rabbi, preferably with a beard (to look like a "real rabbi"), we warmly wish them *mazal tov*, and hope that their children will feel otherwise.

---

[100] It is a well-known truth that having a half-time job means being paid half of a full salary but does not necessarily mean working half-time.

Obviously, we do not always have the patience to engage with this kind of conversation, but our everyday experiences provide us with many opportunities to confront sexist attitudes. We believe that responding to these kind of "petty" questions can affect the whole society, not just the individual. In many cases, prejudice and intolerance vanish when a personal connection exists, and the personal, as we all know, is also the political.

In the last few years, we have experienced a disturbing wave of women's exclusion from the public sphere in Israel. Ultra-Orthodox circles pressure companies and publishers to avoid using pictures of women, not only in commercial advertisements but also in official government publications. Women and even young girls are being harassed for not wearing "modest" clothes, and due to the fear of extreme circles, female singers are not invited to many public events, including military events. These phenomena are not new but they have become more extreme and more frequent in the past few years, and the novelty of the past year or so is that many people openly protest against them. The backlash of these developments is a strong anti-religious sentiment but also endowment of non-Orthodox expressions of religiosity, and especially of women leaders, whose very being is a bold response to the exclusion of women.

A short anecdote to illustrate this: In my own neighborhood in North Jerusalem, the French Hill, a project among many other local initiatives, has recently taken place as a protest against the exclusion of women in our city. The young leadership of the neighborhood has decided to place large posters of women of different occupations all around the neighborhood. Alongside the teacher, the scientist, and the musician, I was asked to participate as a rabbi. Apparently a rabbi is now one of the feminine "neighborhood professions"!

Ironically, the new awareness of the presence of women in the Israeli public sphere, and the dangers to Israeli democracy caused by those who want to eliminate their participation and their images, has begun to cause larger circles of Israelis to appreciate the missing female voices from the generations-old Jewish choir. We women who serve as rabbis in the State of Israel pray that both democracy and pluralism will thrive in the years ahead, so our voices can be raised more in praise than in protest.

5. Opening New Gates

"The definition of what makes a good rabbi," says Rabbi Jacqueline Koch Ellenson, director of the American Reform Women's Rabbinic Network (WRN), "is changing before our eyes."[101] Although it is too soon to make sweeping assessments about the influence of female rabbis on the profession and on Judaism in general, I have tried here to provide some indication of its impact today.

Seeing skirts and pink prayer shawls[102] on the pulpit have contributed to openness and acceptance of other groups within the Jewish community which were formerly marginalized: those who live in alternative family structures; gays, lesbians, bisexuals and trans-gender individuals; Jews by Choice and of unconventional ethnicities; people with special needs; adherents of diverse political and theological views, etc. This significant achievement may be attributed in good part to the many male and female Jewish professionals who are committed to inclusivity and empowerment. Feminism in our time means not only the liberation of women but also the liberation of all people who need to be liberated.[103]

Although the road is still long, it seems that things are indeed changing for Israeli liberal Jews. Of course, this change affects liberal Jews everywhere, and thus it affects Jewish life overall.

Our ancient sages mandated obtaining an etrog (citron) as part of the observance of Sukkot (Feast of Tabernacles).[104] They taught that amongst the ritual four species used in celebrating the festival, the citron is the most favored, since it both tastes good and smells good, and as such is comparable to a person who is both learned and proficient in good deeds.[105] Perhaps we

---

[101] Jacqueline Koch Ellenson, "From the Personal to the Communal," op. cit., 131.

[102] Elyse Goldstein, "My Pink Tallit: Women's Rituals as Imitative or Innovative," Elyse Goldstein, ed., New Jewish Feminism, op. cit., 81-89.

[103] This is often referred to as the "third wave" of feminism. With regard to Judaism, see: Rachel Sabbath Beit Halachmi, "The Changing Status of Women in Liberal Judaism: A Reflective Critique," Moshe Halbertal and Donniel Hartman, eds., Judaism and the Challenges of Modern Life (London-New York: Continuum, 2007), 74-84.

[104] Mishnah, Sukkah 2:10.

[105] Leviticus Rabba 32:12.

can deduce from this metaphor that women do, after all, have a place on the pulpit, just as the orange has a place among the symbols of freedom and liberation on the Passover Seder plate. Like the orange, the citron's sibling, women bring new flavors, fragrances and colors to Judaism, breathing new and vibrant life into it.

There is a long way to go before we can rest on our laurels. Issues like salary discrepancy, professional status, explicit and implicit discrimination, inappropriate remarks in the work place, and gaining acceptance in the wider community have yet to be resolved. But I am convinced that we can look back with pride at what our older sisters and our colleagues have managed to achieve so far. Time will tell how their/our story will continue to unfold.

Wanting a God Who Looked Like Me

Debbie Kozlovich

I AM AN ATHEIST. I came to this realization after a lifetime of searching for a god who looked like me. During twelve years of Catholic school, I realized that the Catholic god wasn't very fond of girls. As I received my first holy communion and attended mass every day, I longed to be up by the altar with the boys but because of my gender, I wasn't allowed. I knew I could never be the Pope or even a priest. God didn't seem to value females the way he did males. Once I graduated, I never went to a Catholic Church again. I felt I was worth much more than that religion wanted me to believe. I needed more than a man god who threatened and shamed women from the sinful mate, Eve, to the obedient virgin, Mary. That kind of god had no relevance in my life. There was nothing to fear because I could not believe in what I considered a myth. I felt the same about Jesus who hung violently on a cross in every classroom and church I entered. His way of shedding blood was different from mine. He didn't teach me how to be a better female, how to relate to sexism, or how to love myself. I was left with a yearning to find a god I could relate to.

I searched other forms of Christianity and found the same thing. Their gods were male and also preferred men. I read the Bible and was appalled at how women were viewed. I studied Islam and Buddhism. I became friends with Thai monks and learned some of their precepts. They all came to the same conclusion: women were second class. That never felt right. Why would a god prefer one gender over another? Why was god a "he"? If this god created us in his image, why didn't I look like him? I had enough of male saviors.

After many years, the answer became obvious. In the beginning, men created god. They made him male and then they gave themselves power over women. I refused to take part in that belief system. It offered me nothing and made me feel irrelevant. I wanted a female god but never found one. I needed a different vision, something that, as a woman, I could relate to. I wanted my daughter to grow up respecting herself and believing that she was equal to any man. The major religions did not offer this perspective. So I raised my son and daughter with

147

the belief that life is sacred and we are all equal. They did not have to fear or worship some distant, male god in order to have morals. They could learn right from wrong by using critical thinking and compassion.

I have surrounded myself with a circle of women who are interested in making the world a better place. We discuss social issues and strive for gender equality and peace. It is in this circle that I learned to love myself as a woman, to value what I have to offer and to like what I see in the mirror. Although I hold many memories and beliefs inside me from my childhood, I have become a woman who does not need a religion to show me how I can become a better person or how to make a positive difference in the world. I can do that on my own. And I do.

My decision to stay away from all religion was a wise one. Now, at 61, I am comfortable in my own skin. I know I am just as valuable as any man. I live my life giving back to the community and promoting women's rights. Women are strong, capable and intelligent, so many of them just haven't been told that yet. We have stories that need to be written. We have the power to change religion and history by writing about these subjects from a woman's perspective. We have been kept silent for too long.

Long ago I decided not to go through life asking, "What's wrong with me?" because I was born female. I prefer to quote Marianne Williamson, "We ask ourselves, 'Who am I to be brilliant, gorgeous, talented, fabulous? Actually, who are you not to be?'" I am grateful to Marianne and the many other women who have inspired, elevated and encouraged me to be the best I can be.

I take wisdom, compassion and love with me into old age. I have no fear of what happens after death. I live each day with joy and the desire to make this a better place. I have learned to embrace my own power and wholeness. I am at peace and I love being a woman.

Led by a Women's Mosque: Space of Our Own

Vanessa Rivera de la Fuente

IMMAN IS AN INITIATIVE for the promotion of inter-religious dialogue between Women of Faith in Chile and other countries. A space for meeting, education and networking for those interested in theological, ethical, and ritual work done by women – a space to facilitate the development of critical thinking about the role of religion in regard to human rights, gender equality, freedom of expression, and peace building.

Since 2013, we have conducted workshops, conferences, and ecumenical meetings that have allowed us to connect with other women and form mutually supportive alliances to strengthen and develop our spirituality from a critical perspective on mainstream narratives that put us at a disadvantage for the reason of gender.

One of Imaan's key activities is developing "A Women's Mosque" project, an initiative that aims to be a meeting place for women and our spirituality.

A Women's Mosque

The idea came after a meeting to discuss Islam and encourage inter-faith dialogue between women from different denominations. They asked me about sex segregation in mosques, which led us to a broader reflection on the position of women in the religious space (both material and symbolic), and how uncomfortable we were with that.

We realized that, in different ways, places of worship displace women – whether to relegate us to separate rooms, not allow us to speak, or limit our participation to "strictly female" issues such as maternity, caregiving, the role of wife. And, of course, clothing, always from a patriarchal "canonical" perspective.

So we decided to join together to create our own space because:

- Despite religious differences, we identify ourselves as feminists and /or hold a very critical view of the narratives about the sacred and the feminine from the elites of our religions.

- We share the conviction that revelations are ossified in a reading of androcentrism and oppression, and they CAN, MUST, and REQUIRE a reading of liberation and this SHOULD and HAVE TO, performed by women across the board of all faiths, from a challenging standpoint to question the religious status quo.

- The traditional places of worship and adoration do not represent us. In those spaces we are silenced, cornered, and invisible; and we have to adhere to a male-centered narrative to gain some respect. The distribution of space, what we can or can't do and the behavior that is expected from us, does not express what we want or expect of ourselves as spiritual beings.

- Patriarchy has taught us to mistrust ourselves, our abilities, and our potential to do so with our sisters. We have to start to trust, believe, support, and recognize the voices, potential, and abilities of other women if we want to tackle patriarchy in religion and open new paths for women in spirituality.

- Every woman has spiritual concerns that are not always met in traditional worship sites. We recover the idea of the view the Mosque as a place of meeting, reflection, and knowledge-sharing to highlight the significant role that women have had in forming and strengthening their communities in the early days of history – a role that was made invisible by patriarchy extensively and, especially, to challenge the cultural imaginary on women believer and the prevailing androcentrism in religious spaces.

"We wanted a space without hierarchy, to come together and share experiences and learn how other women live their faith," said Maria del Carmen, a Lutheran Christian. "I was sick of hearing that we are important only when it comes to listening; to serve coffee; and decorate the hall for worship" states Roxana, a Baptist Christian. Victoria is agnostic and enthusiastically proclaims, "I have been in three meetings. I am not a practicing any religion, but I believe that spirituality goes beyond that; here I meet and connect with women who are different from me in a relaxed and non-judgmental frame, which in other contexts is very difficult."

Breaking the Glass Ceiling

Is this space for women only?

Yes. It will be a space for women only and there are good reasons behind this. I know it's easy for those who have a superficial approach to inequality to accuse this initiative of sexism.

However, in the struggle for equality in all aspects of life, women have to fight on at least two fronts: One, inequality in relation to men by gender. Second, with a solution I consider essential and #1 priority, is the negative socialization we grow up with as girls. This socialism breeds a lack of confidence and isolates women from each other via the competition that patriarchy inspires.

It is important to understand that when I speak of "androcentrism" or "male narratives" I am not referring to men as individuals. Creating a space of spiritual empowerment for women is not intended against men, but on behalf of women.

We are educated in this mistrust since childhood. Just pay attention to fairy tales: *there are always women fighting or competing against each other for the attention of a man.* By considering other women as the enemy, we isolate ourselves and enable the "Culture of Silence" in which women do not talk about our problems; instead, we apologize for our successes and are shamed for being victims of violence.

This competition between women is an extra disadvantage that adds to the existing inequality. Therefore, **to fight the inequality in society, we as women, must first recognize the value in ourselves and work to heal the inequality and distrust between us.**

The negative socialization among women keeps us living separated by a glass wall: We see each other but we don't hear

151

each other, nor do we connect with each other. We believe we are alone because the glass wall keeps us isolated. Maybe you have heard a woman saying, "I never talked about this before because I thought I was the only one suffering with this". This is a common expression of the glass wall.

Solving inequality is not giving to all people the same, but is about giving each person what she needs. In a patriarchal civilization like ours (where women are objects), we need to build our own identities to discover our individuality and do it in sisterhood with other women. Together we are stronger, but that "Us" must be cultivated and encouraged. We are never alone. It is good to have a space to remember and socialize this: WE ARE NOT ALONE. It is education for mistrust, the conditioning to mutual competition and the Culture of Silence that keep us self-censored and isolated from each other.

As women, we must break the glass ceiling that keeps us from moving toward positions of power and decision-making in society. But first, breaking the glass wall is essential to breaking down the walls, cells, and cages that imprison us because of the domestication of Patriarchy.

Breaking the glass wall will help us find our voice and make it heard. Speaking for ourselves is like saying "Open Sesame." The words give life. Unexpected things happen when we break the silence: Like discovering a route to our authentic selves.

Why Spirituality?

Everything starts when you believe. Awareness of our situation must come from internal changes that come before changes in society. Nothing happens in the "real world" unless it happens first in the images we carry in our heads and the feeling of our souls.

The misogyny of religious practices not only affects the exercise of our rights as women and our position in society, but also our self-perception and inner life. Every time a woman discovers her intrinsic value and her inherent dignity, her mood changes, her spirit becomes lighter, and her soul gains new strength. Spirituality is not exclusively religious. What happened is that religion has limited spirituality. Since religion is controlled by

Patriarchy, the Patriarchate is in charge to decide what spirituality is and what it is not.

The Women's Mosque project is an attempt to revive spirituality, to instill the idea of "sacred" as a way to be in this life, and to look at other women and recognize us in them. This initiative challenges the patriarchal discourse about the "Divine Truth" as a monolithic issue, one whose meaning is fixed by male narratives and mediatized by hierarchy; one where women only act as silent and submissive recipients, by engaging in a dialectical and collective construction of "Truth" in spirituality from the voices and experiences of women owning their agency.

Patriarchy starts and ends within. In the fight for our freedom and autonomy, conquering our spiritual life is the beginning of our conquest: Religions that are manipulated by androcentrism have not only hijacked our religious rights, but also have silenced us under a narrative of submission, pushing us toward margins in religious spaces, and declaring non-grata our voices and presence. To own the world we must begin by owning *ourselves*. We must find our voice and give it authority, truth, and value. We must push forward to speak for ourselves.

It is better to do this in sorority. Revelations, and all the ideas they generate, are useless if they do not serve the pursuit of social justice and empowerment to improve our roles as individuals in our communities. Sorority has nothing to do with being friends or agreeing on everything. Overcoming negative socialization and creating sorority is not about loving each other for life (even though it is better when this happens). Instead, it is a strategy to support, promote, and strengthen each other on our individual journeys to spiritual autonomy to develop our talents and abilities. It's as simple and difficult as what the Prophet Muhammad said in a hadith: "Being a true believer is to wish for others what I want for myself."

The sacred and the spiritual are present in everyday life. Our daily prayer is sacred, but also our outrage at social injustice. Our books are sacred, but no more so than our freedom to decide how we want to live. Spirituality can be found in a mantra and in the sincere advice we share with our friends. Sacred are our cultural traditions – as well as our joy, our memories, and moments of solitude. Spirituality is the connection with our

Creator, the finding of our divine feminine, and the multiple possibilities of pleasure our body gives us.

I believe that "The Sacred" is not exemplified in wooden images or in religious declarations burdened with theological ideologies, but in the open dialogue between people who recognize each other as equal. I think that God is seen less in judgments and labels and more in the shared knowledge and experience we have in our everyday lives. "Holy" are our endeavors in finding the truth, making it transcend our ego, and embracing other truths that we assimilate and deconstruct together.

Only if we break the glass wall can we go beyond any "roof" and hold by our own hands the part of heaven that belongs to us all. In this task, Faith has to be a driving force that motivates us to overcome the fear of dissent. Behind all differences, there is something sacred in all women: We are inherently valuable, free, spiritual, and diverse.

The Goddess Within—
Insights into Awakening Her Full Shakti:
Kali-Durga, Lakshmi and Saraswati

Vrinda Jamuna Shakti

Invocation

I invoke Sri Ganesha, remover of obstacles,
Son of Parvati,
Goddess of the Himalayas.
I invoke Goddess Saraswati,
Goddess of learning and literary gifts.
I invoke Sri Bhagavan Gurudev,
The Beloved,
One without a second,
Who reveals the scripture of Goddess
To countless thirsty and hungry ones
For the removal of existential ignorance.
To all, I offer humblest adorations!

Introduction

THE INDIAN GODDESSES TRILOGY appears in the Markandaya Puranas, and its profound mystic meaning and allegorical descriptions are also seen in Her elaborate iconography. The Devi Mahatmya, also known as *Durga Sapta-Shati* and *Chandi*, is the scripture of the Goddess in all Her forms—but the Goddess, who is One, is also formless shakti, energy. The scripture of the Goddess also contains verses found in the *Ratri Sukta* of *Rig Veda*, demonstrating that the Goddess was worshipped from time immemorial. In India, a male god has never been at the center of hegemonic religions because spirituality is a subjective experience more than a social institution.

She appears as Kali-Durga, Lakshmi and Saraswati—though many other goddesses emanate from Her effulgence, just as infinite rays emanate from the effulgence of the sun and moon. She is the interpenetrating presence in the physical, mental and spirit planes of existence. As Shakti, She rules our conscious and unconscious awareness.

The story of the three Goddesses symbolizes the journey through spiritual transformation. This process is all-encompassing, internal and integral, and it covers all aspects of life simultaneously: physical, mental/emotional and unconscious. As such, it leads us to confront the enemies of the soul in the form of egoism (or "I"-ness / mine-ness), mental distractions and ignorance. Though experienced as subjective, closeness to the Divine Feminine has cosmic implications.

The story beings when two bewildered rich men—one a king, the other a merchant—meet in a forest to find a sage who can help them assuage their grief following a tragic separation from their loved ones. Both men learn that their dearest family members had schemed to have them killed in order to inherit their wealth without any delay. Though from different parts of the country, the king was dethroned by his own son, and the merchant's family plotted to have him thrown out of his mansion. Soon they reached the Ashram of Sage Medha; which literally means sharp, untainted intellect. Both complained to the sage that even though their families had caused them intense grief and suffering, they were continually bombarded with memories of joyous times that reminded them of their attachments to the past—but were unable to separate the pain from the good times. After welcoming them, the sage invited them to stay and listen to the glories of the Goddess.

The mysticism of the Goddess is an allegorical description of the expansion of consciousness depicted through a highly symbolic drama. Every gain and loss, depression and elation in our lives is brought under Her divine scrutiny for a loving and empowering connection with Goddess Divine. The mystic transformation that takes place in the minds and hearts of Her devotees—as we question the limits of desire, pleasure, grief, love, and hatred informed by ordinary social constructs—requires the internal enactment of nothing less than a major battle between the conscious and unconscious aspects of the mind.

Many mental concepts, symbolically described as demons in the story of the Goddess, have to be brought out, identified, and completely eradicated in the process of personal transformation. This includes aspects that were previously considered to be "natural" to our character and personality. The demons in the

156

story of the Goddess demonstrate the resilience of the negative tendencies of the mind. Even after being conquered or "slayed" again and again, certain negative tendencies may keep emerging to show their fangs and claws in ways that sabotage our deeper compassionate, loving and creative nature.

The demons, in their arrogance, aspire to take the Goddess by force, and an intense battle ensues in the mind-heart conscience. Taking the Goddess by force is a metaphor that symbolizes intensely harmful psychic imbalances such as low self-esteem, jealousy, egocentricity, greed, anger, hatred, and fear. It also reflects the evil effects of patriarchy from which all negative qualities overpower the qualities of the Goddess in women today. In this struggle, our inner lives are the battlefield where the Goddess restores order, uplifting and empowering Her devotees in the Mother's embrace.

The battle includes instincts and the deepest feelings of love and caring for the land, rivers, oceans, the planet and all beings, as well as conflicting negative qualities, or weaknesses present in almost everyone. In the beginning, the positive and negative qualities appear to be mixed up in the struggle, and whatever happens seems to be random. We are thrown into the battle between the forces of ethical action vs. unethical action— dharma and adharma. However, invoking the Goddess begins a process of discernment that separates the angelic forces within us from negative forces within us.

The journey summons all our passions, considering that it involves an ascending path, as depicted in the systems science and experiential ontology of Kundalini, as well as an integral and systemic meditative movement leading to the awareness of Goddess within—immanent and transcendental.

From Goddess meditations we emerge as each other's keepers.

Goddess is the ultimate radical feminist because She is ready to dismantle the interlocking systems of male oppression against women and all feminine forces in the universe—including, but not limited to, Her children in the forms of fauna and flora, oceans, rivers, mountains, galaxies full of stars, intellectual forces like Sophia and Black Goddesses in Africa and Her sky and lands. She inspires loving devotion and unbound power.

Balancing the spirit energies entrusted to us by Goddess, as the need arises, becomes our daily life mission and central project in life. In India today, Dr. Vandana Shiva and the Gulabi Gang—India Women Warriors—represent Shakti, Goddess power in bold actions and their voices bring women from the most oppressed classes to the center of matriarchal movements.

At a time when the image of God—and his representatives—has been corrupted and distorted by psychopathic religious and secular world leaders, Goddess comes to restore sanity through the compassion of the Divine Feminine in Her most redemptive capacity. She emerges in the caring ways of every woman and man invested in stopping the madness of endless destruction for creating a legacy of life. She appears in women's identity as an empowered and compassionate agency across social, political and personal experiences.

Goddess will test the meaning of love in each and every one, from shallow to deepest love, moment by moment. The mysticism of the Goddess has not been properly understood in western societies, because in order to understand Her love we need to extricate ourselves from layers upon layers of false "needs" and desires considered normal in a consumer-oriented society. History and mainstream religions have silenced Herstory, the stories of the Goddess, as well as women's stories across the planet. She is not appreciated in our discontent with ourselves; She is most exquisitely adored in our appreciation of the "stardust" and galaxies flowing through our nostrils and pores, from the microcosm consciousness energy of our personal experience as compassionate beings to the macrocosm as One with Her. Such is Her lofty nature that She is within us *as us*. Thus being us as Her and Her as us strips us of any artificiality and ordinary adornments, because ultimately, Her most breathtaking adornments emerge in Her dynamic dance and majestic stillness within us.

Goddess mysticism is the gift of India to humanity.

Goddess Durga for Igniting Aspiration

Mantra for propitiating Goddess Durga:
Om Dum Durgayai Namah!

Aspiration

The story of Divine Mother as Durga commences in eternity and infinity, in the ever-present here and now. During the first three days of the Goddess ceremonies, Kali-Durga is worshipped with chants while devotees listen to her stories and engage in conversations about how to apply the symbolic meaning of Her actions to the internal struggles that each and every one confronts in daily life. During these three days we meditate on Durga, usually depicted in a fierce stance, adorned by a garland of skulls with blood dripping from a beheaded demon. The image of an all-powerful mother devouring a demon is intimidating, until we learn that She is the most compassionate Goddess, Mother of all, fiercely combating the evil forces that drive the predominantly male world powers to engage in ongoing wars and the exploitation of natural resources to enrich the coffers of the 1%.

What is it that the Goddess destroys? She is the most tender and formidable Mother—fierce and terrible against the patriarchal hegemony engaged in unending violence against women, children, elders, animals, rivers, mountains, and oceans.

We are aware that the splitting of the atom, and other so called scientific advancements, have contributed to put us closer to the brink of extinction more than once in the last fifty years. The destructive application of nuclear power has made an unprecedented scope of destructive power available to so called developed nations in ways that increases the risks of a global holocaust at the slightest degree of error in judgment by any mentally unstable world leader—most of whom, from what we know, are quite mentally unstable right now. Knowing that we are subjected to these conditions increases the levels of fear and existential angst in most well informed people. How can we cope? From where do we derive the necessary strength and compassion to change our present circumstances? As we become aware of the fiercely protective presence of the Divine Mother in Her terrible form, we gain insight on the subtlest power behind the material universe as basis of our embodiment. When we surrender to the Goddess' divine energy behind mind and matter and Spirit, there is nothing She cannot resolve, in course of time. In spite of the most destructive wars and acts of terror occurring today, Her blessings work in mysterious ways. She comes to the afflicted through healers, peacemakers, and human love and affection overflows right after disaster strikes. She heals us in deep sleep and brings us back into the battle of life in waking consciousness.

She is One and many, the subtlest among all scientific unknowns, immanent and transcendental. Male dominated military forces with weapons of mass destruction may inevitably self-destruct as their demonic strategies confront the formidable power of Goddess. But the enemy is not always external. When the enemies of the soul hide deep in the unconscious She appears as good conscience during the moments of profound insight and meditation to bring about a spiritual transformation in Her devotees. To her devotees She is the sweetest refuge. Close to Her, devotees experience Her influence through transformation in mind and spirit.

On the journey to expansion of consciousness, Kali-Durga manifests to destroy the negative tendencies of the mind. In this simple manner, one commences a most intimate relationship with the Divine Mother as destroyer and remover of obstacles on the path to self-improvement and spiritual maturity. Her power helps us "destroy" and resolve mental errors like egoistic tendencies, anger, fear, greed, and ignorance which cover our true, divine identity.

From the standpoint of Kundalini Shakti the knot of karma, or Karma Granti, in the Manipura Chakra is pierced, and dichotomies of attachment and hatred are resolved. As erroneous mental conditions dissolve and mental faculties sharpen we engage in serving Her in humanity—we see Her presence in everyone. The presence of Goddess grows within us as She establishes a more firm foundation for the most dynamic aspects of the journey to emerge, preparing the "ground" of mind and feelings for the advent of Goddess Lakshmi, Goddess of material and spiritual prosperity.

Goddess Lakshmi for the Blossoming of Divine Qualities

Mantra for propitiating Goddess Lakshmi:
Om Sri Lakshmiai Namah!

Blossoming

The next three days of the feast are dedicated to honoring Goddess MahaLakshmi, who destroys the buffalo demon and his army. This demon constantly changed forms, so the Goddess allowed it to have fun for a while before She discharged the final blow. This demon symbolizes the spirit of distractions, and when Goddess Lakshmi engages it in battle unbound creative powers begin to surge from within.

While Goddess Durga destroyed the negative forces of the mind, by the grace of Goddess Lakshmi a floodgate of creative energies and options opens up in the mind and heart of the devotee. This tidal surge of creativity can be very difficult to manage, at times chaotic and stressful. Even wealth and abundant creative forces can be disastrous in the life of a person who is unable to follow the ways of dharma. Wealthy people can experience intense misery. Talented writers, poets and scientists have come close to losing their minds and some have committed suicide because of the internal chaos stirred up by unrestrained creative forces, emotional storms and dangerous battles between rationality and emotions, mystic and empirical demands, humility and self-assertion against the kaleidoscopic backdrop of an awareness of the demands of body, mind and spirit within.

Unless internal wealth is developed by the grace of Goddess Lakshmi, the goddess of material, spiritual and ethical prosperity, all material attainments become shallow and can even lead to suffering—because in the absence of dharma, material wealth tends to feed selfishness, narcissism, hatred, fear of others, greed for power, and many other demoniac qualities within the individual.

At this stage the Goddess hold divine weapons in some of her arms, these represent various psychic abilities for destroying or dissolving unending aspects of mental distraction—which robs one of spiritual strength and peace, all necessary for concentration, meditation and a disciplined mind— while in Her other arms She holds symbols of the treasures that she confers upon her devotees, i.e., divine wealth in the form of discernment, detachment from adharma or negative habits, and six virtues (tranquility, absence of anger and fear, forbearance, faith, concentration or mindfulness, and an intense longing for liberation). All these energies rage until they find their peace, as it were, during a process of reconstruction, re-creation and transformation of unconscious impressions of the mind. The grace of Goddess Lakshmi brings about an internal transformation toward altruistic values in oneness with Her.

The battle is characterized by a growing awareness of distractions as obstacles to expansion of consciousness, and a keen understanding that the spontaneous flow of meditative awareness (*sahaja* samadhi) represents the blossoming of human existence. The demons at this stage are adept at changing forms, one obstacle is overcome, and it emerges as another. The mind is extremely cunning, and more resourceful than a chameleon. Endless subtle desires from the unconscious keep the mind agitated, and conflicting desires can rob the person of inner peace and a deeper capacity to feel empathy and true love.

The internal battle continues as blind spots are revealed through daily life, in practice and in deep meditations. As meditation deepens what was invisible on the surface level of awareness becomes clearer in conscious states of mind allowing us to enter a feeling of divine subjectivity and profounder self-analysis.

In terms of Kundalini experience, which was the first systems science, Goddess Lakshmi rends asunder the three knots of the heart: desire, anger, and ignorance. The grace of Goddess Lakshmi heralds the end of distractions, anxiety, externalization of mind, and the dawn of spiritual prosperity.

Goddess Lakshmi emerges in loving kindness, and creativity, increasing awareness of ethical integration, and with an ongoing appreciation of personality integration. With Goddess Lakshmi's blessings, all the material wealth one can imagine is little compared to the internal and external resources that the Goddess can shower upon Her devotees. Therefore, She prepares our hearts and minds for the advent of Goddess Saraswati, Goddess of wisdom.

Goddess Saraswati for Ongoing Expansion of Consciousness

Mantra for propitiating Goddess Saraswati:
Om Aim Saraswatiai Namah

Expansion of Consciousness

The next three days of the feast are dedicated to honoring Goddess Saraswati, who destroys the smoky-eyed demon that symbolizes perverted knowledge—or mind and emotions conditioned by egoism. The demon returned with an army of 60,000 soldiers, representing the vast negative ramifications of self-centered desires. As the demon and his army got closer, the Goddess utters the power-charged *bija mantra* "hum," and the demon disappears. A *bija mantra* is a powerful sound wave uttered with subatomic and transatomic one-pointed intention, therefore it is infallible. We do not have to worry about this kind of power, it is not available to ordinary human beings. Since a compassionate person is one with Goddess, when a compassionate being invokes the power of *bija mantra* it results in universal good and is in harmony with the law of karma.

An even more profound meaning of our connection with the Goddess of Wisdom is revealed within us when the **intuitive functions of the mind, intellect and emotions (*Jnana* and *Bhakti*) join forces in** the process of spiritual evolution—an evolution which is not linear, lineal or genetic. As in some forces of nature, our personal and spiritual evolution follows in heuristic cyclical and spiraling patterns. At this stage the Kundalini Shakti moves from the heart center to the throat center and from the throat center to the Ajna Chakra, or third eye between the eyebrows where intuitive wisdom blossoms, ending the knot of ignorance. At this advanced level of personality integration, the mirage of dualistic vision represented by the demons "I-ness and mine-ness" vanishes and the devotee attains spiritual identification or oneness with the Goddess.

Her power to destroy the negative tendencies of the mind shifts from the power to create and recreate new ways of being to the

163

power to transform into new and more evolved identities within this very lifetime—without the need of death and rebirth. In Her story of victory we find the sublimation of the ugly into unbound grace and radiant beauty. She embodies the story of our own spiritual transformation—from a journey sunk in the misery of fear and ignorance, to one with abundant knowledge and divine qualities.

Imagine the Goddess' timeline from antiquity to Her emissaries in empowered women today, "Without stories there is no articulation of experience," Carol P. Christ, author of *Diving Deep and Resurfacing: Women Writers on Spiritual Quest,* reminds us. Without stories, a woman "is lost when she comes to make the important decisions of her life. She does not learn to value her struggles, to celebrate her strengths, to comprehend her pain. Without stories, a woman cannot understand herself. [...] she is alienated from those deeper experiences of self and world that have been called spiritual or religious. She is closed in silence."

Christ calls our attention to empowering stories of the feminine in Ntozake Shange's *for colored girls who have considered suicide/when the rainbow is enuf,* "sing a black girl's song / bring her out..." by elucidating that "What Shange says of song applies equally to story: without articulation, the self perishes. [...] Shange's use of the imagery of death and rebirth [as is the imagery of sublimation and transformation in the story of the Goddess] underscores the urgency of all women's storytelling. Without stories there is a sense in which a woman is not alive." Christ finds echo in what Adrienne Rich calls "the creative potential of storytelling," as if encouraging every woman to write her story. In *Women's Stories, Women's Quest,* Christ elevates storytelling to a consciousness rising ritual, and feminist literary readings to ritual events forging connections by naming the longings, and giving form to our perceptions of the world and its powers. Carol Christ reminds us that "literature created by women," and I suggest that literature about the Goddess, "has both a spiritual and social dimension." The stories about the Goddess intertwine the realms of work, political and personal relationships, bringing us to the central theme of second wave feminism, "the personal is political."

The essence of the *Devi Mahatmya* contains many more insights waiting to be extracted from the story of the Goddess in women's conversations. Separating reality into categories like "the spiritual and the mundane [...], has been typical in Western philosophy." The resulting history of ongoing wars have been devastating. "I believe that women's quest seeks a wholeness that unites the dualism of spirit and body, rational and irrational, nature and freedom, spiritual and social, life and death, which have plagued Western consciousness" explains Carol P. Christ.

And when the metaphors and symbolism are properly understood, I believe that the stories of the Goddess in the *Devi Mahatmya* will contribute even more to unite the spiritual and social quests in a way that intimately speaks of the feminine divine in every woman.

Today, patriarchal and barbaric first world leaders continue their traditions and stories by invading, and colonizing, women and the land. They also colonize the minds of peace-loving people who ignore Her presence within them as raging protector of the value of human coexistence. The "good life" is a myth and cannot last among cultures where leaders lack spiritual maturity about how to control their obsessions about land expansion, technological growth and the accumulation of material goods at the expense of spiritual values. So, the Goddess in Her three forms awaits deep within the hearts of every woman for the ripe moment when She is invited into action, ready to accompany us through the story of our lives. Let us imagine living a life in which the Goddess enacts the drama of expansion of consciousness through every action, every day of our lives as the greatest blessing we can give to people around us. Let our life mission bring all wars and unnecessary miseries to an end.

Goddess Saraswati symbolizes the wisdom that destroys ignorance in its two aspects: the egocentric idea "I and mine" (individuality and its load). Goddess Saraswati emerges in the form of increasing insight and intellectual expansion until She bestows supreme blessedness and liberation from the cycles of births and deaths. When unsure of our steps, let us sit still and invoke Her presence, guidance and inspiration at the center of our hearts. Stillness is a form of angelic action, sometimes nothing needs to be done, this can be a good way to heal by allowing the Goddess within to emerge. She is always with you. Her strength is beyond human imagination.

One of the most dramatic episodes at the beginning of Her story comes when a messenger of a demon king, infatuated with her unparalleled beauty, comes to take her by force to the palace of the king. To this arrogant and crude proposition, Goddess Saraswati calmly responded that since early childhood She had made a vow that She would not marry anyone who does not deserve Her—or defeats Her pride in battle. This is the Goddess' cunning invitation to demons or unethical forces—an invitation to those lacking in intelligence and ethical values to come fight and see if they win, but the fight is in He own terms and conditions, so She always wins. The Goddess will not accept as partner one who is undeserving of Her, and neither should any woman. Anyone who cannot match or excel Her in divine qualities is not a fit match.

The message goes to the heart of problems that women encounter in relationships. But how do we know who is a deserving partner? Are young girls raised in abusive environments, and lacking in self-esteem, able to discern who is a deserving partner, someone who will honor her feminine divine? Every young girl deserves to be encouraged in accomplishing her full potential.

In her stunning and groundbreaking book *The Girl God* Trista Hendren addresses the deepest and most intimate questions by her daughter Helani about what is a girl's social and spiritual identity. Encountering "magic" and "normal" along formative opportunities in conversations, Helani and her mother persist in a most graceful and loving quest for the highest in divine feminine, the Girl God, and Goddess identity. Her beautifully illustrated book is a testament to a mother's power and mission to support her daughter and all daughters in renewal and regeneration across motherlines. The Girl God is on the path to enlightenment, and we hope to read more heroic stories from motherliness inspired by Trista Hendren's contribution to Goddess feminism.

If we miss the opportunity to support the unbound heroic dream identities of young girls, we are left in a world where everyone is blind. As the Goddess potential continues to be obscured by

166

layers upon layers of demeaning voices everywhere a young woman turns, she ends up believing in what passes as "love" in media and films. In our teens, many women literally "fall" in love, instead of rising in true love, the relationships that we weave during a depressed identity can drag us further down into intense grief and degradation.

Every living being is part of Her mystic body. In this mystic vision, She and you are One.

Behold Her in all names and forms,
She is One and many!

The Divine Mother adopts this terrible form as part of Her play, just as mothers put on a scary mask to entertain Her children. While in Her rage, self-controlled and self-directed, she removes barriers and the impositions in patriarchal systems of oppression. Connected to the Goddess within, women tap into sharp discerning powers—making it clear when and how to rage, when and how to relax, when and how to love, when and how to create, and how to live and die for a better world.

Sri Lakshmi is not only Goddess of prosperity and material wealth. She represents, most of all, the qualities that adorn altruistic character, artistic enfoldment, and the wealth of intellectual faculties: good and positive memory, an inquisitive mind, ethical integrity, and the blossoming of compassion for all. All material abundance and prosperity is transient, it is precarious, at least, and one must have good health to enjoy it. In order to secure the grace of Goddess Lakshmi one needs to diligently and sincerely seek ongoing self-improvement. Then, the abundant Grace of Goddess Lakshmi will cascade through the chakras to the body-mind-spirit consciousness.

As mother of creative, intellectual luminosity, and spiritual-emotional expansion, Saraswati Devi informs us of the immanent and transcendental role of spirituality within. This translates into our physical, mental, emotional and spiritual connections with nature, and with one another. It extends to our responsibility to improve the lives of others as integral to us as One. In this spirit, She inspires the fields of social and restorative justice, natural science, servant leadership, women studies and the praxis of learning and education for a better world. She is present in the first comprehensive study of systems thinking, that is: the experiential research of Kundalini Yoga. The Goddess moves the stream of compassion along the mother line stories, and oral traditions that preserve the mother tongues and cultural diversity for our enjoyment and spiritual evolution.

She integrates the arts and sciences wherein all contradictions between caring for oneself and caring for others (including rivers, mountains, oceans and air) cease to exist. She empowers and enriches women through and beyond social, political, class, gender, and personal experiences toward compassionate bonds. The Goddess is the agent of the blossoming in the body-mind-intellect complex. She is also the goal of all spiritual transformation, from the most constricted ignorance to the heights of conscious expansion, i.e., illumination. She emerges in women who embody Her qualities. Honing Her qualities requires immense patience, when dullness is conquered anger emerges, when anger is conquered fear may emerge, when fear is conquered love and compassion shine forth because these qualities are intrinsic, always within us, waiting for us to remove obstacles that appear in the form of unnecessary distractions.

Feminist sisterhood cannot thrive unless women embrace Mother Divine in physical, emotional, and spirit form. Internalizing the talents and powers of Goddess-informed women prepares us to put patriarchal demoniac forces at a comfortable distance, where they are free to self-destruct, by the Grace of Goddess. However, when women fear the power of other women, a whole nation stands to lose because the strength of women is the gift of the divine feminine. When threatened by another woman, one should feel free to ask her, or ask ourselves, what is the gift of strength and positive qualities that she brings to us in spite of the initial mask of fear or anger?

Goddess is One, but, like every woman, She wears many hats. Let us live to express Her beauty, grace, and powers in every facet of our lives. I invite women to seek the company of enlightened women, whether She appears in the form of a graceful feminine guru, or sisters and mothers in other spiritual circles. Her gentleness and powers will emerge in the discerning women birthing and raising daughters and sons in awe of increasing inner appreciation of life's experiences. As women embody the gentle strengths of the Goddess, sisters, mothers, and daughters will no longer witness the downfall of the male child into patriarchal dehumanization.

Some misinformed scholars have expressed their doubt about the benefits of Goddess spiritual traditions in India, considering that rape and aggression against women continue ravaging the lives of Indian women. However, it seems to me that it is very convenient for western women who have internalized Eurocentric male privilege to ignore the destructive influences of 800 years of colonialism in the Indian sub-continent. In the last 200 years India has been under the yoke of British patriarchy and its systemic demonic influences across all class systems, their educational institutions, plundering of its natural treasures, and the deliberate distortion and destruction of Indic/Vedic culture affecting the very identity of its people. Centuries of barbaric invasions and the suppression of Goddess traditions in public spaces has not prevented the uninterrupted oral and written traditions of Enlightened Women and Yogic/Vedic saintly personalities, both male and female, from reaching devotees in the so called west. Here, for space considerations, it is not possible for me to abound on the extensive writings—including stunning poetry—by accomplished Goddess intoxicated saints and devotees from India and other parts of the world. The list of scholars dedicated to Indic Goddess studies keeps growing. I may suggest reading the works of Sister Nivedita, and of mystic poet Janine Canan, Ph.D. Scholars like Dr. Vasuddha Narayan and Tracy Pintchman have written extensively about the social and spiritual influences of male and female monastic *Shaktas* devoted to the Goddess. She is Shakti, mother of the fallen, the grieving, the struggling, as well as the victorious.

Goddess, or the Divine Feminine within, puts on Her terrifying mask to scare the forces of delusion, cowardice, cruelty, and narcissism. Those who honor Her in Her full glory are not afraid of Her many forms, whether She appears as benefactor, as slayer of negative forces, or conferring the boons of wealth, wisdom, and immortality.

**May the three Goddesses endow you with
Love, Bliss and Enlightenment!**

A Woman Who Trusted
Her Own Judgment

Lora Koetsier

HUMAN RIGHTS....do they even exist? In the fundamentalist Christian churches of my childhood and early adulthood, there were so many mixed messages: denial of human rights, then words of men claiming equality for women, actions of men clearly saying otherwise. These men (and women!) would use statements from Apostle Paul to keep women in an inferior position relative to men. For nearly 21 years, these teachings from the Apostle Paul reinforced the problems in my marriage.

Many women who have grown up in fundamentalist Christian churches are familiar with the Apostle Paul's statement describing Eve as the first person to be deceived (I Timothy 2:14). Then there are the common interpretations of Paul's statement: women cannot trust their own judgment, women are so emotional that they cannot think straight, women are emotionally fragile and cannot thrive in a man's world, etc. Ironically, these subtle "Christian" prejudices effectively prohibit many women from seeking and creating knowledge. For this reason, I have decided to explore how this common misinterpretation of Paul's statement interferes with feminist epistemology.

For several years, it was difficult for me to read Scripture and benefit from Christian teachings.

At that time, I started visiting a Messianic congregation where I found support as I separated from an abusive marriage. I started seeking answers from the Hebrew Scriptures because there are so many positive examples of righteous women rising above the oppressive patriarchy of their culture.

In the Christian Scriptures, the Apostle Paul explains the purpose of historical accounts of people in the Hebrew Scriptures as examples for us, written for our admonition (I Corinthians 10:11). If this is true, is there something in the

Hebrew Scriptures that would provide an example of feminist epistemology?

So for women who are trying to overcome their own fundamentalist backgrounds, let's see what can be learned from II Kings chapters 3 & 4 concerning the Shunammite woman and her interactions with the Prophet Elisha and his servant Gehazi. First, a little historical background... In II Kings 3:9, we read about the Prophet Elijah asking the young Elisha: What shall I do for thee, before I be taken away from thee? Elisha responded: I pray thee, let a double portion of thy spirit be upon me. Then, in verse 15, we read that the sons of the prophets recognized the spirit of Elijah resting upon Elisha.

II Kings 4:8-10[1]

Now it happened one day that Elisha went to Shunem, where a notable woman persuaded him to eat some food. So each time he passed by her home, he would turn in there to eat some food.

Notable... KJV says great...
more than likely, women had wealth
and social status – yet had little education?

And she said to her husband, "Look now, I know that this *is* a holy man of God, who passes by us regularly. [10] Please, let us make a small upper room on the wall; and let us furnish a bedroom for him so it will be, whenever he comes to us, he can turn in there."

Woman says: I *know* (KJV says I perceive).
So I ask: How does she know/perceive?
Did she ask her husband if Elisha
was a holy man of God? No.

Okay, so how did this woman come to this conclusion? Perhaps she realized that Elisha was a nice man (faith according to reason) OR perhaps she realized that Elisha was a holy man of God (faith above reason, from the Holy Spirit) OR it could have been both.[106]

II Kings 4:11-16

[11] So one day Elisha went to the upper room and lay down there. [12] Then he said to Gehazi his servant, "Call this Shunammite woman." When he had called her, she stood before him. [13] And he said to him, "Say now to her, 'Look, you have been concerned for us with all this care. What *can I* do for you? Do you want me to speak on your behalf to the king or to the commander of the army?'" She answered, "I dwell among my own people."

Gehazi seems to be serving as an interpreter. Elisha ASKED what he could do for her, without jumping to false conclusions. Elisha speculates that she could be a victim of political oppression. But the woman is honest, stating that she is not a victim.

[14] So he said, "What then *is* to be done for her?" And Gehazi answered, "Actually, she has no son, and her husband is old." [15] So he said, "Call her." When he had called her, she stood in the doorway.

[16] Then he said, "About this time next year you shall embrace a son." And she said, "No, my lord. Man of God, do not lie to your maidservant!"

Even though this woman recognizes Elisha as the man of God, she is skeptical and refuses to believe his promise. Could be a simple lack of faith, OR perhaps she has problems with trusting Elisha due to some past trauma?

---

[106] [106] http://www.biblegateway.com/passage/?search=2+Kings+4%3A8-37&version=NKJV; accessed 20 October 2014. With commentary and some paraphrasing.

172

II Kings 4:17-23

¹⁷ But the woman conceived, and bore a son at the appointed time, as Elisha had promised.

¹⁸ And the child grew. Now it happened one day that he went out to his father, to the reapers.

¹⁹ And he said to his father, "My head, my head!" So he said to a servant, "Carry him to his mother." ²⁰ When he had taken him and brought him to his mother, he sat on her knees till noon, and *then* died. ²¹ And she went up and laid him on the bed of the man of God, shut *the door* upon him, and went out.

²² Then she called to her husband, and said, "Please send me one of the young men and one of the donkeys, that I may run to the man of God and come back." ²³ So he said, "Why are you going to him today? *It is* neither the New Moon nor the Sabbath."

> Her husband's question seems to reflect faith
> according to reason-based on experience,
> he knows that his wife goes to the man of God
> on the New Moon and the Sabbath... So why today?

And she said, "*It is* well."

> So this woman does not tell her
> husband that their son has died.
> Is she lying to her husband?
> Or is she exercising a faith above reason –
> all will be well once she reaches the man of God.

II Kings 4:24-28

²⁴ Then she saddled a donkey, and said to her servant, "Drive, and go forward; do not slacken the pace for me unless I tell you." ²⁵ So she departed to find the man of God at Mount Carmel. So it was, when the man of God saw her afar off, that he said to his servant Gehazi, "Look, the Shunammite woman! ²⁶ Please run now to meet her, and say to her, '*Is it* well with you? *Is it* well with your husband? *Is it* well with the child?'" And she answered, "*It is* well."

So this woman does not tell Gehazi that her
son has died. Is she lying?
Perhaps her statement is related to her
emotional problem with trust?
Or is she exercising a faith above reason -
all will be well once she reaches the man of God.

27 Now when she came to the man of God at the hill, she caught
him by the feet, but Gehazi came near to push her away. But
the man of God said, "Let her alone; for her soul *is* in deep
distress, and the LORD has hidden *it* from me, and has not told
me."

Obviously, Gehazi is judging this woman AND he is
being very disrespectful toward her.

28 So she said, "Did I ask a son of my lord? Did I not say, 'Do not
deceive me'?"

This woman sounds bitter…and she remembers what
she said to Elisha **12 years ago**?
This woman has an incredible memory.

Reflecting on Micah 6:8 and the Lord's requirements for us…to
DO justly, to LOVE mercy,
to WALK humbly before they God…
Elisha's behavior indicates that he
understands the Lord's requirements.
Gehazi's behavior clearly indicates otherwise.

II Kings 4:29-31

29 Then he said to Gehazi, "Get yourself ready, and take my staff
in your hand, and be on your way. If you meet anyone, do not
greet him; and if anyone greets you, do not answer him; but lay
my staff on the face of the child."

Elisha appears to be exercising faith above reason –
that God will work a miracle through the obedience of Gehazi.
Yet, this woman realizes something that
the Prophet Elisha does not yet realize:
Gehazi is NOT a man of God. This woman is
exercising faith according to reason.

³⁰ And the mother of the child said, "As the LORD lives, and *as* your soul lives, I will not leave you." So he arose and followed her.

So Elisha tells the woman to go with Gehazi, but she refuses.
Oh, no! A woman has disobeyed the man of God!
Will he insult her? Will he refuse to help her?
Will he tell her that rebellion is as the sin of witchcraft?
No, the man of God does none of these.
As the man of God, he shows mercy.

³¹ Now Gehazi went on ahead of them, and laid the staff on the face of the child; but *there was* neither voice nor hearing. Therefore he went back to meet him, and told him, saying, "The child has not awakened."

So now, the first "scientific experiment" is complete.
Whereas the woman's disobedience and faith according
to her own reason is validated,

Elisha's faith in Gehazi's obedience is contrary to reason.

II Kings 4:32-37

³² When Elisha came into the house, there was the child, lying dead on his bed. ³³ He went in therefore, shut the door behind the two of them, and prayed to the LORD. ³⁴ And he went up and lay on the child, and put his mouth on his mouth, his eyes on his eyes, and his hands on his hands; and he stretched himself out on the child, and the flesh of the child became warm. ³⁵ He returned and walked back and forth in the house, and again went up and stretched himself out on him; then the child sneezed seven times, and the child opened his eyes.

So now, the second "scientific experiment"
is complete. Elisha has exercised faith
above reason, validating him as a man of God.
Nevertheless, we must remember that miracles AND faith above
reason are both gifts from God.

³⁶ And he called Gehazi and said, "Call this Shunammite woman." So he called her. And when she came in to him, he

said, "Pick up your son." [37] So she went in, fell at his feet, and bowed to the ground; then she picked up her son and went out.

The woman realized that Gehazi was not a man of God.
Ironically, Elisha does not seem to realize
that Gehazi is not a man of God.

The next few chapters indicate that Elisha gradually
realizes that Gehazi is not a man of God.
Then, Gehazi is struck with leprosy.

In II Kings 4 and throughout Scripture, we can observe Elisha's respectful attitude and kind behavior toward women.

As the man of God, Elisha encouraged this
woman to overcome her skepticism.
Although she had her issues with trust, Elisha
respected her faith according to reason.
As the woman observed Elisha's example of faith
above reason, she learned to trust God.

Conclusion

Throughout II Kings 4, it seems to me that the writer repeats "the man of God" as a literary device to make a point. Whereas Elisha is mentioned by name in 5 verses (1, 2, 8, 17, & 32), the writer refers to Elisha as "the man of God" in the 9 other verses. This literary device clearly illustrates the difference between Elisha as "the man of God" and Gehazi who is NOT a man of God.

So let us return to Apostle Paul's statement describing Eve as the first person to be deceived. Since women cannot trust their own judgment, they should trust men to interpret Scripture, leading to the subtle implication that women should also trust men to define reality. Ironically, these common misinterpretations don't leave much room for Christian women to experience the Holy Spirit as Teacher and Comforter in their daily lives as promised by Jesus Christ.

As stated earlier, it was difficult for me to read Scripture and benefit from Christian teachings.

So now, I reflect on statement from the Apostle Paul: God forbid: yea, let God be true, but every man a liar (Romans 3:4a). Based on my background in fundamentalist churches, I believe it would benefit women with a background similar to mine to follow the example of the Shunammite woman, recognizing that a man who respects women is a man of God and discerning that a man who disrespects women is NOT a man of God.

I consider statement from male theologian Gilbert Bilezikian, who reminds us that it was a "satanic scheme, devised at the fall," to make women feel guilty for being women." Carolyn Holderread Heggens continues…"Any religious teachings that imply woman's moral inferiority to man, that infer she is created less in the image of God than is man, and that cause her to trust man's judgment more than her own are not only a heretical distortion of the gospel message, but are tragically dangerous to her and her children" (Kroeger, 20).[107] Reading this book titled *Women, Abuse, and the Bible* edited by scholar Catherine Clark Kroeger has been very helpful to me.

Once I had this deeper understanding, I returned to the statements of Paul that "Christian" men often use to oppress women. As I learned about historical/cultural context from Catherine Clark Kroeger, I realized that Paul was not writing about all women for all time. He was simply protecting the early churches from false teaching coming from the Temple of Diana located in the city of Ephesus.

I experienced these struggles over 10 years ago. Currently, I belong to a small church with a male pastor and women elders. As a true man of God, he respects women. He preaches the Word of God faithfully, using positive examples of women from Scripture to encourage our congregation. Now I can read the Hebrew Scriptures as well as the Christian Scriptures, trusting the Holy Spirit to lead me toward deeper truths.

---

[107] [107] Heggen, Carolyn Holderread. "Religious Beliefs and Abuse"

Kroeger, Catherine Clark & James R. Beck, ed. *Women, Abuse, and the Bible: How Scripture Can Be Used to Hurt or Heal.* Grand Rapids, Mich: Baker Books, 1996.

From ignorance to the feminine wisdom

Zoharah Noy-meir

A S A JEWISH ISRAELI GIRL, the the Hebrew Bible was part of everyday life. The Bible stories were as present in my life as fairy tales like Cinderella and Snow White. My kindergarten teacher read them to us on Fridays before we went home for the weekend and I had books with the Bible stories. In second grade, after a very exciting ceremony, we started reading and studying the Bible.

What I like about the Old Testament and Judaism is that it deals with all aspects of human life, including the physical. The spiritual is very connected with the body's most basic functions. It provides guidance on every aspect of daily life, from what to eat and how to eat it, and hygiene issues from birth to death. It is so specific that you can find detailed descriptions of skin disease in the five books of Moses.

I love that because it means that the body is important, the body matters. I think this is a very feminine approach that I believe comes from the original roots of Judaism that grow on a very deep and vast culture of goddess cultures.

Today, Judaism opposes these faiths as heresy but it was very connected to them when it evolved like a rebellious son who disowns his mother.

In Judaism there are two important concepts "Tame" טמא meaning unclean physically and spiritually and "Tahor" טהור meaning clean and pure, physically and spiritually.

There are many things that are unclean. The dead is unclean and the uncleanness is passed on by touch. Anyone who touches the dead is unclean. It doesn't mean he is a bad person; it means he should wash before he can pray or go to the temple.

The menstrual blood is also "Tame" – meaning that menstruating women are unclean and anything they touch during their bleeding becomes unclean. Religious men should not touch their wives while they are bleeding.

178

Although I grew up in a secular family, the idea that menstrual blood is filthy, shameful, and must be kept hidden was all around me. I learned this from my mother, my friends at school, and tampon ads.

It was something that you don't want anyone to know, and to me, that meant detachment. I was encouraged to ignore it, *a strong woman does not surrender to the limits of her body.* This is an idea that somehow implanted itself in my mind. *If I want to be recognized and appreciated, I should not let my femininity stop me from doing things that men do.*

So detachment was a good solution and when my blood came I dealt with it. Luckily I do not suffer from cramps, so it was easy to ignore it, except for that weird thing that I was not aware of – called PMS – because once in a while I would get these weird mood swings. I would suddenly feel very sad and could start crying because of the most trivial things. In my early 20's I felt like I was going crazy. I started to suspect that this might have something to do with my period, but because I was detached from my cycle and, in general, from my body, I kept "forgetting" each month. I would get these strange moods. Only after the blood came would I understand *"oh, so that is what it was"* and it insulted me in a way... I felt that that my body was uncontrollable – that being a woman had doomed me to having no control over myself.

It was 20 years later, when I participated in my first Red Tent circle, that I learned that that this was not my individual problem, as many women disliked their periods. For many women, menstruation was connected with pain and shame.

Only then did I agree to listen to it. After that circle, I decided I wanted to create an event – a Red Tent festival. Thanks to my teachers, I began to change the way I thought and felt about my cycle, my PMS and my bleeding. I already knew from other practices and experiences that my body was a great teacher; I just did not include my cycle and the feminine aspects of my body as a unique source of wisdom that only women have.

I started tracking my cycle. I still do because I think there is still so much about it, about myself that I don't know. I sense there is so much more to learn and the first requirement is that I stop –

stop my doing in everyday life and listen for a moment to my body and to my womb.

I discovered what I call womb meditations – just sitting and directing my attention to my pelvis and lower abdomen. When I first started doing this, I didn't feel anything, but slowly it changed and became a different way of listening and hearing. It does not come as mindful insights. For me, the wisdom of the womb is mindless and it bypasses my intellectual understanding. Because of that, it is usually very difficult to express it verbally. What I can say is that it connected me deeply to the earth as a spiritual power – as the source of life – and my womb as an extension of this Essence.

I still have a long way to go, after 43 years of ignorance – of ignoring and being unaware of that source of knowledge and intelligence. I need to practice daily and remind myself again to listen to my body – to believe the signs it is sending to me and honor it. But it is worth it. Today I feel grateful to be living my life in a feminine body that holds such wisdom, such magic – an endless field to explore and study.

I still need to find a way to make peace with my origin, with the Jewish tradition and culture that I live in. For me, the way is through connection with the land. The land, the earth itself, holds within it all the layers of human development. In the hills surrounding my neighborhood, there are ancient Catacombs and just beyond are the ruins of the city of Megido – Armageddon. In one of its deepest layers, they found a huge round altar, which I believe was a place to worship the goddess. It is all here, all the knowledge, all the memories – like my body that in its womb and cycles holds the deep wisdom of the goddess of the sacred feminine. The land holds within it all the memories of knowing and honoring the feminine body and wisdom. All I have to do is listen and look, to remove the veils of ignorance of shame and fear. I believe that when we do that— all of us women *and* men— something new and better can emerge.

The Problem with Faith and Fidelity

Lizette Galima Tapia-Raquel

I N THE BOOK OF RUTH, we encounter three women at the crossroads of their lives: they were all widows, had no property, and needed to decide where they wanted to go. The choice of Ruth to journey with Naomi has been interpreted in Christian tradition as a faith conversion experience. Ruth made the right choice: she chose the 'right' God. But a feminist critique of the narrative would expose Ruth's victimization and absence of resistance. Of her own volition, she offers to go to the field to gather grain and find favor with "someone"; falls prostrate with her face to the ground in thankfulness to Boaz's kindness to her and receives his favors; obeys Naomi's direction to uncover and lay down at Boaz's feet, and is acquired along with the land which was acquired by Boaz.

At the end of the narrative even Ruth's son is not hers for "A son has been born to Naomi." Ruth uses her sexuality to ensure security and sustenance and submits to the designs of Naomi and Boaz. Ruth embodies the complex oppression of women: as extensions of husbands and of sons, as properties who can be possessed along with the land, and as women burdened with reproductive labor. Boaz took notice of her but she could have been ignored. Boaz provided Ruth grain for picking but he could also have deprived her. Boaz 'knew' her but could have rejected her to become his wife. Boaz impregnated Ruth and she gave him a son but what if she had been barren? What if he had been sterile? What if there was no land to be possessed alongside Ruth? At every turn of the story, it could have gone the other way, as it does for so many women, and she could have become even more abused and persecuted as she struggled for life. At the end of the story, her bloodline is connected to the bloodline of David. Ruth is not like many women in real life. Ruth is a woman constructed by men in a patriarchal society.

In the Biblical texts, save for the *Song of Songs*, women express no interest in sex. They may be wives, concubines, lovers, prostitutes and adulteresses, but they are incapable of intense desire, pleasure and orgasm. They are desired by men, but do not desire men; whose bodies are offered for the pleasure of men, but find no pleasure in men's bodies. It is in women's sexuality that some women experience the greatest deprivation and perhaps, satisfaction. It is also when she is able to make independent and responsible decisions about her own body that she can begin to feel whole. Sometimes, women are not just in "a man's world,"; women's bodies are thought of as belonging to men.

Faithfulness to God and fidelity to a husband have been held equal in many cultures. The root of fidelity is 'fidelis' which means duty or loyalty to a lord or a master. A person who does not believe or rejects his or her faith is an 'infidel.' Unfaithfulness or adultery is only the sin of women and not the sin of men in biblical culture. It is an ethic that dictates women's lives even today and subjects many to violence and oppression. An ethic that does not apply to men of many cultures and religions.

Behind closed doors:
the complexity of culture and religion in presenting and interpreting the self

Nafhesa Ali

HOW HAS MY FAITH shaped my work as a Muslim feminist? I have to state here that my construction of a Muslim feminist positions me as a Muslim and a feminist researcher, not entirely a Muslim feminist per se. My work and research has not particularly located me with a Muslim feminist agenda, nor do I have the expertise in which I can claim this title, but I have the privilege of being a Muslim woman[108]. With a foundation of belief systems and ideals shaped by my culture and religion, the lens of identifying myself as a feminist researcher gives me a platform on which I am able to explore women within the South Asian diaspora with innovative insights. Therefore, in this anthology I will raise two issues which I have encountered during my work with older South Asian migrant women. Firstly, I will highlight challenges of self-representation in fieldwork and secondly, my motivations for gender equality through constructions of *izzat* (respect and honour).

Feminist thought

South Asian, Pakistani and Indian women for a long time have been constructed under the patriarchal authority of men, whether this has been in the form of cultural, faith or social practices (Shankar et al., 2013). However, Kandiyoti (1988) suggests women have various mechanisms which contest these authorities and are able to exert agency through the use of "patriarchal bargains" (p.274). Further, Shamita D. DasGupta (1998) in her book *A Patchwork Shawl: Chronicles of South Asian Women in America* highlights the role assigned to South Asian women is that which indicates them not only as the bearer, but also the transmitter of culture and therefore, South Asian women living in diasporic locations are thus able to negotiate multiple and often conflicting identities through the use of switching between "cultural voices" (Bhatia & Ram, 2004, p.

---

[108] See also Badran, M. (2008). Between Muslim Women and the Muslim woman' *Journal of Feminist Studies in Religion*, 24(1), 101-106.

224). South Asian women have then become viewed as having the unquestioned task of preserving, but also transmitting cultural and/or religious identity, across borders and over generations, as a result of the multiple identities to which they belong.

However, through the shared experience of being a woman, women from all faith, cultural and social backgrounds feature an overarching gender identity which feminists and feminist thinkers can claim and use in identifying the similarities and differences of women's experience. Feminism is then not solely claimed by women, for women, nor does it claim research by women on women, but is a framework which seeks to question the emancipatory meaning and practices structured in the foundations of our knowledge, and aims to give a voice to those who have been previously overlooked or unheard.

Therefore, working toward gender equality should not solely place focus only on gender in terms of men and women, but also work toward gender equality within representations of women. My work as a researcher, working closely with the South Asian Pakistani and Indian migrant women in the UK has highlighted the ways in which women who are being researched need to be represented, but also needs to highlight representations of the person who is conducting the research. Therefore, motivations for gender equality should be inclusive of those we are seeking to empower, but also the ones who claim the responsibility of doing this. Sariya Contractor (2012) echos this notion and puts forth the role of empowering other women is to narrate their stories, but this cannot be done without the author's own story.

Sandra Harding (1986) further critiques the very notion of feminist thinkers is to challenge the foundations in which intellectual and social orders have been constructed, and thus feminists need to continue to take into account the ways in which representing others, renegotiates the identity battles of both the feminist and the ones they are empowering. The commonalities of women working toward gender equality must therefore be done so with the acknowledgement of representation and interpretation. Mai Yamani (1996) highlights Bouder's (1993) argument that "feminists do not all think the same way or even about the same kind of things" (cited in

Yamani, 1996, p. I), and therefore may utilize subjective interpretations embedded within their cultural and/or religious beliefs.

The complexity of culture and religion

Culture and religion are both key issues within my research with older South Asian Pakistani and Indian women. I would often think about how I could make the women feel at ease, and therefore allow them to open up to me about significant life course experiences. Zubair, Victor and Martin (2012) write about the representation of dress and how the influence of what researchers wear in fieldwork has an impact on research. The way in which I presented myself to participants was also important and highlighted the complexity of culture and religion in fieldwork.

On one occasion during an interview with an Indian Sikh participant in her 60s, I choose not to wear my *hijab* (headscarf). In hindsight, I potentially did this from the fear of being *othered* and thus not wanting to reveal parts of my identity which would potentially stop the participant from opening up to me. Ironically, during the interview Mandeep[109] raised the issue of *izzat* (respect) and mentioned how "younger generations don't cover their heads anymore". Even though this comment wasn't directly aimed at me, it raised questions of how I had chosen to present myself and made me question my representation of myself and the way in which I had chosen not to (re)present my visible religious identity.

The complex nature of the South Asian diaspora with multiple religions, cultures, languages and regional variations highlights how different faiths can be encompassed by shared cultural structures, and how even perceptions of being an *insider*, with a shared community base can be challenged by failing to (re)present yourself appropriately. In addition to presentations of the self, the researcher's subjective belief and value system needs to be taken into account during research.

---

[109] Pseudonym to maintain participant anonymity.

Motivations for gender equality: *Izzat* (respect and honour)

Being respectful and displaying *izzat* (respect) to your elders are South Asian ideals, which are embedded within a significant part of my life teachings and experience. *Izzat* (respect), for me, is created by a bond which binds people together[110] regardless of biological affiliation, ethnic origin and even religion. A bond constructed on the knowledge of shared experience and teachings of multiple cultures, in which a sense of privileged knowledge and attachments to those we do not know are created.

Moreover, concepts of *Izzat* (respect and honour) have shaped my life two-fold, both through respect and honour, but also through its religious and cultural meanings. *Izzat* is a hugely contested word and can be taken in the practical sense of *izzat* (respect) or used to address a woman's *izzat* (honour). It is the former interpretation of izzat which is of interest in this discussion and Amita Handa (2003) considered notions of *izzat* as respect in her book *Of Silk Saris and Mini-Skirts: South Asian Girls Walk the Tightrope of Culture*. Handa brings to light the concept of an auntie/uncle syndrome, which is an unconscious desire to construct anyone from the South Asian community as family and thus referred to as an auntie or uncle.

It is *izzat* (respect) then which has motivated me to work with the South Asian community seeking gender equality and making the voice of older South Asian migrant women heard. During my research, irrelevant of nationality and religion (Indian or Pakistani, Muslim or Sikh) my constructions of these women are embedded within the auntie structure and my participants are often referred to as auntie. *Izzat* (respect) then crosses boundaries and borders, and is not exclusive to gender, religion, caste or ethnic group or to the construction of gendered oppression in which *izzat* is viewed in the traditional sense (e.g., honour crime, patriarchal oppression, domestic violence). Yes, there are undeniably problems with some interpretations of *izzat* which reinforce patriarchal structures and are used as an excuse to exert cultural interpretations of patriarchal power and authority[111] in the form of religious justification. For me however,

---

[110] Handa, A. (2003). *Of Silk Saris and Mini-Skirts: South Asian Girls Walk the Tightrope of Culture*. Ontario: Women's Press.

izzat represents a need to be respectful and honour others, and should be reconceptualised as an altruistic mannerism can motivate feminist research, whether this is in the form of the work we do or the ways in which we represent ourselves, in the field or out.

Conclusion

The motivation for this piece was based on wanting to bring to light the ways in which seeking gender equality needs to take into account the overlapping notions and interchangeable ideals within culture and religion, which may be displayed by both the researcher and researched. I have discussed perceptions of women we are seeking to empower, but also perceptions of how researcher's representations of the self in fieldwork may be presented or repressed in fieldwork. Both the understanding and awareness of representation and interpretation is then important in order to gain a better understanding of how and why we chose to undertake research seeking gender equality and empowerment.

---

[111] Shankar, J., Das, G., & Atwal, S. (2013). Challenging cultural discourses and beliefs that perpetuate domestic violence in South Asian communities: A discourse analysis. Journal of International Women's Studies, 14(1), 248-262.

REFERENCES

Badran, M. (2008). Between Muslim Women and the Muslim woman. *Journal of Feminist Studies in Religion*, 24(1), 101-106.

Batia, S. & Ram, A. (2004). Culture, hybridity, and the dialogocal self: Cases from the South Asian diaspora. *Mind, Culture, and Activity*, (3), 224-240.

Bouder, L. (1993). A lawyer's primer on feminist theory and tort. In M. Yamani (1996). *Feminism and Islam: Legal and literary perspectives*. Berkshire, UK: Ithaca Press.

Contractor, S. (2012). *Muslim Women in Britain: Demystifying the Muslimah*. Oxon, USA and Canada: Routledge.

DasGupta, S. D. (1998). *A Patchwork Shawl: Chronicles of South Asian Women in America*. New Jersey: Rutgers University Press.

Handa, A. (2003). *Of Silk Saris and Mini-Skirts: South Asian Girls Walk the Tightrope of Culture*. Ontario: Women's Press.

Harding, S. (1986). *The science question in feminist critique*. Ithaca and London: Cornell University Press.

Kandiyoti, D. (1988). Bargaining with Patriarchy. *Gender and Society*, 2(3):274-290.

Shankar, J., Das, G., & Atwal, S. (2013). Challenging cultural discourses and beliefs that perpetuate domestic violence in South Asian communities: A discourse analysis. Journal of International Women's Studies, 14(1), 248-262.

Yamani, M. (1996). *Feminism and Islam: Legal and literary perspectives*. Berkshire, UK: Ithaca Press.

Zubair, M., Martin, W. & Victor, C. (2012). Embodying Gender, Age, Ethnicity and Power in 'the Field': Reflections on Dress and the Presentation of the Self in Research with Older Pakistani Muslims. *Sociological Research online*, 17(3), 21.

Divinity, Creativity and Me

Ruth Calder Murphy

I AM AN ARTIST, WRITER AND MUSICIAN. A questioner – an explorer.

Over the years, I've allowed myself to open up and *live* this innate curiosity. I've begun to allow the questions to flow, even when they lead me into difficult places. Places where Divinity is more than I ever imagined and sometimes, even looks a little bit like me.

For a very long time, having been brought up as a Christian, I found it difficult to think in terms of the Divine Feminine.

I didn't – and don't – have a problem with the Divine Father. I adore my own father and have been blessed with many positive examples of male-ness. This makes it relatively easy for me to relate to God as "Father", I think.

It was only as an adult – in fact, as a wife and mother – that I began to realise that my view of God as male *and only male* was damaging my perception of my own role in the scheme of things, and my relationship with the Divine.

I began to wonder whether it was more spiritually and emotionally healthy, and also, even, more theologically intelligent – even from within the religious tradition in which I'd grown up and to which I still feel an affinity – to think of the Divine as, equally, *neither* male nor female, and, at the same time, *both* male and female. (I'd already become more open to other philosophies and traditions, over the years, and had felt a particular kinship with Celtic Paganism, where the Divine Feminine is very much recognised and celebrated.)

I began to look for examples of the Divine Feminine in Judeo-Christian Scriptures and traditions.

I came to realise that a lot of my preconceptions are the result of living in a patriarchal culture, and the consequence of being immersed in Scriptures and religious traditions that were born of a patriarchal culture. (Even though, ostensibly, the Jewish culture is matriarchal in terms of heredity, the dominant interpretations of what I was taught to call the Old Testament is very heavily patriarchal.) Once I acknowledged this, and allowed space for cultural bias in the writings and hermeneutics of the traditions, it became increasingly easy to see how Divinity not only *could* be both male and female – and also neither – but by definition, *has* to be.

This is an ongoing discovery for me. I see the Divine Feminine most strongly as she is made manifest in the Natural world, and through female, or feminine people (whether their bodies are woman-shaped or man-shaped) and deep within my own soul.

Practically, personally, as a feminist in a patriarchal tradition - and as a mother of children growing up in a male-dominated world – it's important for me to own my ideas and perspectives – to respect my interpretations of things and not always look for validation in the approval of other people; specifically women or men who maintain (even in their unconscious actions) that the ultimate authority is male. This is an ongoing effort. I often pull myself up short, realising that I'm not giving my own hermeneutic, experience, intellect, ideas and expression the same respect as I give those of the patriarchal persuasion.

There's a certain sort of person – and, as I said to begin with, I am one – who is, at core, an explorer, a questioner: A "Creative Sort". This isn't defined by whether someone is mathematically minded, or a scientist, or an artist, writer or musician. It's something even more fundamental than that. It's about not being satisfied with having one's questions answered and then enjoying the comfort of those answers. It's about allowing more questions, always, to grow – and to run with them and see where they lead. Creativity, is, I think, in its essence, this innate and persistent childlikeness – this curiosity, and the manifestation or expression of it in art, music, writing, scientific experimentation and so on.

It's in creativity that I find the sweetest release and the most meaningful connections. As an artist, writer, musician and mother, the drive to create and be creative is like air, water and sunlight to me.

It's here, in the creative flow, that I come closest to my own
essence – and closest to Divinity as mother, sister and friend.

Discovering Divinity

You're moon beams and meadows,
the grass beneath my feet.
you're the whisper of the breeze
and profoundest oceans' deep.

You're the turning of the seasons,
the glow of Autumn leaves.
You're the song of the stars,
the embrace of sleep -
singing lullabies under ancient skies
as my spirit soars
and my body lies wrapped
in your lap...

You're spirals and circles,
you're lightning strikes and thunderclaps,
sparking brilliance to mainline my brain.
You're music and laughter and
dancing in the rain.

You flow, in my tears
and breathe, in my sighs -
holding my hopes and fears,
releasing me to rise
to impossible heights on liberated wings,
where the air is thin and sky spins into space
- to find my voice, at last, and sing -
and know for sure,
- secure -
my place
in Everything.

"Aria - Song of Everything" by Ruth Calder Murphy

A Daughter of the Goddess

Susan Morgaine

I AM A WITCH. To be more specific, I am a Feminist Goddess-oriented Witch, which to me means that my feminism is combined with my spirituality, and my spirituality is part of my feminism.

I did not always identify myself as such. I was born and raised a Catholic. I was baptized, had my first communion and my confirmation. I played my guitar and sang at Folk Masses, for any of you who remember what those were. I taught Sunday School once for a year when the church was having trouble finding teachers. I was probably about 15.

I began to have my first feminist leanings at that age. I was at Mass with a couple of friends. The altar boys had not shown up. The priest (our "progressive" priest) picked me and my friend to be altar girls, since he knew we knew what to do. Remember, this was back in the 1970's and it was a huge deal to have women, albeit young women, serving on the altar. When the service was over, we were called in to see the monsignor of the church. He was a big man, big of height and big of breadth. At the time, I didn't realize it as I do now, but he used his size to intimidate, and intimidate he did. How dare we, females, dare to serve the lord? He yelled at us and dismissed us. I could, and can, only imagine what he said to the other priest. Not that it mattered because our progressive priest was gone within a week. This stayed with me. This incident made me realize that the Catholic church did not want me, a female; it also was the birth of a feminist.

Since the Goddess works in mysterious ways, it was around this same time that a book fell into my hands - how or by who I have no recollection. It was called *Diary of a Witch* by Sybil Leek. I was called by the Goddess; it just took me years to realize it that this was my sole path. In hindsight, I think I was a daughter of the Goddess before I was even born.

I was further introduced to what is now called "male privilege" at the age of 16, when I was sexually molested by an older male cousin. Then at 17, I was pulled into a car and driven to an

193

isolated area where some man attempted to rape me. I say attempted because I was fortunate to get away when so many of us are unable to do so for a myriad of reasons. To this day, and I'm in my 50's now, I still somehow believe that both of these incidents were my fault. Intellectually, I know better; they were and are the sole responsibility of the men involved. But that is how pervasive, how insidious our society and culture is with what it teaches women.

I came of age at the tail end of the hippie era and the re-birth of women's lib. I longed to be just a couple of years older, but I learned enough. The feminism and the Goddess started to, very slowly, come together for me. I very easily called myself a feminist in my late teens and early 20's. It was still another 10 years for me to 100% admit to myself that I belonged to the Goddess. I had started to study Wicca after the Sybil Leek book, and I never stopped, to this day. It took me awhile to fully commit myself as Catholic teachings run deep.

My Wicca studies began with very traditional Wicca; Goddess and consort God. However, it did not take me long to begin to work solely with the Goddess. It was, and is, the Goddess that makes me feel fulfilled.

As I was beginning to fully embrace the Goddess in my life, I was ever conscious of the role women played, or did not play, in society. I called myself a feminist, but in the world, it seemed that women were doing, if not great, better. We had birth control; we had the ability to choose what was right for us and our own bodies. While we did not get equal pay, we were making inroads in fields that had been denied us for so long. My own personal choice was to stay home and raise my children, but I loved the fact that other women had these opportunities to do more, if they choose to.

While raising my children, I only kept half an eye on what was going on in the country, as my personal world was one that revolved around PTO, Girl Scouts, Cub Scouts, games, and concerts. I studied in spare moments and completed rituals when I could. Funny thing with kids, though—they grew up and the world started to come back to me in a clearer focus. Things had changed somewhat for women while I was in the throes of raising children. When did we stop moving forward? What happened to the ERA? When did the fight for control over our own bodies begin again? Why were we still not making the wages that men did in the same jobs? Why were we once again fighting for every small step? Rape and domestic violence has increased. Women are blamed for everything that happens to them and men are not responsible for anything because it is the woman's fault. Young girls are being slut-shamed in schools where administrators deem their clothing too seductive and too tempting for the young men. States are attempting to close all of our women's health clinics. Men with no knowledge of the act of creation, no knowledge of the workings of a woman's body are telling us what we can and cannot do with our own selves.

World-wide, women are used as weapons of war, to be raped and discarded or used as shields; their bodies are mutilated by their tribes to subvert their sexuality; and young girls are murdered for trying to get an education. In one of the more ridiculous things I have heard recently, we are told to wear a new nail polish that will tell us if there are drugs in our drinks to help stop rape. Does it not occur to anyone except us that to stop rape, men need to stop raping?

The more news I read and watched, the sadder and angrier I became. I found myself turning to the Goddess more and more, asking *how could this be?* My spirituality was becoming my feminism and my feminism was becoming a part of my spirituality. To me, the Goddess was everything the world could and should be. She was all, She was Light and Dark, She was female and male, She was Creation and Destruction.

I started teaching and have continued to do so for the past 12 years. My teaching evolved into a very women-empowering experience for me, and I hope, for my students. My teaching became a way for me to share my beliefs without proselytizing. My coed yoga class became a women's only class, a place for women to come and nurture themselves, get a brief respite from their daily life and learn Pranic energy for their own healing. My belly dance classes became a way to reach out to both younger and older women, to help them awaken that divine feminine within them; for most, it was the first time they had ever heard of the Goddess.

I have been accused of misandry, even by the man in my life. I do not hate men. But, I do hate the patriarchy. I do hate how women are treated in this country, and in this world. I hate a world where women are used and discarded. I hate a society where it is okay to rape and beat women. I hate a country where men attempt to make decisions for women regarding what is best for her, her body and her life. I hate the political culture of "power over" instead of "power with."

I hate lust for power, for greed, and ambition and those that have a great disdain for the ones they are supposed to represent. I hate a society that is based on the separation of church and state, but allows politicians to use religion to further their own agendas. I abhor a world that looks to war and domination, instead of peace.

I do not believe that individual males (necessarily) view the world be this way; however, I do believe that it is the patriarchy's view of the world and of those who would keep it dominant. Feminism is not the hatred of men. It is not a wish for the world to return to a matriarchal women-rule. To me, feminism is a wish for all to live in peace and equality, with the people working together for the good of all, and the good of Mother Earth.

I have become, in my own way, a women's rights advocate. I sign petitions, I use social media, I use my voice and my wallet. I try to teach others what feminism has taught me, but how can you teach when those around you don't want to learn? How do you explain to men how it is to be a woman in this world, in this society, in this culture? How do you tell a woman, who refuses to see, what is actually going on around her? How do you teach what patriarchy is to those who do not even truly know what the word means.

I don't pretend to know the answers but I do know that I will keep trying. I do know that the fight is not over. I do know that I am still, and always, a Feminist. I do know that I am still, and always, a Daughter of the Goddess.

God is Not a Man

Trista Hendren

THERE IS A WOUND IN THE WORLD that is specific to women and girls. Many of us take a lifetime to figure out what it is, which is grossly unfortunate. You can't heal what you don't recognize.

Every person is born of a woman, but somehow the traditional creation myth was turned around on its head. Women are secondary, if not cursed, via this tradition. The textbooks that our children read are still almost entirely male-dominated filled with male-accomplishments. Our spiritual communities are still mostly male-led and refer to God as "He."

Religious thought seeps in early and is very damaging to girls. If God is a man, and "He" is everything that is good and superior, it is easy to conclude that we as women are, in fact, beneath men. Whether you practice a religion or not, this still has a profound effect on our collective thinking.

> *"There were no religious images in the churches or synagogues of our childhood that celebrated the birthing powers of women. According to religion's myths, the world was brought into being by a male God, and woman was created from man. This reversal of biological process went unchallenged. Most of us didn't even notice the absence of the mother. Although we may not have been consciously aware of her absence in bible stories and sermons, her absence was absorbed into our being. It's painful influence was intensified as we observed the design of our parents' relationship and the treatment of our mothers by our fathers and brothers. Our families mirrored the hierarchical reality of the heavens. In a society that worships a male God, the father's life is more valuable than the mother's. The activities of a man's life are more vital and necessary than the mother's intimate connections with the origins of life. The father is God."*
>
> *Patricia Lynn Reilly*

197

If you doubt why this is important, ask yourself why women today still own only one percent of the world's wealth. That means that men, mostly white Western men, own the rest. Women, by and large, are still dependent on men for that 99 percent. The way we interpret our religious scriptures validate that dependence.

If God is male, men are superior. And women are, by default, *inferior.*

Sadly, I heard this message loud and clear growing up in a Christian home. I vowed that my kids would be raised the opposite way. I hungered to provide my daughter with a different foundation than what I was indoctrinated with. I wanted my daughter to know that she is absolutely wonderful just the way she is. I dreamed of raising her to the heights instead of burying her—as we do with most girls. I didn't want my daughter to spend most of her adult life unburying herself as I have—and continue to do.

I believe that spirituality is the place to start. Whether you are religious or not, the deep cultural roots of our faiths of origin affect all of us deeply. Nearly all world religions practice today on the foundation of patriarchy. But this need not be the case. The feminine divine can be found in all the world religions if you look for Her.

Alice Walker wrote, "...healing begins where the wound was made." I believe most wounds women in the world today experience were brought upon by denying the feminine divine. This is done in both subtle and violent ways. If we want a better world for our daughters, we must begin to re-balance the divine feminine with the masculine.

The divine feminine is unconventional. She does not belong to any one faith tradition. In fact, she belongs to all of them.

She does not come to us as a Savior; rather, she is the force within us who empowers us to save ourselves. She loves indiscriminately; you do not have to be "good" to merit her attention.

As Mary Oliver reminds us:

You do not have to be good.
You do not have to walk on your knees for a hundred miles
through the desert, repenting.

So many women are still waiting for their father or husband to sign permission slips for approval. This has been our indoctrination for thousands of years, so there is no blame in that. When we feel the sense of the divine within us, we learn that we do not need permission for anything. Many of the "rights" we are fighting so hard for are already things we innately possess.

When we recognize, both individually and collectively, our value as women, the world will change. The image of a masculine God is built on patriarchy, which is a vision of control through violence, whether actual or implied. When we honor the divine feminine, beating a woman becomes as unacceptable as burning down a church or a mosque. When we return to the divine feminine, rape will become inconceivable. *How can you pillage what is sacred?*

When we return to the divine feminine, we will stop trying to "save" women in other countries and realize that we have problems of our own to conquer. We will realize that each of us is capable of becoming our own savior. We will re-discover our rich herstory. We will come together as equals and change the world.

Our collective spirituality has largely been tainted to fit the needs of men and those in power. This has a profound effect on the self-esteem of girls and the women they become. This influence can be seen in their life choices, partners and financial security for the rest of their lives. It also has an effect on the way their future partners will view them—and ultimately treat them.

We must radically change how girls are raised from birth. It's so much easier than this never-ending un-doing most women seem to be stuck in. Just that alone is a full-time job. *Something has to change.* The Rev. Dr. Karen Tate recently wrote, "The Dalai Lama said it would be Western women who would come to the rescue of the world. Might it actually be Goddess Thealogy?" I happen to believe she is on to something.

God is not a man. We have been living a blatant lie for thousands of years. Women give life. The Goddess IS life. Until we collectively return to this truth, nothing will improve. Many of the world's problems stem from the attempt to stamp out the truth and kill the Divine Feminine. We are coming into a time now where many women and men are awakening to the Goddess, but we are also seeing a lot of backlash around this. I believe now is the time where we must stand strong or She will be buried forever—and so will the rights, dreams and livelihood of women and girls the world over.

Amy Logan wrote in *The Seven Perfumes of Sacrifice,* "Every time they butcher a woman for honor, they're killing the Goddess." I believe that's true with every rape and murder of a female, and to a *somewhat* lesser extent, every time a woman is hit, verbally abused or forced to live in poverty. It is also true so long as we continue to live under a system that teaches us to hate ourselves.

Harriet Tubman once said, "I freed thousands of slaves, and could have freed thousands more, if they had known they were slaves." Women must break free of their own chains so that our daughters and granddaughters can someday be born free. There is still time for each of us to live a life on our own terms if we have the courage to stand up together now.

It's time for us to become really intentional about what we want for ourselves and our daughters. We can't do it alone. Women must come back together into circles and reclaim what is ours.

> *"It goes on one at a time...*
> *it starts when you say We and know who you mean,*
> *and each day you mean one more."*
> -Marge Piercy, The Low Road

Break a Taboo Today!

DeAnna L'am

"Underneath the color of our skin,
all women bleed the same, red, deep,
ancient flow of life force. It is this power
what makes the blood that naturally
flows through a woman during
her cycle seem taboo."

THIS POWERFUL STATEMENT, made by Marjory Meijia is revolutionary in its depth and implications: **Under all perceived differences between us as women — our blood flows as one.** This profound realization filled my eyes with tears at the first Jewish and Palestinians women's circle I held in 1999 in Israel (my country of origin). Having held many women's circles before, and having been touched time and again by the power of sharing our first blood stories, I was unprepared for the depth of emotions that engulfed us all: Muslim, Christian, and Jewish women, divided by years of political bias, cultural stereotypes, and accumulated fear of each other's nations, we found a common ground that effortlessly bridged any perceived abyss between us!

Raised in small villages or in large urban neighborhoods, by deeply religious or defiantly atheist parents, in close-knit traditional communities or in loosely bound modern ones, our first blood stories differed in details, yet shared profoundly common flavors: those of feeling alone and scared, unprepared, ashamed, fearful, or just plain ho hum, a similar cord ran through our stories — a thread of invisibility, of a Coming of Age lacking in welcome, honor, or celebration.

The potency of our newly found bond was intoxicating! It made all perceived differences between us pale in comparison, dissolve into nothingness in the face of shared monumental experiences of girls who started bleeding with no cultural context, no mentors, and no meaningful acknowledgment; Of women who have been bleeding monthly for years, cycling silently with the moon, bearing cultural judgments and taboos about our bodies and our blood being unclean, gross, unmentionable, and rendering us crazy, lunatic, or sick (as in needing to be medicated).

The liberation we felt was palpable, the bonds we formed unshakeable. Yet it wasn't until I read Marjory Meijia's quote that I realized **we missed something:** Not only does the river of blood we all shed monthly serve as a thread that connects us beyond any divides. Not only is this common experience a dissolving agent for all our culturally cemented differences. But rather it is *because* of this potential bond among *all* women that **our blood became taboo!!!**

As women in indigenous cultures, we sat together in moon huts, moon lodges, or red tents all over the world. Our bleeding times were times of connection and alliance. Making our blood a cultural taboo didn't only create a sense of personal shame, feelings of inadequacy, uncleanliness, and isolation. It didn't only create (over generations) an inner distress that led to physical discomfort and symptoms labeled as 'PMS'. It broke us apart! It created a cultural climate in which every woman bears her bleeding time alone; in which women believe they may be the only ones *so* uncomfortable, *so* out of sorts, *so* disconnected as they feel in any given moment. Women united are so powerful – it may scare the living daylights out of cultures who seek to dominate them!

The taboos around our blood not only disempower us individually, they weaken our collective identity. *They tear us apart*. They sow isolation and alienation. They make us easy to manipulate, medicate, and sell to.

Let's take action to break the taboos (which serve those who wish to keep us in line) by uniting as bleeding women and voicing our blood stories (the good, the bad, the ugly, and the sacred) as the solvents that dissolve cultural taboos. Speaking about our blood, connecting around it, recognizing it as the central experience which defines us as women – are acts of defiance, and as such are revolutionary! Start a revolution today: tell your first blood story!

You are invited to Break A Taboo
right here, right now,
by sharing a Blood Story:
Your first or last blood,
your most or least favorite, your most outrageous,
most embarrassing, most painful, most funny,
or most sacred...
Speaking our silent truth
is an act of revolutionizing
the world!

The Initial Unraveling

Nahida Nisa

And God created humankind, so that we
may be guardians of the Earth.

WHEN LILITH WAS BORN, a quiescent soul in the full formation of a woman, she gazed only at the vast, flower-covered land across her dark eye. In the meadow she saw her destiny unfolded, and she lifted her gleaming halo of hair to the sempiternal reign of movement above her and sighed a quiet aubade. The rush of the stars crowned her with the force of all that would come. And, having no alternative, the weeping willow wept.

Lilith titled her magnificent head, and as she was asked, she Named. She named herself, and all that was around her, and when she had finished, she found pleasure in the likeness of things.

She grouped what she had named together by likeness, so that they might find pleasure in each other and know one another.

It seemed to her, at first, that she had placed these shapes into groups by the most arbitrary method, but even the wildest thing has patterns, its own rhyme and rhythm, and though she was involved more in an artistic concept—she delighted herself in this thought—she supposed that somewhere deep in her mind she had been following an almost unintentional demand. Expressively, she accorded to an inclination that did not consist of categorizing as a basic standard, but rather a hidden one; but human beings themselves, which Lilith had come to understand she was, are uncomfortable with imbalance, so she decided. Even the designs she had created with these shapes—though their categorizing seemed arbitrary—formed to have a certain balance, and balance is one of the important properties of art, declared Lilith. She could not know exactly what she had been thinking, for it was thought so deep it might not have even existed; to be simple she was merely following whatever her heart had desired, and wherever her mind was at the moment is almost thinkable—the categorizing was based on the whims of her design. She was free to do whatever she felt, without apparent form of thought.

In the practice she had found, at the very least, a sense of control; organization, and—if she were to categorize herself with things of her likeness—a sense of belonging. She liked to be in control of what she did, and she liked to see things from certain points of view. Placing objects, ideas, and such things into groups enabled her to take care of these needs and feel a tug of control over herself that put her to peace. Were something to be lost, uncategorized, or imbalanced, she reasoned, it would make her feel discomfort, and she would fidget around with it with a mind that refused to silence itself.

And so Lilith organized the Named Things to care for them, and to Tend to the Earth, but she knew and could foresee that she would soon be at home with loneliness and disorganization. And, having no alternative, the weeping willow wept.

~~~~

She was watching the heavens from a red earthly cave when Lilith heard that she had apparently descended upon the Red Sea; her silvery laugh tinkled like rainwater on glass in sheer amusement. Even before the rumor, she had felt herself fracturing, into—she calculated—at least two pieces. Fate was lining the skies, and the forthcoming desires of men to govern and dictate her would cleave her body into shedding a new being.

"They will call her Eve," she mused, "and Lilith will forever be known to be among the demons."

After a moment, she turned to Adam at her side and smiled, "My own children will say I am barren."

Adam gazed into the distance, his eyes clouded with remorse for the garden. Upon his expulsion he had searched for his love every day, and was at least partially content in finding Lilith at last at the peak of the mountain from which the sun rose. Twice the determined, pining romantic, Lilith had searched both day and night—

"—but it will be Eve who is known to have searched for you," narrates Lilith. "And it will be you who is known as the fearless romantic, the white knight, the trope of the driving lover in the form of the masculine anchor." And she leaned back, with a content smile, as though ready to birth her history. And before the sideways gaze of Adam she transformed into a new woman.

First her face, her hands, her legs, the shift in the darkness of her hair, and sighing at him there, was Eve, with all of the soft femininity of Lilith; Eve, a fully domestic creature, and only a fraction of the wildness that had, over and over, broken his heart.

"Lilith?" he whispered.

The creature looked over her crown of hair and smiled with a strangeness that, with a makeshift spark, belonged at once to the woman he'd remembered, disappeared.

"Lilith," cried Adam.

Eve reached out to comfort him. "We cannot always be wild things."

He shed silent tears for a while, then asked quietly, "Where did you go?"

Eve tilted her head. "The Red Sea, my dear. We will make right among the demons."

~~~~

It is said that Lilith married the Devil, but it is only true that, when the newly she-demon saw her fate written in the stars, she came to visit him in the middle of the Red Sea. Having left Adam with Eve, the Prophetess—the tamer ghostly adaptation of herself—she searched day and night once again for love. It is only true that she offered the devil love. It is only true she came to forgave him for her Fall from the Garden, for she knew what was Written, and so did he. And what soul of God would not pity what she had named as her likeness?

She spoke to him:

You knew, they said, how to Love. The way you worshipped, you were a creature of fire so much like an angel that you practically became of their esteem. There was not a place on this earth, they said, that your forehead had not touched.

Lucifer, how did you fall?

And what need did you have to drag with you this world?

They blame you for all of corruption and it is true that when you have reason to leave me I feel as light and as good and as sweet as though it were what I was created to be. When you are absent the desire to do only good comes quickly, easily, rushing like instinct, instead of the dreary, dragging way I sometimes pull myself up, struggling, foreseeing the afterlife to save myself rather than dropping to my knees out of love. Sometimes, at my weakest, it is only a battle against you in my mentality, because I had refused to let you win.

And most times, even in your presence, I Submit out of Love.

And many times, even in your absence, there is contempt in the world. Have you not seen how I was Broken in Two?

And this is because, Lucifer, as I'm sure you've been aware, that these humans who have struck your jealousy, are corrupt in themselves as well.

They mock you and judge you in their speech and are yours a moment later. And they say this is because they have been possessed by you. The devil, they say, comes in pleasing forms. Like me. Like Lilith.

But you don't.

You never come in disguise.

Murder! Theft! Injustice! When I look you in the face I know it is you.

You are credited too profusely in your work. Or too little in your knowledge. You know mortal beings are weak enough so that disguise would be a waste of time. And some of them cannot see that they are corrupt themselves, but how else would they oblige while knowing it is you?

And so, Lucifer, I, Lilith, will not judge you. If the devil can change one, it is because one is changeable.

And when Lilith finished, Lucifer, the hater of humanity, his eye gleaming, kept his promise to make men dance for his amusement until the world fell, but he promised Lilith that day that he would, from the middle of the barren Red Sea, spare Adam's soul forever.

When Lucifer offered to spare only one other, only hers, she laughed and kissed him. "You fool. I need no sanctuary from the likes of you."

And the barren Lilith birthed a flight of ruthless demons.

"Fire will conquer the world," she sang. "But justice will come. And Guardians will be Appointed."

And, knowing the children of Adam would fail in their original task to tend the Earth, will ravage her instead, Lilith whispered to the Earth, "My Love, I am your Guardian."

II

The creation of Hawwa (translated as *Eve*) and Adam in Islam differs from the one in Christian religious tradition, in that (1) Hawwa is not said in the Qur'an to have formed from Adam's rib, (2) nor is *woman* said to have been created second after man (3) or even Adam disclosed to have been (for certain) the male variant in the couple but for a masculine pronoun utilized of grammatical necessity. God addresses Adam, whose name is interchangeably synonymous with *humankind*, and tells Adam to live with Hawwa (*spouse*) in Paradise, but the sex of each respective figure is not revealed. Hawwa and Adam exist simultaneously, androgynous until they eat from the tree, with neither having been created *from* the other though both are made of the same earth (thus of equal purity), and it is both of them *together* who are tricked into disobeying God's command. But Hawwa is often translated as *Eve*, though this story does not sound like Eve's.

It sounds like Lilith's.

If Muslim readership is unfamiliar with the story of Lilith (except for this slight resemblance, it doesn't exist in Islam by name or detail): she is rumored in Judaism and Christianity to have been Adam's first wife, created not from his rib after he had already been formed, unlike their Eve, but as an original, from (impure) earth. However, as Raphael Patai explains in his article, "Lilith," "Adam and Lilith could find no happiness together, not even understanding. When Adam wished to lie with her, Lilith demurred: 'Why should I lie beneath you,' she asked, 'when I am your equal, since both of us were created from dust?' When Lilith saw that Adam was determined to overpower her, she uttered the magic name of God, rose into the air, and flew away to the Red Sea, a place of ill repute, full of lascivious demons" (Patai, 1964).[112]

The resemblance to Satan, who refused to bow to Adam, citing his fashion of creation as reason, is chillingly striking. But here it is *Adam* who commanded submission, not God. And it is through invoking the name of God that Lilith makes her escape to the Red Sea, uniting with demons, one of whom she becomes.

In Christianity, God then creates Eve from Adam's rib, who naturally does not quarrel with him. In Talmudic tradition, Lilith commands ghostly she-demons that prevent childbirths in human women by causing miscarriages and barrenness: a class of succubae that leave men weak in nocturnal ejaculations. The story of Lilith is the story of a woman who is—quite literally—demonized. And for what? She would not submit to a patriarchal order established by men.

---

[112] Patai, Raphael. "Lilith." The Journal of American Folklore 77.306 (1964): 295-314. Print.

Significantly, in these versions of the story, she returns as the serpent to tempt Eve, "corrupting" the "good woman" who does as she is told. Though she returns to God full-circle, Lilith is the first feminist recognized and defined by patriarchy—a seductress who disobeys men and kills infants as she leaves women barren. She is not only a woman, but a woman so beautiful and monstrous that even nature itself condemns her in this barrenness, an *unnatural* woman: "As Montgomery aptly put it over half a century ago, 'the Liliths were the most developed products of the morbid imagination—of the barren or neurotic woman, the mother in the time of maternity, the sleepless child'" (Patai, 1964).[113]

But Hawwa is a Lilith who was never asked to submit to Adam. Hawwa is a Lilith who thus never felt any need to "abandon" him or to depart. Hawwa is a content Eve, fully and rightfully herself with all the powers to her own autonomy. She is recognized as a Prophetess. With the heavy baggage that Lilith carries, even predating Abrahamic tradition, is it entirely understandable that Hawwa has been translated as *Eve*. She is Lilith's beginning and Eve's end. The truth is that Islam's Hawwa, never asked to submit to Adam, is neither a Lilith nor an Eve. It is possible that both women erupted from the story of the First Woman with the gradual differences accumulated over the retelling of a story for centuries.

Lilith, not entirely human, makes strange and sudden appearances in Muslim theology long after she should have died, though never by that name. When I was young(er) my mother told me a story that took place during the time of Solomon (who had control over humans and jinn [other spirits, made of fire instead of clay]) in which two women fought over the possession of a child. To resolve the issue, the child was brought to King Solomon, who—with the intention of determining the true mother—commanded the child be cut in half. One of the women agreed; the other screamed in agony and exclaimed that she would give up the child so long as it lived. Solomon determined that this was the true mother.

---

[113] Patai, Raphael. "Lilith." The Journal of American Folklore. 77.306 (1964): 295-314. Print.

As a girl the story had left me perplexed. Who was this other woman, and what did she want with the child, if she would only kill it? My mother wondered the same, but had no answers.

And then I encountered this,

"While Lilith and Naamah thus have become unmistakably evil spirits, at least one other time in history they assumed human form—when, in order to try Solomon's wisdom, they assumed the form of two prostitutes and went to Solomon asking for his judgment in their quarrel over the surviving child." (Patai, 1964)

... and felt my heart stop. The woman was Lilith! In Islam she couldn't have been the original Lilith, I don't believe, but it makes sense that she was a jinn, not a human woman. There is also the charge that the Queen of Sheba was none other than Lilith, which is far-fetched, and doesn't fit the Islamic tradition of the story. The Queen of Sheba, according to Islam, is with certainty a human woman, who ruled powerfully— and rightfully, without marrying Prophet Solomon (in the Qur'an), proof that women are entitled to such extraordinary positions.

All I can safely conclude is that Hawwa (or Lilith or Eve) was so torn apart over centuries of patriarchal retellings that she became multiple women with multiple stories, and slandered to have consorted with the devil, all until the introduction of the creation of a second woman out of Adam's rib as an exemplar of the patriarchally preferred model of womanhood to replace her, or to convince human women that disobedience is demonic. Seeing that the purpose of the Qur'an was to restore truth to the revelations that were corrupted by men, it is likely that previously Eve was lessened and Lilith slandered, but these were naturally patriarchal fabrications. Hawwa was not made from Adam's rib, and Lilith did not consort with the devil. Submission to Adam was demanded from neither.

Because woman will not submit to man—

I would not have bowed to Adam, either. Nor to Eve. (They were both the same.) How could I when I submit only to God? For Satan it was pride; for me, love. (Or, if it is not, then make it so.) And if this Divine Love is a sin, my Lord, then damn me to Hell!

211

And let me burn with love so ardent that the Fire itself dies in shame!

And Eve says, "Never submit to anyone but God. I didn't." And Lilith says, "They will slander me. And they will slander you. But remember."

Dreaming Awake In Ceres' Garden

Celeste Gurevich

MY SENSE OF SPIRITUALITY is a swirling amalgamation, a collage of core truths borrowed from a whole spectrum of philosophies and experiences. When I am asked, my answer usually goes something like: "Well, you could call me a tree-hugging, ocean-swimming, Nature-loving pagan humanist, but I've also taken some ideas from Judeo-Christians (such as Jesus' view and treatment of the disenfranchised), Muslims (submission to the power of the transcendent), Buddhists (the tenant of mindfulness), Hindus (the mystical poetry of the Upanishads), and other theologies. Plus, a big ol' chunk of science." A bit confusing to many people, understandably, but what feels truest is to call myself a student of this Wondrous Universe. I feel myself to be one connective strand in the Great Web of Life.

Drift Creek old growth, dappled sunlight
through summerfat leaves. Scent of
pine needle blanket at my feet, baby
pinecone chickens fallen from Mother
Tree's nest of branches. Embraced, by
the warm breeze. Sister Chickadee and
her daily greeting. Teaching me to
speak Bird, coming to check
my progress.
Stellar's jays, robin, wrens, and the
surprise of whee-dee, whee-dee
above my head. Flicker, orange tail
flashing fire, wants in on the
conversation. Dialects. Music.
So much to learn from my
winged siblings.
Sacred, holy. Embraced.
Here, I can tend to my baby chicks, make
a branch teepee on the soft, dry pine
needles. Be hidden. Safe. I want to
be a tree, a hen,
or a squirrel.
Church forest. Sanctuary.

This poem is a scene from when I was five years old, playing by myself in the forest abutting the Pacific Ocean on the Central Oregon Coast. It took almost 40 years to put into language what I experienced that day, and much of my poetry is rooted in my intense relationship with nature.

I grew up in the last generation to run wild in relative safety through the abundance of wildness around us in Lincoln City, then a still lazy town of 6,500 people spread out over 15 miles. My single mother was a child of the '60's, not a full-on hippie, but with the same humanitarian ideals. And a very strong opinion that I learn about religion, history, and art, and most of all, the natural world first hand. "Go out there and search and watch and listen. You'll know what feels true to you," was her mantra during my adolescence.

My mother gave birth to me, just out of her teens, while the American Indian Movement occupied the island of Alcatraz in 1970, a few miles from where we lived. Her emotional connection with that community pushed her toward reclaiming the Cherokee ancestry that my grandmother's family had successfully buried for generations. She was drawn to Native spirituality, as was my uncle who lived in British Columbia at the tip of Vancouver Island, with the Kwakiutl tribe. We spent the summer there after she divorced my father, and the experience had a profound effect on our lives. On the return trip south, we stumbled upon Lincoln City, Oregon, which also has a local tribe, the Siletz, who welcomed us at every gathering we attended. Mom decided to stay, and it was our home for the next fifteen years. I consider myself beyond blessed to have spent so much time with and be so accepted by these communities. They taught me about the world and how to be in it in ways I am still uncovering.

At the top of the list of blessings in my life is the privilege of being raised in the Pacific Northwest. The experience of having my entire being sculpted and infused with a thousand shades of green, year round. Swimming with seals while watching a bald eagle fish in the bay just yards away. Of living my adult life nestled between a rugged and majestic coastline on one side, and the dotted row of Cascade Range volcanoes on the other, in the juicy and fertile Willamette Valley. It is primary to who I am as a spiritual being. This land, this region, has been as much a parent to me as my mother. And more father to me than my own ever was.

I started to read when I was four, and have been a voracious reader ever since. Alice Walker, Nancy Friday, Carl Sagan, and Gloria Steinem became my teachers, and as an only child, their books were my beloved companions. When I was in junior high school, I was introduced to Joseph Campbell, and my fascination with comparative religion began. Not only was he the first male academic that I had seen even acknowledge sacred feminine mythology, but he celebrated the fact that, at the core, all of the branches of religion share a fundamental beauty and wisdom. That all of nature is Our Mother. That free and unlimited access to the Divine is our human right.

With my brain full of Campbell's theories, I wanted to see the inside of organized religion. I started to go with friends to various churches around town, to the denominations that were available in that very Caucasian community: Lutheran, Catholic, Evangelical, Baptist. In these traditions I experienced only repetitious dogma, a dreadful lack of humanism (if there at all, it was the condescending, take-pity-on-the-savages missionary type), and no feeling of sacredness to be found. There seemed to be a disconnected boredom in most parishioner's eyes, not a reflection of divine light. All too businesslike for me. And that business was built upon and thriving on fear, guilt and shame. Not for me. It was a short and frustrating experiment, but vastly illuminating. Whatever sacred truths were to be found in Judeo-Christian theologies, it was up to me to find them on my own. I would explore the texts themselves, without the layers of human application to sully the messages.

Undaunted, I continued to catch up with the enormous backlog of Campbell's work, which lead me first to the big names in prehistoric and contemporary women's history, and feminist spirituality: Marija Gimbutas, Zsuzsanna Budapest, Margot Adler, Merlin Stone. They provided a direct and visceral line back to my European female ancestors, whose indigenous healing traditions I had been studying independently for some time.

I learned how women had been systematically denied access to religion and its institutions, proper education, and most of all, control over their own lives. I began to see the reality of the struggle for gender equality as something that didn't just affect me, in the community where I lived, but as a global issue. And one of extreme importance. The realization hit me that until the balance begins to be restored, our species will continue to limp along, disconnected from our collective history. Never reaching our highest potential: Homo Empathicus, one who lives in a state of divine empathy. I believe wholeheartedly that this is our next crucial step in human evolutionary biology. We are all born from a mother, and we need to remember this.

The work of these fierce women wove a thread through Campbell's mythology, my own Native American-influenced spiritual beliefs, and all the way to contemporary feminist politics. They helped to strengthen my ties to the planet and the connected web of life that She supports and nurtures, and to the Sacred Feminine innate in the Universe and my own body.

Shortly after my 20th birthday, I gave birth to my child using natural methods, with assistance of a midwife, which drove home the lesson of how powerful our life-force and body machines are. Just eight months after that, my mother was killed in a car accident, only 40 years old. Losing her taught me how deeply embedded my beliefs are about life, death, and what comes after. Both experiences fueled my determination to live a life as close as possible to the forests, rivers, and beaches that were the genesis of my intense connection to the natural world.

I've been able to achieve this, living in Portland, Oregon for more than 20 years. I was fortunate to be able to raise my son here, to share my childhood loves with him. To expand his experiences beyond mine, of growing up in a very small town. In this city, my church has many names: Forest Park, Oaks Bottom, Reed Canyon, Tryon Creek. Powell Butte. For the past five years, the love of my life has magnified my sense of worship and awe with his own. We visit the trees to be renewed and recharged. The varieties of nature also come to us, our home. Raptors and Great Blue Heron fly over our house, and flickers hang out in the giant fir tree in the backyard. The abundant maple trees flame and die each Autumn, reminding us of the turning of the wheel of time, as midlife, our bodies are reminding us that we too are part and parcel in that cycle.

I will turn 45 years old just as the first spring crocus buds show their purple and white faces. Many people, and especially women in American culture, have a hard time celebrating their aging. I look forward to it as I am learning exponentially about myself and the world with each year. The gift of nature I am experiencing through the roller coaster of peri-menopause brings as many new insights and freedoms as it does confusion and discomfort. It is a delight in my life to have a partner who is also determined to age with grace and gratitude, and honors the changes in us both.

It's been challenging at times, living and trying to thrive in this culture. Regardless, I and my beloved have chosen to walk through our lives with our hearts and minds open, curious, searching. For the sacred in each and every one of us.

* * *

I am the cream-colored foam at the tip
of a salty wave, hurling toward blackred rock.
I am the racing heart of a chickadee,
singing, singing.
I am the glint in the midnight eye of a harbor seal.
I am the keening cry of a bald eagle fishing the bay,
perched on a log
seasoned by sun and time.
I am a pine needle on a wind-stunted tree,
roots holding firm at the ocean's edge.
I am a shimmering drop of the mist dancing away from
the collision of wave and rock, toward clouds on high
that will rain me back to
Mother Pacific.

CONCLUSION

This book is just one beginning to a conversation I hope that will spread around the globe. I sincerely hope that each reader will take a look at the list of books that follows and read prolifically.

... to be continued ...

Contributors

Dr. Amina Wadud is Professor Emerita of Islamic Studies, now traveling the world over seeking answers to the questions that move many of us through our lives. Author of *Qur'an and Woman: Rereading the Sacred Text from a Woman's Perspective* and *Inside the Gender Jihad*, she writes about her life journey and anything that moves her about Islam, gender, and justice, especially as these intersect with the rest of the universe.

Trista Hendren (editor and contributor) is author of *The Girl God* series. She lives in Portland, Oregon with her children where her Norwegian husband visits as often as he can. You can read more about her projects at www.thegirlgod.com.

Pat Daly Kendall (editor) is an aspiring Goddess, mother of three daughters, and proud grandma. With a spiritual journey that includes an Irish Catholic upbringing, a rebellious bout with atheism, and a Christian coffee house conversion, Pat is on an ongoing quest for spiritual wholeness. A published author / writer on career and job search issues, Pat lives in Portland, Oregon and is planning to build a tiny house.

Rev. Dr. Karen Tate is an independent scholar, speaker, radio show host, four-time published author, and social justice activist. Karen's body of work blends her experiences of women-centered multiculturalism evident in archaeology, anthropology and mythology with her unique academic and literary talents and travel experience throughout the world. She's been named one of the 13 Most Influential Women in Goddess Spirituality and a Wisdom Keeper of the Women's Spirituality Movement. Tate's work has been highlighted in the *Huffington Post, Los Angeles Times, Seattle Times* and other major newspapers. Her first book, *Sacred Places of Goddess: 108 Destinations* has garnered prestigious endorsements, while her second book, *Walking an Ancient Path, Rebirthing Goddess on Planet Earth*, was a finalist in the National Best Books of 2008 Awards. Her newest books, *Goddess Calling, Inspirational Messages and Meditations of Sacred Feminine Liberation Thealogy,* and the anthology, *Voices of the Sacred Feminine: Conversations to ReShape Our World* came out in 2014. She is interviewed regularly in print, on television and on national public radio and hosts her own long-running radio show, *Voices of the Sacred Feminine Radio* considered a treasure trove of insight and wisdom for our time. Her work has segued into writing, producing and consulting on projects which bring the ideals and awareness of the Sacred Feminine into the mainstream world through television and film. She can be seen in the documentary, *Femme, Women Healing the World* produced by actress Sharon Stone and Emmanuel Itier of Wonderland Entertainment. Karen and her husband, Roy, her life partner for more than thirty years, are the creators, artists, and caretakers of the Isis Temple of Thanksgiving and Sekhmet's Mountain Grotto. (www.karentate.com)

Soraya L. Chemaly writes about gender, feminism and culture for several online media, including Role Reboot, The Huffington Post, Fem2.0, RHReality Check, BitchFlicks, and Alternet among others. She is particularly interested in how systems of bias and oppression are transmitted to children through entertainment, media and religious cultures. She holds a History degree from Georgetown University, where she founded that schools first feminist undergraduate journal. She later studied post-grad at Radcliffe College.

Neorah Garcia is a Jewish woman with French Canadian / Native American (Abenaki) roots. She was born and raised a Catholic in the French Catholic Church in Manchester, New Hampshire and later raised her children as Christian. A few months before the death of her daughter (at age 19 from Cystic Fibrosis) she started searching for God. With the help of her desktop computer (and very strong inner spiritual voice), something finally clicked and she found her new path in Judaism. Her daughter passed away on the morning before Passover, 14 Nisan, and she knew that day that God was telling her something... that she was headed in the right direction. Her marriage ended and she converted to Judaism nine years ago. She later met her feminist soul mate at her synagogue; she has been happily married for the last eight years. She has a 27 year old son she is very proud of, who stood by her side throughout her journey. She is an active member of a Conservative synagogue in El Paso, Texas and also serves as a Board Member of her synagogue and the local Jewish Family and Children's Services. She is a women's healing drum circle facilitator and has recently become active as an educator in Jewish Feminist studies, focusing on the Divine Feminine in Judaism. In addition to currently studying with the Darshan Yeshiva to become an ordained "para Rabbi" and Jewish lay Chaplain, she is planning to study for the Kohenet Hebrew Priestess program

Shehnaz Haqqani is a PhD Student of Islamic Studies at the University of Texas at Austin. She specializes in gender and sexuality in Islamic law, and her interests include Islamic feminism, female authority in Islam, and Pashtuns in the western diaspora. Shehnaz keeps a personal blog where she discusses questions and problems related to Muslims (particularly Muslim Americans), Pashtuns and Pashtun culture, and current events affecting women, Muslims, and/or Pashtuns.

Priestess Bairavee Balasubramaniam, PhD is a scholar-researcher, Goddess worshiper, motivational speaker, intuitive astrologer and poetess. She sees the Movement of Spirit in every waking moment, every form, every Chapter in this Divine Dance of Life and Existence. She runs three Facebook pages devoted to the Rising Consciousness of the Divine Feminine and writes extensively on her blog. As 'a Priestess with a PhD', Bairavee weaves her intuitive knowledge-through-gnosis, along with her academic commitment to in depth-research and analytical rigour together. Seeing spirituality as 'not just something you do for a few minutes a day' or 'not just what is written in texts', she explores the intersections between the spiritual, social, political, ritual, cultural and transcendental. Some of her topics of interest are: the breaking of spiritual stereotypes, the difference between the text and embodiment of spiritual understanding, the notion of 'cultural appropriation' and the challenges of cross-cultural interpretation of spiritual insights – and – living, speaking, writing and embodying 'The Path of the Dark Goddess'. She is also the host of 'Astrology with Priestess Bairavee Balasubramaniam PhD' and 'The Dark Mother's Show' on WGTR Radio.

Monette Chilson, author of *Sophia Rising: Awakening Your Sacred Wisdom Through Yoga,* has lived her yoga on and off the mat for 20 years. She writes and speaks about the melding of faith and yoga. She's written for *Yoga Journal, Integral Yoga Magazine, Om Times* and *Christian Yoga Magazine.* Her book was recently awarded an Illumination Book Award Gold Medal, as well as the Hoffer Small Press and First Horizon Awards. Connect on Twitter and Instagram (@MonetteChilson) or explore her work at www.SophiaRisingYoga.com.

Rebecca Mott is an exited prostitute, activist abolitionist and writer. She was prostituted when she was 14 and the severe mental, physical, and sexual torture continued until she was 27. After leaving, she blocked out her experiences for around ten years, and only remembered when she had a severe mental breakdown. Rebecca suffers from severe PTSD, but credits her memories for making her a passionate abolitionist. She blogs at http://rebeccamott.net.

Sarah Ager is an English teacher living in Italy. She describes herself as an 'Anglo-Muslim hybrid' having converted to Islam in 2011. She runs Interfaith Ramadan, an online interfaith initiative bringing together writers and contributors from different faiths and backgrounds during the month of Ramadan. As well as her passion for interfaith dialogue, Sarah writes about education, language, and Italian culture on her blog, 'A Hotchpotch Hijabi in Italy' (www.interfaithramadan.com).

Metis is a wife, mother, academic, and a writer on topics related to Religion and Feminism.

Susan Mehegan is a 67-year-old spiritual counselor living on the south coast of Lake Ontario in Upstate New York. Her family is a mix of three generations as well as three generations of 11 cats. Susan has been married to her high school sweetheart for nearly 50 years, has two children, eight grandchildren, and three great-grandchildren. Her days include walks in the country and identifying and harvesting wild plants, which she uses dried and in tinctures for remedies and magical purposes.

The Reverend Jacqueline Hope Derby is an ordained minister in the United Church of Christ. She has served primarily as a healthcare chaplain working with trauma victims, young mothers, and children. Subsequently, Jacqueline's professional interests include bioethics, Neonatal Abstinence Syndrome, self-care for the healthcare professional, healing and meaning making. She is a national speaker and writer, and her work can be found at TheSophiaCollective.com. Jacqueline lives in

Kentucky with her husband, young daughter, and their beloved Springer Spaniel.

Jen Raffensperger has been writing since she could, talking since she could, and seeking since she was old enough to ask questions. She is actively engaged in her Unitarian Universalist congregation, still writing, still talking, still seeking. Her writing can be found on her blog, examorata.com.

DeAnna L'am is an internationally established expert on Menstrual Wellness, author of 'Becoming Peers – Mentoring Girls Into Womanhood' and 'A Diva's Guide to Getting Your Period'; Founder of Red Moon School of Empowerment for Women & Girls™, and of Red Tents In Every Neighborhood – Global Network. Fondly known as 'Womb Visionary', DeAnna has been transforming lives worldwide for over 25 years, teaching women and girls how to love themselves unconditionally! She helps women dissolve PMS symptoms by drawing spiritual strength from their cycle; guides women in the art of welcoming girls to empowered womanhood; and inspires women to hold Red Tents in their communities. DeAnna L'am was the first to bring Menstrual Empowerment work to Israel / Palestine, her country of origin, where she helped Jewish and Palestinian women surpass political and religious differences by deeply bonding as cycling women. Visit her at: www.deannalam.com.

Visual artist, writer and cultural visionary **Pegi Eyers** is occupied with smashing icons, contributing to the paradigm shift and working with the decolonization process in herself and others. A Celtic Animist who sees the world through a spiritual lens, she is a devotee of nature-based culture and all that is sacred to the Earth. Author of Ancient Spirit Rising: Reclaiming Your Roots & Restoring Earth Community, she examines cultural appropriation, the interface between Turtle Island First Nations and the Settler Society, rejecting Empire, social justice work, cultural reclamation, earth rights, sacred land and the holistic principles of sustainable living. She is an advocate for our interconnection with Earth Community and the recovery of authentic ancestral wisdom and traditions for all people. Pegi Eyers lives in the countryside on the outskirts of Peterborough, Ontario, Canada on a hilltop with views reaching for miles in all directions. www.stonecirclepress.com .

Elizabeth Hall Magill has been blogging about feminist issues at Yo Mama since 2011 – and her posts have been featured on BlogHer (Spotlight BlogHer), Miss Representation's Sexy or Sexism campaign, and Girls Re(write) Herstory. A video reading of her piece "Reclaiming the Sacred Feminine: Venus" is featured in the May 2013 issue of *Spaces* literary magazine. Elizabeth holds degrees in English from the College of William and Mary and James Madison University. She has been a technical writer for IBM and taught college-level writing and gender courses. She is currently researching a nonfiction book, *American Sexism: Questions and Answers.*

Liona Rowan is Founder and Priestess in Residence of 10K Sanctuary Goddess Temple and Retirement Community. Liona Rowan completed a traditional year and a day apprenticeship in Eclectic Wicca in 1995 and was initiated as a priestess in July of that same year. Ms. Rowan has a master's degree in Humanities with a Women's Studies emphasis from Dominican University in San Rafael, California and a terminal master's degree in Philosophy and Religion with an emphasis in Women's Spirituality from California Institute of Integral Studies in San Francisco, California. She is a co-founder of OCHRE Journal of Women's Spirituality (www.ochrejournal.org). Ms. Rowan has participated in planning and priestessing both public and private rituals for more than 18 years. Ms. Rowan is also a beekeeper.

Patty Kay is a retired bookkeeper in Lake Charles, Louisiana. She has studied ecology and world religions for the past forty years. Retirement has offered her the opportunity to delve further in her interests.

Zoe Nicholson has been standing in front of a room and in the public square with one message: WAKE UP. And with each day, each event, each year, waking up to something new has led to a dynamic life that unfolded sharply, quickly, deeply. Marching against the Vietnam War in 1968; organizing opposition to the California Briggs Initiative, working in the American Women's Movement, fasting for the ERA; NOW liaison for the National Equality March. In the middle of these decades of activism, Zoe formally studied Buddhism for 12 years and was initiated as a Buddhist monk and teacher, January 24, 1989. Leaving the ashram and silent meditation, she continued her passionate practice as an Engaged Buddhist. Zoe Ann Nicholson can be reached at Zoe@Zoenicholson.com. You can find more about her work at http://zoenicholson.com.

Erin McKelle is an activist, writer, and student at Ohio University, studying for a degree in Women and Gender studies. She has written for a variety of publications and worked for a variety of non-profits, including Everyday Feminism, Adios Barbie, and Stop Street Harassment. Erin divides her time between Athens and Cleveland Ohio, and enjoys reading, black tea, and HGTV.

Rabbi Dalia Marx (PhD) is an Associate Professor of Liturgy and Midrash at the Jerusalem campus of Hebrew Union College-JIR, and teaches in various academic institutions in Israel and Europe. Marx, tenth generation in Jerusalem, earned her doctorate at the Hebrew University and her rabbinic ordination at HUC-JIR in Jerusalem and Cincinnati. She is involved in various research projects and is active in promoting liberal Judaism in Israel. Marx writes for academic and popular journals and publications. She is the author of *When I Sleep and When I Wake: On Prayers between Dusk and Dawn* (Yediot Sfarim 2010, in Hebrew), *A Feminist Commentary of the Babylonian Talmud* (Mohr Siebeck, 2013, in English) and the co-editor of a few books. Marx lives in Jerusalem with her husband Rabbi Roly Zylbersztein (PhD) and their three children.

Debbie Kozlovich is a professional Ballroom Dance Instructor, writer, mother, grandmother, mentor, wife, sister, supporter of those in need, vegan, women's rights and gay rights activist, adventurer and happiness seeker, interested voter and runner.

Vanessa Rivera de la Fuente is a media analyst, gender journalist, writer and specialist in social development projects. She is a lecturer in Feminism, Islam and Interculturality. Her work focuses on Gender, Identity, Media Representations and Religious Fundamentalism. She has lectured in Universities and International Conventions in México, Equator, Peru, Argentina, France, England, Spain, Brazil and Chile. A pioneer on Islamic Feminism in Latin America, she is the Founder and Director of Imaan: Center for Gender Studies in Religion and Dialogue

Islam-Society. You can reach her at
vriveradelafuente@gmail.com.

Vrinda J. Shakti is a yogic mystic, scholar practitioner and student of the Goddess in motherline Vedic traditions. She is an initiate in Samkhya and Vedanta—duality and nonduality. Vrinda trained as a nun with honorable mentors who embody the Divine Mother in her three forms. After two decades immersed in the practice, studies and beauty of Integral Yoga at Revered Bhagavan's ashram, she continues the beloved teachers' mission and research with a focus on the ways that Goddess traditions from antiquity presently inform spiritual activism for societal transformation and the ongoing expansion of consciousness.

Lora Koetsier grew up in Indiana and served three years in the military. As she raised her children, Lora earned Bachelor of Science and Master's degrees. Lora published her first book, *Natural Law and Calvinist Political Theory*, in 2004. She currently works as a technical writer.

Zoharah Noy-Meir lives in Israel. In 2010, she started the Red Tent movement in Israel by creating with many women Red Tent gatherings 1-4 times a year. In 2012 she started a monthly local Red Tent in her home town of Tivon. Since then, more Red Tents have been created and are now held regularly, in Tel-Aviv, Jerusalem, in the south of Israel and more. She is now working on a Hebrew feminine anthology, with writings translated from English, about the sacred feminine.

Lizette Galima Tapia-Raquel is an Assistant Professor for Feminist and Contextual Theologies, Christian Ethics, and Ecumenics at Union Theological Seminary (UTS), Philippines. She earned her Master of Divinity from UTS in 2005 and her Master of Theology in 2010 from the Southeast Asia Graduate School of Theology. She is a member of the Ecumenical Association of Third-World Theologians. An ordained deacon of the United Methodist Church, she is an advocate for human rights, gender and climate justice.

Nafhesa Ali is author of *Asian Voices: First generation migrants* (2010) and is currently completing her PhD studies at the University of Huddersfield, UK where she is researching older

South Asian migrant women and their experiences of ageing, migration and wellbeing in later life.

Ruth Calder Murphy is a writer, artist, music teacher, wife and mother living in London, UK. Her life is wonderfully full of creativity and low-level chaos. She is the author of two published novels, *The Scream* and *The Everlasting Monday,* several books of poetry and one or two as-yet unpublished novels. She is passionate about celebrating the uniqueness of people, questioning the unquestionable and discovering new perspectives on old wonders. She is learning to ride the waves that come along—peaks and troughs—and is waking up to just how wonderful life really is. You can visit Ruth and view more of her art on her website at www.arciemme.com.

Susan Morgaine is a Witch, Healer, Teacher, Feminist, Yogini, Belly Dancer and Writer. She focuses her classes and workshops on awakening the Divine Feminine in each woman and in women-empowerment. She is the Meditation and Goddess Columnist at PaganPages.Org. Her blog can be found at https://shaktiwarrior.wordpress.com. Susan can be reached at ShaktiWarriorSpirit@gmail.com.

Nahida Nisa enjoys wisteria trees, writing, red lipstick, astrophysics, garden path sentences, deceptive boxes, Islamic architecture, Toni Morrison, and can sing from G3 to E6.

Celeste Gurevich grew up on the Central Oregon Coast and currently lives with her husband, Andrew, in Portland. After experiencing a trauma-induced decade-long writer's block, she started taking writing and film classes at Mt. Hood Community College and experienced a literary rebirth. A Social Artist in training, her goal is to teach others about the transformative nature of sharing our stories with one another, and the collective healing that comes from revealing our deepest inner selves in community. Her work has appeared in: *Perceptions: A Magazine for the Arts,* The Manifest-Station.net, and *The International Journal of Gender, Nature, and Transformation.* She is currently a member of the Dangerous Writers workshop with Tom Spanbauer, and is working on her first book.

Further Reading

A selection of books suggested by contributors

21st Century Motherhood: Experience, Identity, Policy, Agency – Edited by Andrea O'Reilly

A Diva's Guide to Getting Your Period – DeAnna L'am

A Feminist Commentary of the Babylonian Talmud – Rabbi Dalia Marx (PhD)

A God Who Looks Like Me – Patricia Lynn Reilly

A History of God – Karen Armstrong

A Jihad for Justice: Honoring the Work and Life of Amina Wadud – Edited by Kecia Ali, Juliane Hammer and Laury Silvers

A Woman Awake – Christina Feldman

All About Love: New Visions – bell hooks

An Anthology of Sacred Texts by and About Women – Serenity Young

Ancient Spirit Rising: Reclaiming Your Roots & Restoring Earth Community – Pegi Eyers

Asian Voices: First generation migrants – Nafhesa Ali

Be Full of Yourself: The Journey from Self-Criticism to Self-Celebration – Patricia Lynn Reilly

Becoming Peers – Mentoring Girls Into Womanhood – DeAnna L'am

Believing Women in Islam: Unreading Patriarchal Interpretations of the Qur'an – Asma Barlas

Beyond God the Father: Toward a Philosophy of Women's Liberation – Mary Daly

Blood & Honey Icons: Biosemiotics & Bloculinary – Danica Anderson

Breaking up with God – Sarah Sentilles

Buddha's Daughters – Edited by Andrea Miller

Buddhism after Patriarchy – Rita Gross

Cave in the Snow – Vicki Mackensie

Composing a Life – Mary Catherine Bateson

Cultures of Peace: The Hidden Side of History – Elise Boulding

Daughters of the Goddess – Linda Johnson

Dance of Days – Ruth Calder Murphy

Enduring Grace – Carol Lee Flinders

Enduring Lives: Portraits of Women and Faith in Action – Carol Flinders

Feminism is for Everybody – bell hooks

Feminism Without Borders, Decolonizing theory, Practicing Solidarity – Chandra Talpade Mohanty

Feminist Theory: From Margin to Center – bell hooks

Gender Hierarchy in the Qur'ān: Medieval Interpretations, Modern Responses – Karen Bauer

Goddesses and the Divine Feminine: A Western Religious History – Rosemary Ruether

Goddess Calling, Inspirational Messages and Meditations of Sacred Feminine Liberation Thealogy – Rev. Dr. Karen Tate

Goddesses, Goddesses – Janine Canan

Grounding Human Rights in a Pluralist World – Grace Kao

Gyn/Ecology: The Metaethics of Radical Feminism – Mary Daly

Heartbreak – Andrea Dworkin

Hildegard of Bingen: A Saint for Our Times – Matthew Fox

Holy Women Icons – Angela Yarber

229

Illuminations: A Novel of Hildegard von Bingen – Mary Sharratt

In Memory of Her: A Feminist Theological Reconstruction of Christian Origins – Elisabeth Fiorenza

In Search of Our Mothers' Gardens: Womanist Prose – Alice Walker

Inside the Gender Jihad – Dr. Amina Wadud

Living Beautifully: with Uncertainty and Change – Pema Chodron

Living in the Lap of the Goddess – Cynthia Eller

Longing for Darkness – China Galland

Making a Way Out of No Way – Monica A. Coleman

Marriage and Slavery in Early Islam – Kecia Ali

Matri: Letters from the Mother – Zoe Ann Nicholson

Missing Mary – Charlene Spretnak

Mitting the Great Bliss Queen – Naomi Klein

MotherWit – Diane Mariechild

Muslima Theology: The Voices of Muslim Women Theologians – Edited by Ednan Aslan

Natural Law and Calvinist Political Theory – Lora Koetsier

New Jewish Feminism: Probing the Past, Forging the Future – Edited by Rabbi Elyse Goldstein

Nine Parts of Desire: The Hidden World of Islamic Women – Geraldine Brooks

Not Alone – Monica A. Coleman

Of Woman Born: Motherhood as Experience and Institution – Adrienne Rich

On Observing the Pain of Others – Susan Sontag

Opening the Lotus – Sandy Boucher

PaGaian Cosmology: Re-inventing Earth-based Goddess Religion – Glenys Livingstone

Passionate Enlightenment – Miranda Shaw

Pedagogy of the Oppressed – Paulo Freire

Progressive Muslims: On justice, Gender and Pluralism – Edited by Omid Safi

Qur'an and Woman: Rereading the Sacred Text from a Woman's Perspective – Dr. Amina Wadud

Rebirth of the Goddess: Finding Meaning in Feminist Spirituality – Carol P. Christ

Recovering the Sacred: The Power of Naming and Claiming – Winona LaDuke

Relational Reality – Charlene Spretnak

Religious Imagination of American Women – Mary Farrell Bednarowski

Sacred Pleasures – Riane Eisler

Secret Lives – Barbara Ardinger

Sexism and God-Talk – Rosemary Radford Ruether

Sexual Ethics in Islam: Feminist Reflections on the Qur'an, Hadith, and Jurisprudence – Kecia Ali

She is Everywhere!: An Anthology of Writings in Womanist/Feminist Spirituality – Mary Saracino and Mary Beth Moser

She Rises: Why Goddess Feminism, Activism or Spirituality? – Edited by Dr. Helen Hwang and Dr. Kaalii Cargill (June 2015)

She Who Changes: Re-imagining the Divine in the World – Carol P. Christ

She Who Is – Elizabeth A. Johnson

Siddur haKohanot: A Hebrew Priestess Prayerbook – Rabbi Jill Hammer and Holly Taya Shere

Sister Outsider – Audre Lorde

Sisterhood is Forever – Robin Morgan

Sisterhood is Global – Robin Morgan

Sisters at Sinai: New Tales of Biblical Women – Jill Hammer PhD

Societies of Peace: Matriarchies Past Present and Future – Edited by *Heide Goettner-Abendroth*

Sophia Rising: Awakening Your Sacred Wisdom Through Yoga – Monette Chilson

Sophia - The Feminine Face of God: Nine Hearts Path to Healing and Abundance – Karen Speerstra

Spirit Song – Ruth Calder Murphy

Stepping Into Ourselves: An Anthology of Writings on Priestesses – *Edited by Anne Key and Candace Kant*

Teaching Critical Thinking: Practical Wisdom – bell hooks

Teaching to Transgress: Education as the Practice of Freedom – bell hooks

The Bond Between Women – China Galland

The Book of Blessings: A New Prayer Book for the Weekdays, the Sabbath, and the New Moon Festival – Marcia Falk

The Chalice and The Blade – Riane Eisler

The Church and the Second Sex – Mary Daly

The Civilization of the Goddess – Marija Gimbutas

The Color Purple – Alice Walker

The Creation of Feminist Consciousness – Gerda Lerner

The Creation of Patriarchy – Gerda Lerner

The Dance of the Dissident Daughter – Sue Monk Kidd

The Dinah Project – Monica A. Coleman

The Divine Consort – Edited by John Hawley

The Gospel of Mary Magdalene – Jean-Yves Leloup

The Graceful Guru – Karen Pechillis

The Great Cosmic Mother – Monica Sjoo & Barbara Mor

The Hidden Lamp – Caplow/Moon

The Language of the Goddess – Marija Gimbutas and Joseph Campbell

The Lives of Muhammad – Kecia Ali

The Living Goddess – Linda Johnson

The Living Goddesses – Marija Gimbutas and Miriam Robbins Dexter

The Mother's Songs: Images of God the Mother – Meinrad Craighead

The Pedagogy of Hope – Paulo Freire

The Places that Scare You: A Guide to Fearlessness in Difficult Times – Pema Chodron

The Real Wealth of Nations – Riane Eisler

The Sacred Hoop: Recovering the Feminine in American Indian – Paula Gunn Allen

The Secret Legacy of Biblical Women: Revealing the Divine Feminine - Melinda Ribner

The Spiral Dance: A Rebirth of the Ancient Religion of the Goddess – Starhawk

The Veil and The Male Elite: A Feminist Interpretation of Women's Rights In Islam – Fatima Mernissi

The Woman with the Alabaster Jar: Mary Magdalen and the Holy Grail – Margaret Starbird

The Women's Spirituality Book – Diane Stein

Wings of a Thousand Tigers – Ruth Calder Murphy

Transgender Warriors: Making History From Joan of Arc to RuPaul – Leslie Feinberg

Voices of the Sacred Feminine: Conversations to ReShape Our World – Edited by Rev. Dr. Karen Tate

Walking an Ancient Path, Rebirthing Goddess on Planet Earth – Rev. Dr. Karen Tate

Weaving the Visions: New Patterns in Feminist Spirituality – Judith Plaskow and Carol P. Christ

When God Was a Woman – Merlin Stone

When I Sleep and When I Wake: On Prayers between Dusk and Dawn – Rabbi Dalia Marx (PhD)

When Things Fall Apart: Heart Advice for Difficult Times – Pema Chodron

When Women Were Priests - Karen Torjesen

White Fire – Macka Drucker

Why Not Become Fire – Evelyn Mattern

Wise Women: Over Two Thousand Years of Spiritual Writing by Women – Edited by Susan Cahill

Woman as Healer – Jeanne Achterberg

Woman Prayer, Woman Song: Resources for Ritual – Miriam Therese Winter

Womanspirit Rising: A Feminist Reader in Religion – Judith Plaskow and Carol P. Christ

Women and Gender in Islam: Historical Roots of a Modern Debate – Leila Ahmed

Women and Human Development: The Capabilities Approach – Martha Nussbaum

Women and Redemption – Rosemary Radford Ruether

Women and Religion – Majella Franzmann

Women and the Vatican – Ivy Helman

Women of Sufism – Edited by Camille Helminski

Women of Wisdom – Anne Bancroft

Women of Wisdom – Tsultrim Allione

Women's Buddhism – Edited by Ellison Findley

Women's Spirituality: Contemporary Feminist Approaches to Judaism, Christianity, Islam and Goddess Worship – Johanna H Stuckey

Women's Spirituality: Power and Grace – Mary Faulker

Acknowledgements

Endless thanks to my mother (and co-editor) Pat, who has always believed in me. You've been a great partner in so many ways over the years, mom. I love you!

Love and appreciation to my beloved husband, Anders, who has been my rock and my soul mate. Thank you so much for your tremendous contributions to all of my books and websites, and your never-ending support of my work.

Eternal love for my children, who continually inspire me.

Heartfelt appreciation to Dr. Amina Wadud for agreeing to write the preface for this book despite her busy schedule—and many additional thanks for her input on the book itself.

Many thanks to Liz Hall Magill for reading the introduction many times and offering input.

Love and thanks to Elisabeth Slettnes for allowing us to use her gorgeous art on the cover.

I am forever grateful to my attorney, Chris, and his associates, who helped lift an endlessly heavy weight off my shoulders.

Heartfelt gratitude to Hussein, who encouraged me to find my faith again and continues to be a huge support in so many ways.

Special thanks to my best friend since Jr. High, Tanya Lamb. You have done more for me and my children over the years than I can ever begin to repay. I also thank Tanya for her help in editing and reviewing the last-minute addition on money to this anthology.

Thanks and appreciation to all the women who have offered support, love, prayers and a shoulder to cry on over the years. In particular, I'd like to thank Bridget, Alyscia, Desiree, Liz, Haseena, Rhonda, Soraya, Bridget, Danica, Susan, Jerin, Melissa, Ruth, Jessica, Sumayya, Wendy and Mary. I love each of you tremendously.

~ Trista

Made in the USA
San Bernardino, CA
05 June 2015